HORRIBLE
AND
FASCINATING

HORRIBLE
AND
FASCINATING

JOHN BOORMAN'S
EXORCIST II:
THE HERETIC

DECLAN NEIL
FERNANDEZ

BearManor Media

2022

Horrible and Fascinating: John Boorman's Exorcist II: The Heretic

© 2022 by Declan Neil Fernandez

Published in the United States of America by:

BearManor Media
1317 Edgewater Dr #110
Orlando FL 32804
bearmanormedia.com

Printed in the United States.

Typesetting and layout by John Teehan

ISBN—978-1-62933-948-1

Table of Contents

Hypnotherapy in *Exorcist II: The Heretic*. L-R: Regan MacNeil (Linda Blair), Dr. Gene Tuskin (Louise Fletcher), and Father Philip Lamont (Richard Burton).

"I hated The Exorcist… *It was a film about torturing a child. I made this fundamental error of trying to make not a sequel, really, but a kind of riposte, a film about spirituality."*

– John Boorman, director of *Exorcist II: The Heretic* [1]

"I did see a great deal of Exorcist II… *I sat through maybe forty minutes of it. It's the worst piece of shit I've ever seen. It's a fucking disgrace. It is so damn dumb and idiotic, and what it does is, it takes Blatty's great creation and tries to reverse it and trash it, and on that level alone it's idiotic and stupid, but on the level of filmmaking it is talentless. And, God, what a cast it had—Richard Burton, Louise Fletcher, plus Linda Blair, James Earl Jones… It's the worst forty minutes of film I've ever seen, really, and that's saying a lot."*

– William Friedkin, director of *The Exorcist* [2]

1. J Boorman, quoted in P Horne, "John Boorman: interview." *The Telegraph*, Mar. 24, 2013, https://www.telegraph.co.uk/culture/film/starsandstories/9946641/John-Boorman-interview.html

2. W Friedkin, quoted in "The Movies That Made Me: William Friedkin." Jan. 8, 2019, https://trailersfromhell.libsyn.com/william-friedkin

My introduction to *Exorcist II: The Heretic*.
The Australian 1991 VHS re-release by
Warner Home Video.

Prologue

From Kallaroo
To Pazuzu

I SHOULD BE HONEST from the start by confessing I have no firsthand experience of *Exorcist II: The Heretic*'s original theatrical run, much less its production: the film was made and released years before I was born. I do, however, have some personal history to share, peripheral though it is to *Exorcist II*.

My family and I emigrated to Western Australia in 1986. By the following year, my parents owned and operated a restaurant in Kallaroo, a suburb sixteen miles north of the state capital city of Perth and less than one mile from the beach.

The restaurant was called Spicy Den. House of aroma and taste. Specializing in home-made curries. My father played jazz piano for the clientele. (Don't look for it, it's not there anymore, as Marty Di Bergi would say. Spicy Den closed its doors in 1991.)

For approximately four years, Spicy Den was home-away-from-home for me and my two brothers. My parents' restaurant was part of Springfield Shopping Centre, a business property bordered by a public park on one side and residential housing on the other three. The center comprised a parking lot and two L-shaped buildings: one containing a newsagency, liquor store, and delicatessen; the other housed, from left to right, Dial-a-Dino's Pizza, a hairdressing salon, a fish & chips shop, Spicy Den, and… a video rental shop.

The video shop. That once-ubiquitous industry. Movies! *Next door* to *me*, and this was one of those non-franchise, mom-and-pop VHS rental stores boasting a more eclectic range of titles than the likes of Blockbuster Video would provide years later.

(For people reared on streaming and downloading films, the era of renting movies in plastic boxes from shops and returning them might as well have taken place when dinosaurs roamed the Earth... but for an older generation of film enthusiasts, *iucunda memoria est.*)

A video shop next door. In retrospect, this was an idyllic, seed-planting childhood for a future obsessive of cinema (and inveterate collector of films on physical media).

It's screwy the things that fascinate you when you're a kid, but I awed at the video shop's storefront movie posters, periodically changing to herald the latest new releases. I still remember many of them specifically: *The Mission. The Name of the Rose. Masters of the Universe. Superman IV: The Quest for Peace. Crocodile Dundee II. Funny Farm. Young Einstein.* The Shelley Long/Bette Midler comedy *Outrageous Fortune*, for some reason.

If the outside of the video shop impressed, it had nothing on the interior—a labyrinth of VHS-adorned shelves, posters on the walls, cardboard stand-up displays, and store-issue snacks (including the obligatory popcorn) on sale in the corner. In other words, a perfectly average 1980s suburban video rental store—but to me it was practically Disneyland.

Since the Springfieldian shopkeepers were on friendly terms, the owners of the video shop didn't mind one of their business neighbors' sons idling away time inside their store, and idle away time I did. When I wasn't in the restaurant or playing in the adjacent Bridgewater Park, I'd be in the video shop. I'd putter around the children's section, and wherever *Ghostbusters* and the *Star Wars* and *Indiana Jones* films were located... but where I *really* liked to go was the shelf just to the left of the counter, near the back of the store.

The horror movies.

Like the metaphorical moth to the figurative flame, I was drawn to this shelf, resplendent with video cassettes in chunky plastic cases with paper sleeves bearing scary titles, creepy taglines, and grisly, garish pictures of vampires, werewolves, zombies, skeletons, aliens, goblins, demons, maniacs with axes and knives, and their bloodied victims.

Alien. The Blob. Children of the Corn. Evil Dead II. The Fly. Fright Night. The Gate. House. Night of the Creeps. Poltergeist. The Return of the Living Dead. Return to Horror High. Silent Night, Deadly Night. Stephen King's Silver Bullet. TerrorVision. Vamp. Innumerable *Halloween* and

Nightmare on Elm Street and *Howling* sequels. And there were many others. Those videos *beckoned* to me, fairly grasping at my eyes, *begging* to be seen.

Understand, this was when I was 5-8 years old. Back then I would not have been allowed to actually *watch* any of these bizarre, violent, mostly R-rated movies. I was renting G and PG-rated fare like *Teen Wolf*, *Mac and Me*, Disney's *Condorman* and *The Last Flight of Noah's Ark*, and episodes of *The Transformers*. When it came to the horror films, I had to settle for holding the video boxes and drinking in the sight of the lurid artwork and photographs. Of course, there's nothing so appealing to a child as what they can't have. This was forbidden fruit, and I was years away from being able to take a bite.

(Incidentally, I have no memory of spotting any *Exorcist* videos back then. I assume they were in-store but their minimalist sleeve designs were too subtle for me to notice.)

Flash-forward.

As a teenager in the 1990s with over a half-dozen video shop memberships, access to cable TV 24-hour movie channels, and a lot of spare time, I gave free rein to my desire to watch almost horror film available to me. Many of those films impressed; others were lamentably schlocky and didn't live up to the video sleeve art I pored over years before. Inevitably, I rented William Friedkin's *The Exorcist*, which I was aware of via cultural osmosis and felt primed to see after having watched *The Omen* and *Rosemary's Baby*. I knew *The Exorcist* was required viewing. *The Exorcist* was important. It *meant* something.

Incidentally, I read and re-read the behind-the-scenes book *William Peter Blatty on The Exorcist: From Novel to Film*—which I bought at a *Doctor Who* fan club meeting, of all places—before I watched *The Exorcist* for the first time. Knowing the film's script practically off by heart didn't diminish the impact of actually *seeing* the movie: I was blown away by *The Exorcist*, regarding it as one of the best horror films I'd seen, and surely one of the best films of *any* genre—an opinion I maintain to this day. I obtained my own copy of *The Exorcist*, viewed it repeatedly and, unsurprisingly, felt duty-bound to watch its sequels.

Enter *Exorcist II: The Heretic*.

I didn't go unawares into *Exorcist II*. I realized nobody talked about that film as much as they did about *The Exorcist*, and I gleaned from various books and film guides that it was generally regarded as one of the *worst* films ever made. I expected no masterpiece.

No masterpiece I got. I watched *Exorcist II...* and I re-watched it, again and again. (I later learned this was the revised, shorter version of the film, which was the only version of *Exorcist II* commercially available in Australia for two decades. I didn't view the original theatrical version until after its Australian home video release in 2001.)

Now, I knew *Exorcist II: The Heretic* clearly wasn't in the same league, quality-wise, as *The Exorcist*. I knew it wasn't a *good* movie, let alone a *great* one, and to me it failed a horror film's basic requirement of being *scary*. Yet... I didn't *hate* it.

Nor did I have a problem accepting it as a legitimate *Exorcist* sequel. *The Heretic* had Linda Blair; it had Max von Sydow; it had flashbacks to *The Exorcist*; and its onscreen credits shared the first movie's *font*. (The last point, weirdly, counted for a lot with me.) I also didn't have a problem with *Exorcist II* repeatedly citing the name of the demon Pazuzu—after all, William Peter Blatty had named the demon as such, in print if not in film.

So, if liking *Exorcist II* was out of the question... but I didn't *hate* it outright... nor did I regard it as a lesser-but-worthy sequel... what *was* it, exactly? An unintentional comedy? A puzzle to be solved? A blatant rebuke to the habitues of horror? A 100-minute bafflement-engendering cinematic crime-scene? All of the above?

Flash-forward again.

I have seen enough movies, I believe, to have expanded my knowledge and—I hope—my taste in film. Although I can no longer state emphatically that horror is my *favorite* film genre, it is perhaps the one for which I retain the most nostalgic affection.

For all its faults, *something* about *Exorcist II* stayed with me for years—a fascination with its manifest *wrongness*, coupled with the nagging question: *why* did the movie turn out the way it did? My attempts to find out, and what I learned, coalesced over the years into a creative project of which this book is the result. It has answered a lot of my questions, and, if you have an interest in the *Exorcist* series, I hope it answers a lot of yours.

Another question remains, touching upon the implications of causality. If my parents *hadn't* owned that restaurant next to that video shop, and I *didn't* loiter around the shop's horror section at an impressionable age, what path would I have gone down? Would this book exist without the lure of that shelf of forbidden videos near the back of the store?

I would like to dedicate this book to my parents, Dennis Joseph Fernandez and Teresa Ann Fernandez. I thank them not only for their unswerving love, guidance, and support, but for the path they set me on unintentionally, beginning in a small video shop many years ago.

Early *Exorcist II* theatrical release poster by Warner Bros. (1977)

Introduction

"It was horrible. Utterly horrible... and fascinating."
– From *Exorcist II: The Heretic* by William Goodhart

ON WEDNESDAY, DECEMBER 26, 1973, Warner Brothers' supernatural horror film *The Exorcist* was released to movie theatres across America. Directed by William Friedkin and produced by William Peter Blatty (who scripted the film, based on his 1971 bestselling novel), *The Exorcist's* graphic depiction of a little girl afflicted by demonic possession attracted large enough crowds to force Warners to expand the film into wide release quicker than had been planned. *The Exorcist* went on to play around the world and become one of the highest-grossing and most controversial films in history. It also became the first instalment of a media franchise—encompassing sequels, prequels, and a television series.

In his 1999 book *The Exorcist: Out of the Shadows*, Bob McCabe devotes one chapter to *The Exorcist's* first sequel, John Boorman's *Exorcist II: The Heretic* (1977). Addressing *Exorcist II's* status as "one of the most notorious disasters in film history," McCabe wonders where the blame ultimately lies: "Boorman's illness and constant revising of the script can't have helped, but these events alone are not enough to explain the film's almighty failure."[3] In fact, *all* of *The Exorcist's* sequel films were dogged by production difficulties, and none of them, in critical and commercial

---

3.   B McCabe, *The Exorcist: Out of the Shadows* (London: Omnibus Press, 1999), p. 165.

7

terms, were especially successful. Yet the most contentious instalment of the series remains *Exorcist II: The Heretic*. Released in June 1977—three and a half years after the premiere of *The Exorcist*—*Exorcist II* fell far short of the first movie's quality, impact, and commercial success, "a failure on the grandest scale possible," in the words of Boorman biographer Brian Hoyle.[4] When *Exorcist II* is cited and discussed in pop-culture circles, it is usually in the context of its reputation as a *bad* movie.

Let there be no mistake on that last point. *Exorcist II: The Heretic* is *not* a great movie. On the contrary, it is one of the most unintentionally silly films ever released by a major studio. Many multi-instalment film franchises suffer from decreasing quality over a course of sequels; the *Exorcist* saga took a rapid plunge into full-blown farce with its *first* sequel. Departing from the taut narrative of its predecessor, *Exorcist II* is a barely coherent, globe-trotting mess involving half-baked mysticism, dubious science, tap dancing, and locusts. *Exorcist II* is an unworthy follow-up to *The Exorcist* and a misguided film in its own right; practically every facet—script, production design, direction, acting—is stunning in its wrongness, coalescing into a film that achieves a bizarre grandeur. That *Exorcist II* failed is, perhaps, not surprising—what *is* surprising is the *manner* in which the film failed. This was not a case of a studio employing a hack director to churn out a bland re-tread. *Exorcist II* was no cheap knock-off, like so many horror sequels that have littered the cinema landscape. It was a big-budget, major studio picture; the sequel to an Oscar-winning film; and a legitimate bid for quality by an award-winning, freewheeling, and critically praised film director. A prestige vehicle, subject matter notwithstanding. To that end, *Exorcist II* starred A-list actors, was shot in multiple locations, utilized huge interior sets, and employed state-of-the-art special effects. Audiences and critics were aghast at the result: ineptly assembled, and bloated with self-important ideas, *Exorcist II* fell off the cliff of competent filmmaking to drown in a pool of schlock. While it is staggering how much unintentional humor can be found in *Exorcist II*, there is no merit in simply dismissing the film with mordant commentary. After all, *Exorcist II* elected—rather boldly—to *not* copy *The Exorcist*. However, it is possible for a sequel to distinguish itself from its predecessor without *declaiming* it. *Exorcist II* is a denunciation of *The Exorcist*, showing disdain towards Friedkin's film. To John Boorman, *The Exorcist* was a *bête noire*, a harmful and destructive film about "torturing a child" and nothing more. As far as Boorman was concerned, *Exorcist II* would be didactic—a healing movie,

---

4.   B Hoyle, *The Cinema of John Boorman* (Lanham: Scarecrow Press, Inc., 2012), p. 102.

a work of overarching moral purpose that would curve audiences away from profanity and gore to a sequel of restorative spiritual value. Under the auspices, then, of a filmmaker who wanted to take what worked in *The Exorcist* and do the *opposite* of it, *Exorcist II* stands as something unique and unprecedented in history: the film sequel as corrective. Yet, while *The Exorcist* holds up five decades after its release, *Exorcist II* cannot help but show its age. It is very much a film of its time—displaying the self-help pop-psychology, trendy ESP fringe beliefs, and roomy trousers that were rampant in the 1970s.

The 1970s was a seminal decade for horror films. Not only did *The Exorcist* make the gothic fare of Hammer Films, Amicus Productions, and AIP Films practically obsolete, the decade also yielded many landmarks of the genre: Robin Hardy's pagan/folk horror *The Wicker Man* (1973); Nicolas Roeg's supernatural-tinged psychodrama *Don't Look Now* (1973), Tobe Hooper's gritty, proto-slasher *The Texas Chain Saw Massacre* (1974); Steven Spielberg's blockbuster *Jaws* (1975); Brian De Palma's high school horror *Carrie* (1976); Richard Donner's satanic pulp-thriller *The Omen* (1976); Dario Argento's impressionistic *Suspiria* (1977), George A. Romero's zombie masterpiece *Dawn of the Dead* (1978); John Carpenter's trendsetting slasher *Halloween* (1978); Werner Herzog's elegant, stylish *Nosferatu the Vampyre* (1979); and Ridley Scott's sci-fi/horror blockbuster *Alien* (1979). Horror *auteurs* Dario Argento, Wes Craven, and David Cronenberg rose to prominence in the genre, and—thanks to the immensely profitable *Halloween*—John Carpenter became inadvertently responsible for the "slasher film" craze of the 1980s. Horror films proliferated in the 1970s thanks to the influence of the counterculture, the loosening of censorship restrictions on violence, advances in make-up and special effects, and growing recognition of the genre's viable commercial appeal beyond the B-crowd fringe. It was into this fertile field that Warner Brothers released *Exorcist II*. Originating as a studio cash-grab and drawing upon characters and situations created by William Peter Blatty, *Exorcist II* had developed into an *auteuristic* work on the part of John Boorman, operating in a triple-threat role of director/producer/co-writer (although Boorman received no official credit for his contributions to the film's screenplay).

Exorcist II: The Heretic occupies a very different cultural place to its predecessor. *The Exorcist* is an R-rated horror film that has inspired devotion from a subset of genre fans, but it was also a huge *mainstream* success; Friedkin's film made a tremendous amount of money, won numerous awards (including two Oscars from ten nominations), and instantly penetrated popular culture. *The Exorcist* has been widely imitated and specific elements of it have been endlessly referenced and parodied. (Pea soup, head-spinning, "The power of Christ compels you!" etc.) *Exorcist II*, on the other hand, has made relatively little impact on the cultural consciousness; generally speaking, the film's debased reputation (and not any scenes or dialogue from the film itself) is what is most remembered about it. Beyond the general audience, *Exorcist II*'s more specific attributes are celebrated by admirers and derided by its detractors. In this respect, *Exorcist II* is a "cult" film in a way its predecessor is not. "Some people do like it and others don't" is *Exorcist II* star Linda Blair's weary, and not inaccurate, assessment of Boorman's film.[5] Fans of *Exorcist II* are prepared to defend the movie as misunderstood as well as an example of extravagant, go-for-broke 1970s filmmaking, the sort of film that would not have been made by the more risk-averse film industry of the following decade.

Whatever else it is, *Exorcist II* is *not* the worst film ever made. It is not the worst sequel ever made; nor is it even the worst film Warner Brothers released in 1977. (*Viva Knievel!* preceded *Exorcist II* by a fortnight.) If *Exorcist II* is no longer generally considered to be the worst sequel of all time—a tag it has lived with for years—that might say less about re-evaluation of its reputation than it does about the general quality of film sequels in subsequent years. *Exorcist II* has endured—if that is the right word—far longer than many other maligned sequels. More than four decades after its release, *Exorcist II* remains a *fascinating* film, and the question of how and why it became a disaster is what this book seeks to answer. The making of *Exorcist II* is a troubled story, characterized by hubris and miscalculation, and comprising a tumultuous pre-production; a six-month shoot beset by catastrophes (including the director contracting a near-fatal infectious disease); and a controversial theatrical release that resulted in multiple versions of the film playing during its first-run engagement to scathing reviews, audience riots, and box office indifference. This account is also the story of two highly idiosyncratic filmmakers, one American and one British, both roughly the same age –William Friedkin and John Boorman—locked in a mutual loathing of each other's work that has persisted to this day. Boorman, essentially, made *Exorcist II* to denounce *The Exorcist*, implicating the very audience he needed to make his own film a hit. Inevitably, the production of *Exorcist II* was a recipe for disaster.

---

5. Linda Blair interview on Suicide Girls.com, Oct. 8, 2010, suicidegirls.com/interviews/2732/Linda-Blair---The-Exorcist/

The first part of this book is an overview of the history of *Exorcist II* from its inception in 1975 to its release in 1977; the second part is an analysis of the film itself and an examination of what went wrong. There will be much comparison between *Exorcist II* and its more famous predecessor. The more redemptive reading of *Exorcist II* might involve considering the film solely on its own merits, free of comparison to Friedkin's film. Certainly, the argument has been advanced that *Exorcist II* is appreciated best as an entirely separate piece from *The Exorcist*. However, scrutinizing the relationship between both films is necessary, since *Exorcist II* co-opts, and actively seeks to undermine, *The Exorcist*—contributing, inexorably, to its own ultimate failure.

Part One

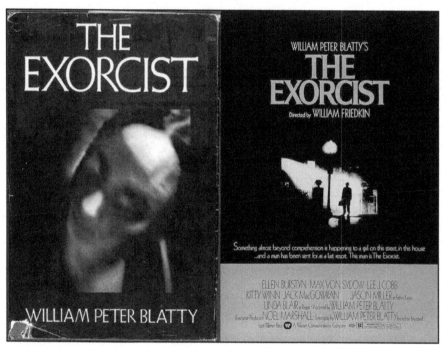

L: Harper & Row's first edition hardback of William Peter Blatty's *The Exorcist* (1971), jacket design by Frederick Cantor; R: Warner Bros' theatrical release poster of William Friedkin's *The Exorcist* (1973), poster design by Bill Gold.

1

The Exorcist

"I have no recollection of intending to frighten anyone at any point in time... It was all an accident."

– William Peter Blatty [6]

"It's a story that can perhaps make you question your own value system, even your own sanity, because it strongly and realistically tries to make the case for spiritual forces in the universe, both good and evil... Over the years I think that most people take out of The Exorcist *what they bring to it."*

– William Friedkin [7]

IN 1950, WILLIAM PETER BLATTY—a junior at Washington, D.C.'s Jesuit institution of Georgetown University—came across a four-page article published by the *Washington Post* on August 20, 1949. Titled "Priest Frees Mt. Rainier Boy Reported Held in Devil's Grip," Bill Brinkley's article reported that a 14-year-old Lutheran boy from Mount Rainier, Maryland

---

6.   WP Blatty, quoted in "After 40 Years, Grisly 'Exorcist' Book Gets A Rewrite." NPR Books. Oct. 29, 2011, http://www.npr.org/2011/10/29/141683620/after-40-years-grisly-exorcist-book-gets-a-rewrite

7.   W Friedkin, quoted in his introduction to the 1998 home video release of *The Exorcist*.

was the victim of demonic possession and that a team of Catholic priests successfully freed the boy after multiple performances of the rite of exorcism in St. Louis, Missouri. (The alleged victim was assigned the pseudonyms "Roland Doe" by the Catholic Church and "Robbie Mannheim" in Thomas B. Allen's 1993 account of the case, *Possessed: The True Story of an Exorcism*. The plausibility of the case has been contested, most notably by investigative journalist Mark Opsasnick in "The Cold Hard Facts that Inspired *The Exorcist*," an article published by *Strange Magazine* in 2000 and reproduced in the 2011 book *Studies in the Horror Film: The Exorcist*. In 2021, *Skeptical Inquirer* magazine revealed "Roland Doe" to be Ronald Edwin Hunkeler, who died in 2020 at the age of 86.) For Blatty, a young Catholic undergoing a not-uncommon crisis of faith, the 1949 story was a revelation: "The article impressed me. And how coolly understated that is. I wasn't just impressed: I was *excited*. For here, at last, in this city, in my time, was tangible evidence of transcendence. If there were demons, there were angels and probably a God and life everlasting."[8]

Blatty made the Roland Doe story the subject of a senior paper, and by 1963 the idea of writing a book about demonic possession had crystallized in his mind. He was already a published author by this time, due in no small part to a windfall in 1961: winning $10,000 as a contestant on Groucho Marx's TV quiz show *You Bet Your Life* enabled Blatty to quit his regular job and devote himself to writing full-time. However, neither Blatty's agent nor his publisher, Doubleday Books, expressed interest in his idea for a book about exorcism. By 1967, Blatty had a string of comic novels and screenplays—including the successful *Pink Panther* sequel, *A Shot in the Dark* (1964)—to his name, but the recent death of his mother strengthened his resolve to write something in a more serious vein. He returned to his idea of a book about exorcism and, encouraged by Marc Jaffe of Bantam Books to pursue the idea, Blatty contacted one of the priests who conducted Roland Doe's exorcism. With sufficient research and Bantam's $10,000 advance, Blatty began writing the book in 1969. He finished it nine months later, in the summer of 1970. Blatty titled his novel *The Exorcist*.

The Exorcist begins in Northern Iraq. An archaeological excavation led by an elderly Jesuit priest, Father Lankester Merrin, leads to the retrieval of a statue of the Assyrian/Babylonian demon Pazuzu. Merrin recognizes this discovery as a portent of a confrontation with the demon. The story

---

8. WP Blatty, *William Peter Blatty on The Exorcist: From Novel to Film* (New York: Bantam Books, 1974), p. 6.

moves to Georgetown, Washington, D.C., where film actor Chris MacNeil lives with her twelve-year-old daughter, Regan; her secretary, Sharon; and her housekeepers, Willie and Karl. Chris is currently shooting a film in Georgetown under director Burke Dennings. Regan becomes ill. Her behavioral changes are accompanied by a gradual series of poltergeist activity. Medical specialists are baffled by Regan's worsening and inexplicable condition. Left alone in the MacNeil house with Regan, Burke Dennings is murdered, his head twisted backwards. After Regan undergoes a series of unsuccessful medical and psychiatric treatments, Chris—an atheist—is advised by doctors to turn to a Catholic priest to perform the rite of exorcism, which might work as a force of suggestion if Regan believes herself to be possessed. Chris sees Regan's head turn backwards and speak with Burke Dennings' voice. Chris engages Father Damien Karras, the psychiatric counsellor at the local Jesuit seminary, who is secretly undergoing a crisis of faith stemming from feelings of guilt over the recent death of his mother. Karras fends off questions from homicide detective William Kinderman, who is investigating the recent murder of Burke Dennings; Kinderman thinks the murderer might be the same person who has committed a series of religious desecrations in the area and Karras might know the culprit. After examining Regan, Karras tells Chris he doesn't believe she is possessed by the devil or a demon; Chris tells Karras that Regan murdered Burke Dennings. Although he is unconvinced, Karras asks Church authorities for permission to perform an exorcism. It is decided the rite should be performed by an experienced exorcist with Karras assisting. Father Merrin, who has returned to America, is summoned. Merrin arrives at the MacNeil house, convinced Regan is possessed by the demon he once encountered in Africa. The demon recognizes Merrin. The exorcism in Regan's bedroom is grueling for the priests: the supernatural phenomena intensify as the demon verbally abuses everyone in the house. Karras breaks down when he hears his dead mother's voice coming from Regan. Merrin excuses Karras from the room; Karras returns to find Merrin has died from a heart attack. Enraged, Karras goads the demon into inhabiting him. The demon leaves Regan and enters Karras, but Karras regains control and throws himself out of the bedroom window, rolling down the long staircase below. A crowd gathers, and Karras dies after receiving the last rites from his friend and colleague, Father Joe Dyer. A recovered Regan does not remember her ordeal; she and Chris leave Georgetown. A friendship forms between Kinderman and Father Dyer, reprising the banter that existed previously between Kinderman and Karras.

The Exorcist was published in hardback by Harper & Row in 1971—to dismal sales. "I got very nice reviews," William Peter Blatty recalled. "I did a 26-city tour with twelve to thirteen interviews a day. But nobody was buying the book."[9] Fate intervened in mid-1971 when Blatty made a guest appearance on television's popular *The Dick Cavett Show*—a last-minute arrangement after (as the story goes) the scheduled guest, actor Robert Shaw, was deemed to be too drunk to participate in a pre-taped interview. In the course of his interview with Blatty, Cavett confessed he hadn't read *The Exorcist*, giving the author the opportunity to discuss his novel by way of what he later described as "virtually a monologue interrupted only by commercials."[10] Ten days after the interview aired, *The Exorcist* rocketed to #4 on *The New York Times* bestseller list; a week later it was #1, holding that position for over four months. The book went on to sell 13 million copies in two years and spend 57 weeks on the bestselling list.

Warner Brothers acquired the rights for a film adaptation of *The Exorcist* which Blatty, wary of ceding too much control, insisted on writing and producing. For various reasons, Stanley Kubrick, Arthur Penn, and Mike Nichols declined offers to direct *The Exorcist*. Refusing Warners' suggestions (including Mark Rydell, who had directed the 1972 John Wayne Western *The Cowboys* for Warners), Blatty insisted upon William Friedkin, with whom he had worked on an unrealized adaptation of his 1966 novel *Twinkle, Twinkle, "Killer" Kane!* Warners did not believe *The Exorcist* was appropriate for Friedkin, whose feature films thus far comprised the musical comedies *Good Times* (1967) and *The Night They Raided Minsky's* (1968) and the stage adaptations *The Birthday Party* (1968) and *The Boys in the Band* (1970), but the studio relented after the release of Twentieth Century-Fox's police thriller *The French Connection* (1971): the year's second highest-grossing film and the winner of five Academy Awards, including Best Director for 36-year-old William Friedkin. Hired to direct *The Exorcist*, Friedkin found Blatty's first-draft screenplay overwrought and requested a rewrite. The revised screenplay duly provided by Blatty was reasonably faithful to the novel, albeit with some supporting characters minimized and several subplots condensed or eliminated entirely. Filmed on location in Georgetown, New York,

9. WP Blatty, quoted in S King, "William Peter Blatty reflects on 40th anniversary of 'The Exorcist.'" *L.A. Times*, Oct. 8, 2013, http://www.latimes.com/entertainment/movies/moviesnow/la-et-mn-william-peter-blatty-exorcist-20131008,0,2078194.story

10. WP Blatty, quoted in McCabe, p. 25.

Winner 10 Academy Award Nominations!

Best Picture
Best Actress—Ellen Burstyn
Best Supporting Actor—Jason Miller
Best Supporting Actress—Linda Blair
Best Director—William Friedkin
Best Screenplay—William Peter Blatty
Best Film Editing
Best Sound
Best Cinematography
Best Art Direction

Publicity for *The Exorcist*'s ten Academy Award nominations (1974).

A unique version of the Warner Bros. ident designed by Saul Bass
as it appears onscreen in *Exorcist II: The Heretic.*

and Iraq, *The Exorcist* starred Ellen Burstyn as Chris MacNeil, Max von
Sydow as Father Merrin, Lee J. Cobb as Kinderman, Kitty Winn as Sharon, Jack MacGowran as Burke Dennings, Jason Miller as Father Karras,
and Linda Blair as Regan.

After a two-year production, including filming between August 1972
and March 1973, *The Exorcist* was released to cinemas in December 1973.
People lined around blocks to see it. Playing to packed theatres, *The Exorcist* became a huge box office success, quickly earning a reputation as
the scariest film since Alfred Hitchcock's *Psycho* (1960). Audiences were
shocked by the prepubescent Regan's transformation from a sweet-faced
girl to a coarse-voiced monster, and newspapers reported the adverse effects *The Exorcist*'s most viscerally repellent scenes had upon filmgoers,
claiming patrons would scream, faint, vomit, or run out of theatres. (The
more lurid accounts alleged the film caused heart attacks and miscarriag-
es.) *The Exorcist* drew condemnation *and* praise from spiritual leaders of
various denominations, giving rise to debate within a religious context.
(With Biblical epics going out of fashion in the mid-1960s, Christianity
was expressed through more eclectic film genres in the 1970s. *The Exorcist* was released in the same year as the film adaptations of two then-con-
temporary Jesus musicals: the vaudevillian/hippie devotional *Godspell*
and the more cynical rock opera *Jesus Christ Superstar*.) Psychologists
and sociologists also weighed in and echoing the response to Stanley Kubrick's *A Clockwork Orange* two years before, *The Exorcist* was blamed for
inspiring violence. The film was nominated for ten Academy Awards, in-

cluding Best Picture, Best Director, and nods for actors Ellen Burstyn, Jason Miller, and Linda Blair (William Peter Blatty took home an Oscar for his screenplay; *The Exorcist* also won an Oscar for Best Sound). The film was condemned by many as banal and trashy sensationalism—but there were those who absolutely loved it. *The Exorcist* had become the most controversial horror film in history—a milestone in cinema, a box office phenomenon, and a *cause célèbre*. Warner Brothers wanted a follow-up.

But what could top *The Exorcist*?

John Boorman, director/producer of *Exorcist II: The Heretic.*

2

Low-Budget Rehash: Preparing *The Heretic*

". . . the only free act in the creation of a film is the decision to make it. After that, you become a slave for a year or two, and you simply can't escape."

– John Boorman[11]

THE SEQUEL TO *THE EXORCIST* was initiated in 1975 by John Calley, Warner Brothers' President in Charge of Worldwide Film Production. According to William Peter Blatty, it was Calley who was primarily responsible for Warners obtaining the film rights to *The Exorcist* after the other major studios had turned it down:

> John told me he was alone in his home reading *The Exorcist* in bed on a windy night with lots of tree branches rustling and sighing against the roof... At a certain point in his reading, he got so spooked that he called for his German shepherd to get up on the bed with him. The dog had previously been forbidden to ever do so, so there ensued a titanic struggle with John trying to drag the dog onto the bed by his collar, and the dog whining and digging his claws into the wood pine floor. John said to himself, "My God, if it's this scary, we've got to make it!"[12]

11. J Boorman, quoted in M Ciment, *John Boorman* (London: Faber & Faber, 1986), p. 177.

12. WP Blatty, quoted in D Konow, *Reel Terror: The Scary, Blood, Gory, Hundred Year*

For the head of a major film studio, John Calley was a maverick, albeit an unassuming one. Eschewing the dictatorial approach that was *de rigueur* for old-time studio chiefs, Calley was an affable and erudite man with an uncommonly artistic approach and a reputation for trusting and supporting film directors. (Mel Brooks claims Calley was the only Warners executive to laugh at the screening of the *Blazing Saddles* rough cut.) The son of a used car salesman, Calley was raised in poverty by his single mother, and throughout his childhood and teenage years in Jersey City he worked factory and janitorial jobs to make ends meet. Calley's Horatio Alger-like rise in the entertainment industry began in 1951. After two tours of duty in the U.S. Army, the 21-year-old Calley joined NBC television's New York headquarters as a mail clerk. Working his way up the ranks of film and television advertising and production, Calley became Vice President of Martin Ransohoff's Filmways Inc. in 1960—co-producing *Ice Station Zebra* (1968) and *Castle Keep* (1969)—before receiving an invitation from Ted Ashley, the new chairman of Warner Brothers, in 1969. Calley's tenure at Warners, which lasted until 1981, was immensely fruitful. Calley's predecessor, Kenneth Hyman, oversaw a qualitative upbeat trend, but with some exceptions—most notably Arthur Penn's *Bonnie and Clyde* (1967) and Sam Peckinpah's *The Wild Bunch* (1969)—the films Hyman greenlighted did not generate noteworthy revenue for the studio. However, Warners' fortunes would change. The success of the taboo-breaking, trend-setting *Bonnie and Clyde*, the waning influence and 1969 retirement of founding mogul Jack Warner (who had tried to block *Bonnie and Clyde*'s production), and the nous of John Calley led to the studio's finest and most commercially successful era since the 1940s. Under the stewardship of Ted Ashley and John Calley, Warners' output included a veritable cavalcade of classic films: *Woodstock* (1970), *McCabe & Mrs. Miller* (1971), *Klute* (1971), *The Devils* (1971), *A Clockwork Orange* (1971), *Dirty Harry* (1971), *The Cowboys* (1972), *What's Up, Doc?* (1972), *The Candidate* (1972), *Deliverance* (1972), *Jeremiah Johnson* (1972), *Scarecrow* (1973), *O Lucky Man!* (1973), *Enter the Dragon* (1973), *Mean Streets* (1973), *Badlands* (1973), *Blazing Saddles* (1974), *Alice Doesn't Live Here Anymore* (1974), *The Towering Inferno* (1974), *Night Moves* (1975), *Dog Day Afternoon* (1975), *Barry Lyndon* (1975), *All the President's Men* (1976), *The Goodbye Girl* (1977), *Superman* (1978), and *The Shining* (1980).

And there was *The Exorcist*: the box office champion of 1974 and winner of two Oscars and four Golden Globes. *The Exorcist* re-invigo-

---

rated the horror genre, spawning numerous imitations—none of which matched its quality. In America, *The Exorcist* inspired the Blaxploitation film *Abby* (1974) and the pornographic *The Sexorcist* (1974). More *Exorcist* rip-offs came from abroad: Turkey's *Seytan* (1974) was a shot-for-shot remake of *The Exorcist*; Spain released *Demon Witch Child*, *The Devil's Exorcist*, and *Exorcismo* in 1975; West Germany contributed *Magdalena, Possessed by the Devil* (1976); and in Italy, exorcism scenes were added to Mario Bava's *Lisa and the Devil* (1972) before its international release as *House of Exorcism* (1975). Italy practically made an industry out of possession-themed movies in the 1970s, churning out lurid shockers like *Who Are You?* (1974), *The Antichrist* (1974), *Enter the Devil* (1974), *Naked Exorcism* (1975), *The Exorcist: Italian Style* (1975), *The Night Child* (1976), and *Malabimba: The Malicious Whore* (1979). Warners was so keen to exploit its biggest commercial success, John Calley turned down David Seltzer's satanic-themed screenplay *The Antichrist*, opting to make *Exorcist II* instead. (*The Antichrist* went to Twentieth Century-Fox and was filmed as *The Omen*, the USA's fifth-highest grossing film of 1976.) In the 1970s, sequels rarely matched or surpassed the success of their predecessors and were far less common than they are today. Major studio films tended to not lead to franchises (the James Bond, *Planet of the Apes* and *Airport* pictures notwithstanding). The *Dirty Harry* sequel *Magnum Force* (1973) and *French Connection II* (1975) were lucrative but neither matched the acclaim of their respective predecessors. For the best sequel of the 1970s—Francis Ford Coppola's Academy Award-winning *The Godfather Part II* (1974)—Paramount Pictures had retained most of the key personnel behind *The Godfather* (Coppola, Mario Puzo, Gray Frederickson, Fred Roos, Dean Tavoularis, Gordon Willis, and Peter Zinner) as well as many of the first film's stars. Warners would attempt to do the same for its *Exorcist* sequel.

William Friedkin's *The Exorcist* had a solid story to work from: William Peter Blatty's novel, which Blatty and Friedkin streamlined to translate to film. *Exorcist II* required a story to be created from scratch and Warners was keen to resecure the services of Blatty and Friedkin. Friedkin recalled, "I was asked to direct it, and I respectfully declined. I said "I'd rather direct my nephew's Bar Mitzvah!""[13] In fact, Friedkin was planning *The Devil's Triangle*, a film about the Bermuda Triangle—later

---

13. W Friedkin, quoted in S Biodrowski, "William Friedkin at the Fangoria Weekend of Horrors, Part Two," Aug. 27, 2000, http://www.mania.com/william-friedkin-fangoria-weekend-horrors-part-two_article_23746.html

abandoned it in favor of *Sorcerer*, a remake of Henri-Georges Clouzot's *The Wages of Fear* (1953). Blatty, for his part, had no interest in producing a sequel to *The Exorcist*, literary or cinematic, insisting the ending of *The Exorcist* was conclusive: "Warners did approach me and at that time I thought: the story is over... Karras fell down the steps; he's dead—the story is over. There is no sequel possible. So I declined."[14] He later admitted, "Warner Brothers offered me a lot of money if I would agree to write the sequel to *The Exorcist*. I didn't. But frankly speaking, I wish I'd done it now. Then at least we would never have had *The Heretic*."[15] Blatty's involvement in the film would amount to an early version of the screenplay being run past him.

Facing the prospect of an *Exorcist* sequel made by an entirely new production team, Warners appointed Richard Lederer as producer of the film. For fifteen years, Lederer had been Warners' Executive Vice President of Advertising and Publicity and in that role he had been heavily involved with the marketing of *The Exorcist*. "Once [Warners] had the book they were scared to death they had it," Lederer recalled. "There was tremendous interest, more interest than ever before on any movie in my time. There was very little for me to worry about it in the marketing because it was gonna go bang... I can recite [the marketing plan] in about a dozen words. We open the theater doors and get the fuck out of the way."[16] Lederer insisted *The Exorcist* would be huge and advised Warners to open the film in one hundred theaters. The studio opted for a more cautious twenty-four but scrambled to expand the film's release once the film's mass popularity became obvious. Lederer's savvy regarding *The Exorcist* placed him in good stead for the sequel, his first film as producer, which was conceived as a low-budget affair:

> *The Heretic* was first envisioned as a very inexpensive effort...
> What we essentially wanted to do with the sequel was to redo
> the first movie—have the central character, an investigative
> priest, interview everyone involved in the first exorcism,
> then fade out to unused footage, unused angles from the
> first movie. A low-budget rehash—about $3 million—of

---

14. WP Blatty, quoted in McCabe, p. 156.

15. WP Blatty, quoted in DE Winter, "The Horror Fiction of William Peter Blatty," *A Dark Night's Dreaming: Contemporary American Horror Fiction* (eds: T Magistrale & MA Morrison, Columbia: University of South Carolina Press, 1996), p. 91.

16. R Lederer, quoted in Konow, p. 155.

The Exorcist, a rather cynical approach to moviemaking, I'll admit. But that was the start.[17]

Given that *The Exorcist* was a high-profile major studio film, it might seem odd that its sequel was originally planned with a budget $2 million cheaper than that of the average studio film. Warners' attitude at the time reflects a naivety about sequels that would be unthinkable today, but this was years before the blockbuster success of the *Star Wars*, *Indiana Jones*, *Rocky*, and *Superman* sequels. The low-budget *Exorcist* sequel envisioned by Warners might have made a good profit for the studio, but the project gradually evolved into something far more elaborate and far more expensive, with a budget over four times greater than was originally planned.

In lieu of William Peter Blatty, John Calley and Richard Lederer turned to William Goodhart, a playwright they both admired, to write the *Exorcist* sequel. Goodhart, a Yale physics major and World War II veteran, wrote the stage comedy *Generation* (which ran on Broadway in 1965-1966, starring Henry Fonda) and its 1969 film adaptation (starring David Janssen). Goodhart was a curious choice to write the *Exorcist* sequel, but it is worth remembering that William Peter Blatty was known as a comedy writer before hitting pay dirt with *The Exorcist* (which practically ended Blatty's reputation, though not his career, as a humorist). Goodhart, Calley, and Lederer brainstormed the basic concepts of the *Exorcist* sequel. Goodhart admired *The Exorcist* and was intrigued by the theories of Pierre Teilhard de Chardin (1881-1955), the French Jesuit priest/philosopher/paleontologist/archaeologist upon whom Blatty had partly based the character of Father Lankester Merrin. (Some aspects of Merrin were based on British archaeologist Gerald Lankester Harding, whom Blatty had met in Beirut.) In his posthumously published pseudo-scientific treatise *Le Phénomène Humain* (1955), Teilhard theorized that the evolutionary process will, in a teleological fashion, become conscious of itself, and humankind's increasingly complex collective consciousness will eventually culminate in a state of divine unification:

We have seen and admitted that evolution is an ascent towards consciousness... Therefore it should culminate forwards in some sort of supreme consciousness. But must not that consciousness, if it is to be supreme, contain in the highest

---

17. R Lederer, quoted in B Pallenberg, *The Making of Exorcist II: The Heretic* (New York: Warner Books, 1977), p. 12.

degree what is the perfection of our consciousness—the illuminating involution of the being upon itself?... Because it contains and engenders consciousness, space-time is necessarily *of a convergent* nature. Accordingly its enormous layers, followed in the right direction, must somewhere ahead become involuted to a point which we might call Omega, which fuses and consumes them integrally in itself... The Future-Universal could not be anything else but the Hyper-Personal—at the Omega Point.[18]

Lederer explained how, as Goodhart integrated Teilhard's ideas, the screenplay took shape:

Goodhart's [concept] was the World-Mind-Teilhard de Chardin approach, that one day all our minds will evolve to a point where they'll be able to join, like atoms, into a huge telepathic entity. Our concept was more down-to-earth and centred on the Vatican investigation. Calley imagined that two groups would still be interested in the exorcism and the deaths of the first movie—the cops, because of the murders, and the Church, because an ecclesiastical heavyweight had lost his life. The Church, maybe, would be worried about ridicule, especially now that they would be unable to keep abreast of the times—something they have always done brilliantly, in the past... Well, we wound up with a very good script, which met with a whole lot of enthusiasm.[19]

Goodhart's script was titled *The Heretic*, a name designed to echo *The Exorcist*, and centered on the investigation by a priest, Father Philip Lamont, into the exorcism that had been performed on Regan MacNeil. Regan was now being treated by a (male) psychiatrist, Dr Gene Tuskin. *The Heretic* sought to clarify why Regan had been possessed (a question left ambiguous in *The Exorcist*) and how this was connected to the ideas of Teilhard de Chardin. (The notion of the Catholic Church impounding Father Merrin's writings and questioning his reputation echoes Teilhard's writings being censored by the Church on the grounds they contradicted ortho-

---

18. P Teilhard de Chardin, *The Phenomenon of Man* (London: Harper & Row, 1965), pp. 258-260.

19. R Lederer, quoted in Pallenberg, pp. 12-13.

doxy.) Goodhart contended that Regan was spiritually unique—capable of telepathic communication and healing—and was as one of those who would help usher in the next phase of human evolution; she would attract evil, as Satan would have a vested interest in doing away with her. Like *The Godfather Part II*, *The Heretic* would incorporate prequel aspects: Goodhart's script brought back Merrin, who had died in *The Exorcist*. Flashback sequences would depict Merrin's encounter with the demon during an exorcism in Africa, an event mentioned briefly in *The Exorcist*. Exorcising the demon from a boy named Kokumo began Merrin's quest to find others targeted for possession. Goodhart's script also featured *The Exorcist*'s Detective Kinderman, and "the Synchronizer," a machine designed for mutual hypnosis, allowing people to enter each other's minds. By tapping into Regan's mind, the Synchronizer unwittingly unleashes the demon that had been dormant since the exorcism. With a tentative script, Warners sought a director for *The Heretic*.

In June 1975, *The Hollywood Reporter* announced *The Heretic* would begin shooting in January 1976 with Sam O'Steen directing William Goodhart's script. O'Steen was one of the most respected film editors in the business, with credits including *Who's Afraid of Virginia Woolf?* (1966), *Cool Hand Luke* (1967), *The Graduate* (1967), *Chinatown* (1974), and Roman Polanski's *Rosemary's Baby* (1968). Editing Polanski's satanic melodrama was almost certainly the reason Warners considered him a viable director for *The Heretic*. By July 1975, O'Steen had finished shooting his first motion picture as director, the Warners musical *Sparkle*, and on September 24, 1975, *Variety* reported he was still attached to the *Exorcist* sequel. In fact, O'Steen never officially signed on to *The Heretic*. He later directed the TV sequel *Look What's Happened to Rosemary's Baby* (1976) and edited *Amityville II: The Possession* (1982)—a possession-themed potboiler with a last act that rips off *The Exorcist*.

Figuring the scale of *The Heretic* required a director with sufficient experience, John Calley and Richard Lederer decided upon English filmmaker John Boorman. Born in Shepperton in 1933 and raised as a lower-middle-class Londoner, Boorman had aspired from a young age to a career in filmmaking. He joined BBC Radio Bristol in the early 1950s and contributed articles to *The Manchester Guardian* before spending several years as a National Conscript infantryman. Boorman resumed his broadcasting career in 1957 by joining Southampton's Southern Television, where he honed his film directing and editing skills. "I was only 24 years old and found that I had fifty people working for me, at the same time responsible for three hours of television every week. It was totally exhausting," Boorman recalled.[20] He joined the BBC in 1961, became head of the Documentary Unit in 1962, and by 1965 he made his feature film directorial debut with *Catch Us If You Can*, a vehicle for the British pop group, the Dave Clark Five. (Incidentally, the nascent phase of Boorman's career bore notable similarities to William Friedkin's. Boorman and Friedkin both directed documentaries for television; like Boorman, Friedkin's first motion picture as director was a pop-music vehicle—*Good Times* [1967], starring Sonny and Cher.) Released in the USA as *Having a Wild Weekend, Catch Us If You Can* received some good notices, although it failed to replicate the success of its most obvious antecedent, Richard Lester's Beatles film *A Hard Day's Night* (1964). Boorman was offered the job of controller of BBC2, but he declined the position to concentrate on his filmmaking career.

Boorman's first Hollywood film was the crime drama *Point Blank* (1967), adapted from Donald E. Westlake's 1962 novel *The Hunter*. Filmed partially in California's disused Alcatraz prison, *Point Blank* starred Lee Marvin (as a vengeance-minded anti-hero) and a strong supporting cast (Angie Dickinson, Keenan Wynn, John Vernon, Lloyd Bochner, and Carroll O'Connor). Boorman elevated the film's source material with an energetic style: alternately stark and dazzling, combining elements of classic *film noir* with unusual touches characteristic of the French New Wave. A critical, though not a commercial, success for Metro-Goldwyn-Mayer, *Point Blank* anticipated tough urban thrillers like *Bullitt* (1968), *Dirty Harry* (1971), and *The French Connection* (1971).

In mid-1967 Boorman was reported to be working with producers Irwin Winkler and Bob Chartoff to adapt Tom Wolfe's *The Kandy-Kolored Tangerine Flake Streamline Baby* for MGM, a film that never eventuated. Boorman's next film, the World War II drama *Hell in the Pacific* (1968), told the story of an American pilot and a Japanese navy captain stranded on a deserted island in the Pacific Ocean, their mutual distrust and conflict giving way to grudging cooperation. Starring real-life WWII veterans Lee Marvin and Toshirō Mifune—the only two actors to appear in the entire film—*Hell in the Pacific* was filmed, rather gorgeously, on location in the Rock Islands of Palau. Boorman returned to England to produce and direct the inventive, if uneven, Marxist tragicomedy *Leo the Last* (1970), adapted by Boorman and Bill Stair from George Tabori's one-act play *The*

---

20. J Boorman, quoted in M Thrift, "John Boorman on Kubrick, Connery and the lost Lord of the Rings script." *Little White Lies*, Jan. 18, 2018, https://lwlies.com/interviews/john-boorman-lost-lord-of-the-rings-script/

Prince. Starring Marcello Mastroianni as an *ennui*-ridden European aristocrat who becomes an unlikely liberal revolutionary in a London ghetto, *Leo the Last* won Boorman a Best Director Award at Cannes and was a hit for United Artists in France, but a financial failure elsewhere.

During post-production of *Leo the Last*, Boorman approached United Artists with his idea of a film about King Arthur and the Knights of the Round Table. The studio's counteroffer was an adaptation of J.R.R. Tolkien's three-part fantasy novel, *The Lord of the Rings* (1954-1955), which had become a cultural phenomenon by the mid-1960s. Over six months, Boorman wrote a *Lord of the Rings* screenplay in collaboration with Robert "Rospo" Pallenberg, a young Italian-English architect student with filmmaking aspirations whom Boorman had met in New York in 1969. "We spent months not only writing it, but trying to research how we were going to do the effects, to make those little fellows work," Boorman recalled. "By the time we'd finished, United Artists had lost a bunch of money and simply didn't have enough to make it."[21] After financial setbacks and a management reshuffle prompted United Artists to pass on Boorman and Pallenberg's screenplay, the project evolved eventually into the 1978 animated film directed by Ralph Bakshi. (Boorman dismissed Bakshi's incomplete rendition of Tolkien's epic, but his own live-action version would not have been better: Boorman planned to truncate Tolkien's three volumes into one film, with Hobbits to be played by children with facial hair and dubbed adult voices.) Stinging from this rejection as well as *Leo the Last*'s dismal box office, Boorman opted to make a more commercial-minded film: the violent thriller *Deliverance* (1972), adapted from James Dickey's novel, and released by Warner Brothers. (Sam Peckinpah was Warners' original choice to direct *Deliverance* before the studio fell out with the mercurial filmmaker; Peckinpah directed *Straw Dogs* [1971] instead.) *Deliverance* depicts four city men—played by Jon Voight, Burt Reynolds, Ned Beatty, and Ronny Cox—whose canoeing trip down a remote river in the North Georgian backwoods turns into a harrowing ordeal of survivalism. Noted for its "Dueling Banjos" musical sequence and dangerous whitewater stunts, and its notorious "Squeal like a pig" scene in which Beatty's character is raped, *Deliverance* was a huge commercial hit. It was also nominated for three Academy Awards, including for Best Picture and Best Director.

Boorman's next project was a self-written film, but he had difficulty finding a studio to finance it. "Nobody wanted to do it," he claimed. "Warners didn't want to do it, even though I'd made a shitload of money for

---

21. J Boorman, quoted in Thrift.

them."[22] It was Twentieth Century-Fox that chose to fund Boorman's film: the allegorical, post-apocalyptic science-fiction fantasy *Zardoz* (1974). Written, produced, and directed by Boorman, and starring Sean Connery and Charlotte Rampling, *Zardoz* was a commercial failure and found little favor amongst film critics, many of whom dismissed the film as pretentious, self-indulgent, dull, and weird. Critic Pauline Kael remarked, "Everybody is entitled to a certain amount of craziness, but John Boorman may have exceeded the quota."[23] Boorman spent two years working on *Zardoz* but made no money from it: he forewent his fee, expecting that the film's low, $1.57 million budget would ensure him a profit share. *Zardoz* eventually found an appreciative cult audience, but its initial failure meant Boorman did not have the clout to produce his King Arthur film. In October 1975 he travelled to Los Angeles where he was asked by John Calley to read William Goodhart's script for *The Heretic*. Disinterested at first, Boorman took the script to the Racquet Club in Palm Springs, and after some tennis, he read it.

On paper, John Boorman was a feasible choice to direct *The Heretic*. He made money for Warners with *Deliverance*; his films demonstrated great range and visual imagination; he had an interest in filming the fantastical; and, with *Hell in the Pacific* and *Deliverance*, he demonstrated an aptitude for the rigors of location filming. There was just one problem.

John Boorman hated *The Exorcist*.

John Calley was not unaware of this. When he secured the film rights to Blatty's novel for Warners, Calley offered the project to Boorman, whose stock was high in the aftermath of *Deliverance*. Boorman recalled, "Calley asked me to make [*The Exorcist*]. Would I read it and give him a fast answer? I found it repulsive. I told Calley it would be a film about a child being tortured. Calley said, 'You're such a snob.' This was a huge bestseller. What business did I have to moralize?"[24] Boorman told Michel Ciment,

> I replied that not only would I refuse [to direct *The Exorcist*], but that I didn't think Warners should produce it. It seemed to me a very difficult film to make, since everything depended on the performance of a twelve-year-old child.

22. J Boorman, quoted in Thrift.

23. P Kael, "O Consuella!", *The New Yorker*, Feb. 18, 1974. Reprinted in *Reeling* (New York: Warner Books, 1976), p. 376.

24. J Boorman, *Adventures of a Suburban Boy* (London: Faber & Faber, 2003), p. 204.

The problem of rendering the story credible was enormous. And, as a father, I found the book extremely tasteless, cruel and sadistic towards children.[25]

(Had Boorman felt otherwise, he still would have been no guarantee to direct *The Exorcist*. To protect his material, William Peter Blatty had insisted on producing the film in addition to scripting it. Blatty had input on who Warners hired to direct and it is unlikely he would have approved of Boorman. William Friedkin was Blatty's first choice but it took the success of *The French Connection* for Warners to hire the outspoken director.)

After turning down *The Exorcist*, Boorman directed his own project, *Zardoz*: released in early 1974, the film crashed and burned while *The Exorcist* was enjoying its lucrative theatrical run. Throughout his autobiography, Boorman makes repeated references to *The Exorcist*'s supposed advocating of child torture, and his condemnation of Friedkin's film is an inadvertent confession of his unsuitability to make the sequel. Why *did* Boorman agree to make the sequel to a film he hated? Perhaps he *had* convinced himself *The Heretic* would be "not so much a sequel as a response to *The Exorcist*"[26] and that "far from being destructive, the story was an optimistic one, which reinforced one's faith in life."[27] It could be reasonably assumed that Boorman, once again chastened by box office failure, sought to regain his standing by filming a more commercial property. After *Leo the Last*, Boorman made *Deliverance*; after *Zardoz*, he agreed to make *The Heretic*. As the sequel to *The Exorcist*, *The Heretic* had advantages such as brand recognition and a readymade audience. Boorman hated *The Exorcist* but he had no qualms about commandeering its fan-base:

The idea of making a film which drew on the expectation of an existing audience was what I found exciting. Every film has to struggle to find a connection with its audience... Pale plagiarism is what Hollywood's mostly about. One of my difficulties is finding this connection, because my work always tends to be somewhat experimental. Here I saw the chance to make an extremely ambitious film without having

25. J Boorman, quoted in Ciment, p. 164.

26. Boorman, p. 213.

27. J Boorman, quoted in Ciment, p. 164.

to spend the time developing this connection. I could make assumptions and then take the audience on a very adventurous cinematic journey."[28]

When *The Heretic* went into production, Boorman toed Warners' line, conceding "there is no doubt that Billy Friedkin displayed extraordinary skill in pulling [*The Exorcist*] off the way he did. I think very few directors could have done it."[29] (Friedkin received no mention in Boorman's memoirs, *Adventures of a Suburban Boy*. Returning the favor, so to speak, Friedkin doesn't mention Boorman—or *Exorcist II*, for that matter—in his own memoirs, *The Friedkin Connection*.) In his autobiography, Boorman is candid as to why he agreed to make *Exorcist II*, implying, condescendingly, that people who liked *The Exorcist* were sadists:

> I was tempted. I would get a substantial fee. I would have a large budget and resources at my disposal to make what amounted to an experimental metaphysical thriller involving innovative special effects and huge sets. Millions of people had enjoyed watching a child being tortured in *The Exorcist*. *The Heretic* would be the antidote, a film about goodness rather than evil. I should have known better. [Stanley] Kubrick told me the only way to do a sequel to *The Exorcist* is to give them even more gore and horror than before. No one is interested in goodness.[30]

(Incidentally—in a 1980 interview with future Boorman biographer Michel Ciment—Stanley Kubrick named *The Exorcist* as a horror film he liked and confessed to having not seen *The Heretic*.) Boorman believed Goodhart's story to be "extremely compelling" and was intrigued by the device of the Synchronizer and its philosophical applications:

> What appealed to me was the Teilhard de Chardin idea of people coming together into a new sort of contact with each other, which could be a force for either good or evil—an apt description of what is actually going on in the world. We're

---

28. J Boorman, quoted in Pallenberg, p. 82.

29. J Boorman, quoted in Pallenberg, p. 82.

30. Boorman, p. 215.

seeing this happening, for instance, in communication—
the telephone, television—is a new science-created kind
of nervous system. In the script, the machine called the
Synchronizer, which is actually based on experiments in metal
hypnosis done in the thirties, carries that communication a
step further.[31]

Boorman was also intrigued by the story's lead male character, Father
Lamont: "I had a Jesuit education, and the idea of making a metaphysical
thriller was terribly seductive to my psyche. I was also intrigued by the
idea of a relationship between a young girl and a priest, the poignancy of
unresolvable sexuality."[32] Boorman's claim of "a Jesuit education" is not
quite true: he was educated at the Salesian School in Chertsey, Surrey. In
his memoirs, Boorman dismissed the Salesians as "a blander, less intel-
lectually rigorous version" of the Jesuits.[33]

Boorman outlined his conditions to Warners: he would produce as
well as direct *The Heretic* and, wary of studio interference, he would answer only to John Calley. These demands were accepted. "Calley made
John Boorman an offer he couldn't refuse, and with his coming on board,
the whole picture changed, in both senses of the phrase," said Richard
Lederer.[34] Now co-producer, Lederer took charge of *The Heretic*'s marketing and distribution, leaving the film's other aspects to Boorman. On November 11, 1975, *Daily Variety* reported that John Boorman would direct
The Heretic. After his announcement as director, Boorman described the
project to *The New York Times* as "a fascinating story dealing with spiritual evolution and the need for God. I intend to investigate the characters
and ideas more thoroughly and make the story more terrifying and profound. Some people felt that the first *Exorcist* was destructive. I think of
this one as a healing movie."[35] *The Heretic* was reported to begin shooting
on January 3, 1976, with an $8 million budget.

Although Boorman professed admiration towards William Goodhart's screenplay, he regarded it largely as a springboard for his own ideas,

31. J Boorman, quoted in Pallenberg, pp. 14-15.

32. J Boorman, quoted in Pallenberg, p. 15.

33. Boorman, p. 29.

34. R Lederer, quoted in Pallenberg, pp. 12-13.

35. J Boorman, quoted in Oalar Hendrek, "What Will 'Jaws' and 'Exorcist' do for an
     Encore?" *The New York Times*, Jun. 27, 1976.

and by tailoring *The Heretic* to suit his personal vision, Boorman asserted himself, to all intents and purposes, as the "author" of the film. The relegation of Goodhart's authorship was, in essence, a fulfilment of film theorist Peter Wollen's interpretation of *la politique des auteurs:*

> Incidents and episodes in the original screenplay or novel can act as catalysts; they are the agents which are introduced into the mind (conscious or unconscious) of the auteur and react there with the motifs and themes characteristic of his work. The director does not subordinate himself to another author; his source is only a pretext, which provides catalysts, scenes which fuse with his own preoccupations to produce a radically new work.[36]

Even so, Boorman had no desire at this stage to exclude William Goodhart from rewrites of *The Heretic*. In Ireland—his home since 1969—Boorman began reworking the script with Goodhart, later admitting that little progress was made: "Although Goodhart is a man of formidable intelligence and powerful imagination, he writes slowly and carefully. In discussion he would resist my ideas, and only after a couple of days would be prepared to consider them."[37] In the midst of rewriting *The Heretic*, Boorman flew to Rome to meet with Rospo Pallenberg's father, Corrado Pallenberg—the Rome correspondent for *The London Evening Times* and author of *Inside the Vatican* (1960). The purpose of Boorman's visit to Rome was twofold: research for the script, and inquiries into the possibility of shooting parts of the film in the Vatican. Boorman explained that Corrado Pallenberg "took us around the Vatican. We spent time talking to the Jesuits in Rome, getting background on the character of the priest, Father Lamont. We wanted to work out the hierarchical system within the Vatican—who, for instance, would be sending Lamont on his investigation? At the same time, it became obvious we wouldn't get permission to shoot our movie in the Vatican, so building Vatican sets became a necessary alternative."[38] Boorman also hoped to film location footage in Ethiopia, but this proved to be logistically impossible, as Boorman later admitted:

---

36. P Wollen, *Signs and Meaning in the Cinema: New and Enlarged* (Bloomington: Indiana University Press, 1972), p. 113.

37. J Boorman, quoted in Pallenberg, p. 16.

38. J Boorman, quoted in Pallenberg, p. 16.

In Ethiopia there was civil war, and famine, and plague, and it would have taken several days by mule train to get to the fantastic churches of Lalibela, where much of the action would take place. There, isolated communities were practicing Christianity as it was in the first century, with the same vividness and simplicity. We wanted to contrast that with the decadence and pomp of the Vatican. So now I knew I'd have to do Africa in the studio, as well.[39]

Although the reasons for not filming in Africa were practical and budgetary, Boorman provided a more fanciful explanation in his memoirs: "To give the film a heightened dream-like style, we decided to the shoot the outdoor African sequences in the studio rather than on location."[40] In any case, plans to film in North Africa, Italy, and Georgetown were scrapped. Africa would be replicated in the Warner Brothers Studio in Burbank, California, supplemented by some exterior shots in Page, Arizona. There would be some exterior filming in New York City, but almost all of the story's locations would be filmed in Burbank. Hollywood had a long history of shooting exterior scenes in soundstages, but the more recent trend had been to film on location. Warners preferred to have *Exorcist II* filmed at Burbank to save money, and Boorman embraced the notion; shooting indoors would facilitate his desire to create a more distorted, stylized reality. The curtailing of exterior photography would heavily influence the overall look of the final film. Even the Mac-Neil house in Georgetown had to be simulated in the studio, as after six months of fruitless negotiations, Warners was refused permission by homeowner Florence Mahoney to film inside the 3600 Prospect Street house used for *The Exorcist*. Boorman also had to replicate the infamous "Hitchcock Steps" adjacent to the house, as Washington city officials forbade the filmmakers to shoot scenes by the real steps. Multiple soundstages in the Warners lot would host *The Heretic*'s various interior and exterior locations. Dr Tuskin's institute, Regan's bedroom in the MacNeil house, and the Prospect Street exterior were filmed in Stage 4/11; the Vatican interior in Stage 12; the massive Ethiopian rock chimney (built horizontally, shot vertically) in Stage 15; the Ethiopian rock church, the Hitchcock Steps, and the mud city of Jepti in Stage 16; and the South American shantytown chapel in Stage 25.

---

39. J Boorman, quoted in Pallenberg, p. 16.

40. Boorman, p. 219.

By late 1975, John Calley had vacated his position at Warners—temporarily, as it turned out. His replacement was Guy McElwaine. A former professional baseball player who pitched in the Minor Leagues, McElwaine moved into show business in 1955 when he joined Metro-Goldwyn-Mayer's publicity department. He left MGM in 1959 to go into management and public relations; his clients included Frank Sinatra, Judy Garland, and Warren Beatty. In 1969, McElwaine joined the talent agency Creative Management Associates, where he became the first agent to sign a young filmmaker named Steven Spielberg. McElwaine was still working for CMA when he joined the Warners board. Since John Boorman did not enjoy with McElwaine the same sort of relationship he'd had with John Calley, it was decided he would answer directly to Ted Ashley and his aide, Alan Shayne, both of whom exerted tremendous influence upon some of the key casting choices of the film.

The Heretic began as a film designed by committee, and had Warners employed a journeyman director—a mere orchestrator of resources—the finished product would likely have been impersonal and unchallenging, but lucrative. With the idiosyncratic John Boorman at the helm and intent on remolding the script, *The Heretic* was reconfigured into a more personal and ambitious project—but by asking for and receiving almost total creative freedom, Boorman would bring massive problems down upon the film, and upon himself.

3

Pazuzu's Players: Casting *The Heretic*

Tom Snyder (**Dan Aykroyd**): *Linda, you could say you're a gal who's been through the mill at the age of nineteen, you've been around the block a few times. Now, you did a picture called* The Exorcist... *Now, here you are: you're a gal of thirteen, you're strapped to a bed, you're using language that's—to say the least—a bit raw! You spend a year of your life portraying the very embodiment of evil—Satan incarnate, the Antichrist... How the heck did you keep up with your schoolwork??*

Linda Blair (**Carrie Fisher**): (laughs) *Well, Tom, you know— I didn't! And I'm suffering for it now, you know? I mean, there's a lot of stuff I don't know! I can barely read English!...And I can name, like, only three states! And you know, sometimes, when I'm in an airport or something, I pick up a magazine and I see my picture... I really miss being able read what they're saying about me!*

– Parody of *Tomorrow with Tom Snyder* on
Saturday Night Live, November 18, 1978

WITH WILLIAM GOODHART WORKING on *The Heretic's* script in New York, John Boorman returned to California to cast the film. Warner Brothers, unsurprisingly, sought to retain as many stars from *The Exorcist* as possible. However, Ellen Burstyn, who received top billing in *The Ex-*

The principal cast of *Exorcist II: The Heretic*. Top row, L-R: Linda Blair as Regan MacNeil, Richard Burton as Father Philip Lamont, and Louise Fletcher as Dr. Gene Tuskin. Bottom row, L-R: Max von Sydow as Father Lankester Merrin, Kitty Winn as Sharon Spencer, Paul Henreid as Cardinal Jaros, and James Earl Jones as Kokumo.

orcist as protagonist Chris MacNeil before winning a Best Actress Oscar for Martin Scorsese's *Alice Doesn't Live Here Anymore* (1974), declined to appear in *The Heretic*, opting to make Alain Resnais' *Providence* (1977) instead. "I turned down a lot of money for *The Exorcist 2*," Burstyn later recalled. "You can't make a brand out of *The Exorcist*. It's just ridiculous."[41] Burstyn's refusal to participate was known to Warners months before John Boorman joined the project. In the revised script, Chris MacNeil is referred to but not seen; the story explains that Chris (an actor) is filming a movie overseas, leaving her daughter in New York.

Warners had better luck with Linda Blair, who agreed to reprise her role of Regan MacNeil. Before the notoriety of *The Exorcist*, Blair enjoyed a successful career in child modeling but was, by Hollywood standards, an unknown. Picked out of allegedly thousands of child actors, Blair un-

---

41. E Burstyn, quoted in B Lee, "Ellen Burstyn: 'Women on screen were prostitutes or victims—I wanted to embody a hero,'" *The Guardian*, Apr. 27, 2018, https://www.theguardian.com/film/2018/apr/26/ellen-burstyn-women-on-screen-were-prostitutes-or-victims-i-wanted-to-embody-a-hero

derwent four months of auditions and screen tests and acquitted herself admirably in a difficult role. For her portrayal of the twelve-year-old Regan, Blair won a Golden Globe Award and was nominated for an Oscar (which she lost to Tatum O'Neal for *Paper Moon*). *The Exorcist* made Blair the subject of tabloid speculation and bizarre innuendoes ranging from merely untrue (she was psychologically damaged by the film!) to plainly ridiculous (she *really was* demonically possessed!). In the immediate years following *The Exorcist*, Blair's acting credits were limited to a supporting role in *Airport 1975* (1974) and lead roles in the TV movies *Born Innocent* (1974), *Sara T: Portrait of a Teenage Alcoholic* (1975), and *Sweet Hostage* (1975). As far as the wider public was concerned, Blair was still the *Exorcist* girl, even if Blair herself was now a young woman navigating the paparazzi-strewn path of female celebrities under the media spotlight. (For example, Blair's relationship with Australian singer Rick Springfield, ten years her senior, inevitably garnered tabloid scrutiny.) Blair agreed to play the now-teenage Regan in *The Heretic*, and her involvement in the film was announced by reports in January 1976. Although *The Heretic* would not alleviate typecasting concerns, Blair's initial doubts in the project were allayed by the script she was presented with. "I just couldn't see anyone writing something that could measure up to the original," Blair told *People Weekly*. "Where could they possibly find another whopper of a story? But after a year of talking about it, they have finally come up with a good script."[42] Not only did Blair like the screenplay of *The Heretic*, but the film shoot would take her mind off her parents' recent divorce and, for the first time, she would receive top billing in a major studio motion picture—with a significantly larger paycheck than she had ever received for anything before. Blair was paid $750,000 upfront to star in *The Heretic* with reports indicating she stood to make up to $2 million in total should the film replicate the profits of *The Exorcist*. However, wary of her experience with Dick Smith's extensive effects in *The Exorcist*, Blair refused to wear demon make-up again. A double would therefore be used for the demonic Regan scenes in *The Heretic*.

Another star of *The Exorcist* secured for the sequel was Max von Sydow, the Swedish actor who played Father Merrin, who died attempting to exorcise Regan. Von Sydow came to international prominence for his portrayal of the knight Antonius Block in *The Seventh Seal* (1957)—the first of eleven films von Sydow appeared in for director Ingmar Berg-

---

42. L Blair, quoted in B Lardine, "Peaches and cream Linda's second trip with the Devil for $2 million." *People Weekly*, Jul. 8, 1976.

man—and his most high-profile role was as Jesus Christ in George Stevens' biblical epic *The Greatest Story Ever Told* (1965). The actor was in his early 40s when, augmented by Dick Smith's make-up, he portrayed the elderly Father Merrin in *The Exorcist*; in *The Heretic*, he would portray both old and young versions of Merrin, in flashbacks and dream sequences. According to John Boorman, von Sydow was initially reluctant to appear in *The Heretic*:

> He hated the first film, the torturing of the child, and thought it was morally destructive. The links with the first film were diminishing. I was getting desperate. I met Max and argued that by making the sequel he could perhaps repair the damage he had helped to inflict. He said that Jesuitical sophistry made no sense to a practical Swede. He had a goodness and a kindness that I felt was vital to the film and eventually I talked him round.[43]

Von Sydow's feelings about *The Exorcist* were complicated. According to William Friedkin, the actor pursued the role of Merrin vehemently, beating out Paul Scofield for the part. However, von Sydow developed an antipathy towards the film after its release, believing it conveyed a resentment of young people: "I was shocked by the perspective it opened for me, about our days, and our attitude to a younger generation, to children."[44] However, von Sydow had no qualms working with Friedkin again, in the stage play *Duet for One* (1981), and many years later he spoke of *The Exorcist* in admiring terms: "It's a brilliantly made film. Very well done, and of course very scary… William Peter Blatty's novel is very good, also."[45]

As conceived by William Goodhart, Father Philip Lamont, the priest who conducts the Church's investigation into Regan MacNeil's exorcism, was a young man: compulsive, wrestling with his faith, and in awe of the teachings of his late mentor, Father Merrin. Boorman described Lamont as "disaffected—a familiar dilemma among modern priesthood. Not

43. Boorman, p. 219.

44. M von Sydow, quoted in *The Fear of God: 25 Years of The Exorcist*. BBC, 1998.

45. M von Sydow, quoted in S Reynolds, "Max von Sydow interview: 'I was never scared by *The Exorcist*,'" *Digital Spy*, Feb. 14, 2012, http://www.digitalspy.co.uk/movies/interviews/a365668/max-von-sydow-interview-i-was-never-scared-by-the-exorcist.html

close, really, to God or man, he discovers a spiritual connection through the Synchronizer that religion cannot give him. But in doing so, he confronts enormously powerful forces of evil... At the time the priest in the script was a young man, fierce in his beliefs, a fighter."[46] Boorman's choice for the role was 37-year-old Jon Voight, Best Actor nominee for *Midnight Cowboy* (1969) and the top-billed star of Boorman's *Deliverance*. Voight had returned to the stage when Boorman approached him for *The Heretic*: "[He] was playing Hamlet at that time. He was extraordinary, one of the very best of the dozen or more I have seen in my lifetime. It was a painful, tormented portrayal, and the madness utterly convincing. It is an overwhelming ordeal for any actor."[47] The role of Father Lamont intrigued Voight, who had been raised Catholic and educated in New York's Archbishop Stepinac High School and Washington D.C.'s Catholic University of America. In late January it was reported that Voight had joined the cast of *The Heretic*. According to Boorman, the actor alienated William Goodhart further:

> Goodhart came back and we put together a draft, dated December 22, 1975. After Christmas we had a meeting, Jon, Bill, and I, at my bungalow at the Beverly Hills Hotel. Bill was upset, I think, at the kind of freewheeling improvisation that Jon was indulging in, and he became very defensive. Conversely, I am always stimulated by the input of actors and other collaborators. A movie grows out of this convergence; this is how one breathes life into it.[48]

Goodhart's resentment was unsurprising. His script was being altered by someone who had not formally committed to the film, and for all this, Voight eventually opted *not* to play Father Lamont. In 1977, Boorman claimed that "a strong divergence grew up between us. [Voight] wanted character scenes showing the priest's background; I thought these had no place in a metaphysical thriller."[49] This would demonstrate narrow thinking on Boorman's part—after all, *The Exorcist* emphasized the tortured nature of Father Karras by depicting his background and guilt over his in-

---

46. J Boorman, quoted in Pallenberg, p. 15.

47. Boorman, p. 216.

48. J Boorman, quoted in Pallenberg, p. 17.

49. J Boorman, quoted in Pallenberg, p. 17.

ability to take care of his impoverished, sickly mother during her terminal decline. However, Boorman was probably being discreet with his earlier explanation: in 2003, he revealed a different reason for Jon Voight turning down *Exorcist II*:

> Jon was a kind and caring husband. He is a deeply spiritual man, but he has a dark, shadow side. Father Lamont's wrestle with evil was something that he connected with and feared. Yet he could not make up his mind... He was still in the grip of Hamlet. He had fallen in love with the young actress playing Ophelia. She was a wild free spirit, a redhead with a fierce temper and unpredictable sexual appetites. She found his obsession with her oppressive. She was fickle. She would come and go. Jon was demented. He had always been devoted to his family and now he was torn apart. The dark side was demanding its due... Father Lamont's contest between his goodness and his evil was close to Jon's own, too close. After much agonising, he decided not to play the role.[50]

By 1976, Voight's relationship with Stacey Pickren had ended his marriage to Marcheline Bertrand. (Voight and Bertrand married in 1971 and had two children, actors James Haven and Angelina Jolie. Their divorce was initiated in 1978 and finalized in 1980.) The relationship between John Boorman and William Goodhart was also in a state of deterioration, which took its toll on *The Heretic's* production. Nobody was satisfied with the script, and by December 1975, the film had fallen behind its planned November 1975-February 1976 shoot. With filming postponed until April, Boorman decided to develop the script "in parallel" with Goodhart, meaning the two men worked apart. Boorman then turned to Rospo Pallenberg, his *Lord of the Rings* co-writer and general assistant on *Deliverance*. "We talked about the script; he had a lot of ideas, and he developed a structure which I approved, and we got out a new version of the script, which was done much too fast," Boorman said. "It was rambling, which often happens when you rewrite and impose new information on an old structure. We gave it to Goodhart, who didn't like it at all, of course."[51] Goodhart, who had already felt marginalized by John Boorman and Jon Voight, also resisted the input of Rospo Pallenberg. According to

---

50. Boorman, pp. 216-217.

51. J Boorman, quoted in Pallenberg, pp. 17-18.

Boorman, Goodhart refused to rewrite the script based on the structure proposed by Pallenberg:

> He couldn't get a foothold on it; he couldn't get started. It was too different, he thought, from his own sensibilities. We began to spend hours arguing over a single line of dialogue, which as everyone involved in the making of a picture knows, will probably be changed two or three times during rehearsals, or on the set the day it is being shot, or even in post-production, in re-recording the dialogue. Finally, Goodhart and I separated. It was rather painful for me, because I like him a great deal. He resented Rospo, he resented Voight, he resented any external input. He's a playwright—*Generation* was his big success—and playwrights rent their words. Screenwriters sell them outright, whether for a few thousand or a few hundred thousand dollars. The words of a play are rarely altered. But the essence of a screenplay is that it must have a strong structure but be totally flexible.[52]

A film script must be subject to change, and Goodhart, a relatively inexperienced *screen*writer, would have been naïve to think otherwise. However, Goodhart's sense of propriety is understandable: his involvement with *The Heretic* preceded Boorman's; his script was good enough for John Calley and Richard Lederer; and since Goodhart liked *The Exorcist* and Boorman did not, it would be reasonable to assume Goodhart resented how far *The Heretic* was straying from *The Exorcist*. In any case, Rospo Pallenberg's imposition ended William Goodhart's active involvement in *The Heretic*. The schism between Boorman and Goodhart did not help the film. (Friedkin and Blatty had their disagreements over *The Exorcist*, especially during post-production, but theirs, generally, was a mutually beneficial collaboration.) "I was distressed at this development with Goodhart because of my great admiration for him and for the brilliant story he had written," Boorman said. "I told him that the film would remain true to the spirit of his tale but that I had to re-express it in cinematic terms. So now I had Rospo come in in earnest to spend all his time writing, and the movie started to grow and take shape."[53]

---

52. J Boorman, quoted in Pallenberg, p. 18.

53. J Boorman, quoted in Pallenberg, p. 18.

Pallenberg exerted a tremendous influence on the creative direction of *The Heretic*. Revised drafts of the script were credited to "William Goodhart and Rospo Pallenberg," but as Goodhart was contractually obliged to receive sole screenwriting credit, *Exorcist II* was officially written by William Goodhart with Pallenberg credited as "Creative Associate," industry code for an uncredited writer. (Similar credit, for instance, was given to Carl Sandburg for *The Greatest Story Ever Told* [1965] and to Tom Mankiewicz for *Superman* [1978].) Pallenberg's wife Barbara, who had worked as a secretary for Boorman during the making of *Deliverance*, was commissioned to write a book on the making of *The Heretic*. Boorman remarked there was more horror in the book than in the film itself. "Rospo's wife, Barbara, was always at my side, watching, sharing the tribulations. We were in daily intimate contact, as close as lovers," Boorman later recalled. "She had seen all that I had seen and felt it as deeply. It struck me that the probing interview, the professional study of one person by another, is the post-modern relationship. Barbara and I became bonded by what she knew of me, and the journey we had taken together through the making of the movie."[54]

The death of actor Lee J. Cobb on February 11, 1976, led to a massive rewrite of *The Heretic*. Cobb portrayed the rumpled, *Columbo*-esque Detective William F. Kinderman in *The Exorcist*, and the character was intended to have a more central role in *The Heretic*. Cobb's fatal heart attack occurred, reportedly, the day the script of *The Heretic* arrived at his home. His part was written out of *The Heretic* without any publicity. Boorman later claimed Cobb's death caused "a bigger story problem. No sooner did we shore up the story, when down it would tumble on our heads."[55] One might well ask why Cobb's death necessitated a drastic rewrite. If Kinderman was so central to *The Heretic* that the character's absence caused such a problem, why didn't Boorman simply recast the role? Lee J. Cobb turned in a fine performance in *The Exorcist*, but his was a supporting role: Kinderman was a major character in Blatty's novel, but a minor one in Friedkin's film. Would audiences have objected to a new Kinderman? (One can't imagine cinemagoers refusing to see *Exorcist II* on the grounds that a relatively minor character from the first movie was played by a different actor in the second.) In lieu of recasting Kinderman, or assigning his narrative role to a new character, the entire police investigation subplot was removed from *The Heretic*. Since Lee J. Cobb died only two months before principal photography began, the

---

54. Boorman, p. 228

55. Boorman, pp. 218-219.

script was overhauled at relatively short notice, symptomatic of Boorman's tendency throughout the production to "solve" problems by creating *bigger* problems. The absence of Kinderman in *Exorcist II* left the character free for William Peter Blatty to use in his novel *Legion* (1983), subsequently filmed as *The Exorcist III* (1990)—in which Kinderman was played by George C. Scott. (Interestingly, George C. Scott played the bullish Juror #3 in William Friedkin's 1997 remake of *12 Angry Men*—in Sidney Lumet's 1957 original, Juror #3 was played by Lee J. Cobb.)

The third player from *The Exorcist* to sign on for *The Heretic* was 31-year-old Katherine "Kitty" Winn. An actor of considerable stage experience—with roles including Shakespeare's Ophelia, Miranda, Desdemona, Juliet, and Cordelia—Winn was awarded Best Actress at the 1971 Cannes Film Festival for her performance opposite Al Pacino in Jerry Schatzberg's *The Panic in Needle Park*. Winn was cast in *The Exorcist* as Chris MacNeil's young secretary, Sharon Spencer; after *The Exorcist*, she had a lead role in Noel Black's supernatural horror film *Marianne* (which was filmed in 1974 and released in 1978 under the title *Mirrors*). Winn also co-starred with Michael Caine and Natalie Wood in Peter Hyams' comedy/mystery flop *Peeper* (1975). John Boorman was reluctant to include Sharon in *The Heretic*, believing the character didn't register enough in the first film to justify a return appearance and it was dramatically wrong for her to return. (At the conclusion of *The Exorcist*, Sharon left Chris' employ, shaken by the ordeal of Regan's possession.) However, Ted Ashley insisted Sharon be added to *The Heretic*, in order to maintain as many links as possible to the first film. Also, without her mother in the story, Regan needed a guardian. (Boorman later told Michel Ciment that Winn assumed certain functions of Cobb's role, but besides accompanying Lamont to the MacNeil house, Sharon does little in the finished film one can imagine Kinderman doing.) After meeting with Kitty Winn, Boorman and Pallenberg came around to the idea of using her in *The Heretic*. Pallenberg explained that Winn "had this incredibly haunted, expressive face. We became more and more excited about working with those qualities."[56] Boorman recalled being struck by Winn's "extreme nervousness, her tension and vulnerability... a neurotic quality she had, as though she were permanently on edge. I was quite disturbed by that. We therefore decided to include this character, as she seemed an ideal means of conveying the strangeness of someone grazed by the shadow of evil."[57]

---

56. J Boorman, quoted in Pallenberg, p. 20.

57. J Boorman, quoted in Ciment, p. 165.

In *The Heretic*, Sharon has returned to watch over Regan for reasons she is not entirely sure of—drawn by Regan's spiritual aura.

With the departure of Jon Voight, *The Heretic* did not have its male lead. In April 1976, *Daily Variety* reported that Christopher Walken was in talks to appear in *The Heretic*. Walken, a relative unknown at the time, auditioned for the part of Father Lamont, and Boorman found the 33-year-old actor convincing: "There was something brittle about him that I found interesting. You always felt that Walken could break at any point, that he could snap. And that was something that could be used."[58] However, the studio executives were not satisfied by Walken's screen-test and Ted Ashley wanted a bigger star for the part. (In retrospect this was a twofold miscalculation. *The Exorcist* did not rely on big-name stars, and Christopher Walken's talents are considerable; he won an Academy Award for *The Deer Hunter*, released a year after *Exorcist II*.) Jack Nicholson was suggested but ruled out: his salary was too high, and Boorman claimed, "Much as I admired Nicholson, I couldn't see him in the role. If Jack made a pact with the devil, you'd think that was where he belonged."[59] (Nicholson's rakish *mien* had also disqualified him for the role of Mia Farrow's clean-cut-but-treacherous husband in Roman Polanski's *Rosemary's Baby*; Polanski, fortunately, had no qualms casting Nicholson in *Chinatown* five years later.) David Carradine, a consideration for Father Lamont *or* Dr Tuskin, was unavailable due to contractual obligations to his television series *Kung Fu*.

Eschewing the idea of Lamont as a young man—apparently because there were few young male actors with the star power *The Heretic* supposedly required—Ted Ashley and Alan Shayne suggested 50-year-old Welsh actor Richard Burton for the part. An accomplished stage actor in Britain, Burton successfully transitioned to Hollywood in the 1950s and was nominated for a Best Supporting Actor Academy Award for *My Cousin Rachel* (1952). Burton became a Top 10 box office draw in the 1960s, starring in big-budget epics like *The Robe* (1953) and *Cleopatra* (1963), as well as domestic dramas like *Look Back in Anger* (1959) and *Who's Afraid of Virginia Woolf?* (1966). His four Actor Academy Award nominations in the 1960s included nods in three consecutive years, for *Becket* (1964), *The Spy Who Came in from the Cold* (1965), and *Virginia Woolf*. (Burton turned down

---

58. J Boorman, quoted in S Abrams, "Director John Boorman on Young Christopher Walken, *Lord of the Rings*, and Violence in Film." *Vulture*, Nov. 26, 2014, https://www.vulture.com/2014/11/director-john-boorman-on-violence-in-film.html

59. Boorman, p. 218.

the lead role of Sir Thomas More in Fred Zinnemann's *A Man for All Seasons* in 1966; Paul Scofield accepted the role, for which he won a Best Actor Academy Award.) After headlining (with Clint Eastwood) the successful World War II derring-do action movie *Where Eagles Dare* (1968), Burton's career went into creative decline in the 1970s, with the actor spiraling into alcoholism, receiving more notices for his tempestuous marriage to Elizabeth Taylor than for his acting, and gaining a reputation for appearing in projects beneath his talents. "The press have been sounding the same note for many years," Burton wrote in 1971. "That I am or was potentially the greatest actor in the world and the successor to Gielgud, Olivier, etc., but that I had dissipated my genius, etc., and 'sold out' to films and booze and women. An interesting reputation to have and by no means dull but by all means untrue."[60] Later in the decade, however, Burton professed, "I've done the most unutterable rubbish, all because of money... There have been times when the lure of the zeros was simply too great."[61]

Burton's mid-1970s career was not without its successes. In 1975, the actor won a Best Children's Album Grammy Award for his recording of *The Little Prince*. Then there was his turn in Peter Shaffer's *Equus* during the play's 1976 Broadway run. Returning to the stage for the first time in a decade, Burton played psychiatrist Martin Dysart in *Equus* between February and April 1976, to great acclaim: "The Best Work of Burton's Life," proclaimed *The New York Times*. John Boorman stated, "Ashley asked me to go to New York to see [Burton] on stage in *Equus*. Everyone was impressed that he could get himself on stage every night in such a demanding role. I had to admit he was mesmerizing."[62] Burton was offered the role of Father Lamont and he accepted—to the delight of Linda Blair, a fan of Burton's films *Becket*, *Anne of the Thousand Days*, and *Cleopatra*. Blair praised her new co-star to *The New York Times*, asking "How many people my age would get the opportunity of working with Richard Burton?"[63] Burton joining *The Heretic* was reported in April 1976, and the actor later told Barbara Pallenberg,

60. R Burton, quoted in C James, "Book of the Times: Burton's Life and His Love Affair With the Press." *The New York Times*, Feb. 22, 1989.

61. R Burton, quoted in J Maslin, "Burton: 'In Trouble All My Life." *The New York Times*, Oct. 5, 1977.

62. Boorman, p. 218.

63. L Blair, quoted in Oalar Hendrek, "What Will 'Jaws' and 'Exorcist' do for an Encore?" *The New York Times*, Jun. 27, 1976.

To be perfectly frank, I did this picture because, although I already had the film of *Equus*, and they didn't want me to do another one in between, I needed the ready cash for my divorce, which I knew would come up soon. Among all the projects that were offered me, I liked this one the best, and I had never played in a film like it or even seen one like it. And I wanted to work with John. Lee Marvin told me what a spectacular director he was.[64]

The salary of $750,000—equaling the fee Boorman and Blair each received—was Burton's primary motivation, but not his only one; Burton told *The New York Times* that *Exorcist II* "wasn't strictly done for money, I did it for my children. They were all terribly excited by *Exorcist I*."[65] Burton later told biographer Michael Munn,

I can't resist playing priests. I have a fascination for them. What makes them tick? And what is it in me that film directors see that makes me a priestly figure? What do I see in myself that makes me think I can play them? Because I'm a Christian, perhaps? Well, I'm not. Maybe it takes a good atheist to play a convincing priest… How can [priests] go through life without sex? That makes no sense to me. Not that I can accept that they are all celibate. It isn't in man's nature to be celibate. I find a wondrous sense of irony in the fact that I, who love to fuck, get chosen to play men who can't.[66]

Burton also wanted to prove he could be relied upon to handle a major studio film to ensure his casting in the film adaptation of *Equus*. Boorman claimed casting Burton "made the screenplay a lot better. New elements came in, but what remained to be seen was whether the compromise could work. I felt uncomfortable having given up on my "young" idea, but the idea of Burton was growing on me. Something positive nearly always comes out of clashes with Ted Ashley."[67] These remarks were made while

---

64. R Burton, quoted in Pallenberg, p. 196.

65. R Burton, quoted in J Maslin, "Burton: 'In Trouble All My Life.'" *The New York Times,* Oct. 5, 1977.

66. R Burton, quoted in M Munn, *Richard Burton: Prince of Players* (London: JR Press, 2008), p. 220.

67. J Boorman, quoted in Pallenberg, p. 23.

The Heretic was in production and must be considered in the context of promoting the film and supporting the studio's decisions. Freed from such obligations a quarter-century later, Boorman in his autobiography confessed that "letting Voight slip through my fingers and casting Burton against my instincts was [a] mistake."[68] He also bemoaned that "the passionate young priest became a weary and burnt-out one... What had been an original character became something of a cliché."[69] Indeed, the "poignancy of irresolvable sexuality" between Lamont and Regan would be largely obliterated by the lack of onscreen chemistry between Burton and Blair.

> *"Ellen Burstyn I still confuse with the other actress, who won for* Cuckoo's Nest, *I forget her name... Yeah, Louise Fletcher. Don't you mix them up?"*
>
> – Bill Murray, *Saturday Night Live*, April 7, 1979

The Heretic had its Father Lamont, but still not its Dr Tuskin—the only major character John Boorman had a free hand to cast, as Linda Blair and Max von Sydow were required by the dictates of the script, and Richard Burton and Kitty Winn were mandated by Ted Ashley. Boorman wanted a "practical, down-to-earth counterpart" to the "ascetic, tortured, otherworldly" Richard Burton. Rospo Pallenberg had suggested Chris Sarandon, who received an Oscar nomination for his portrayal of the transgender partner of Al Pacino's Sonny Wortzik in *Dog Day Afternoon* (1975) and played a rapist in the revenge thriller *Lipstick* (1976). Although Guy McElwaine was in favor of Sarandon, Boorman deemed the actor "too introspective" for the role of Tuskin. (Sarandon went on to headline the 1980 television films *The Day Christ Died* and *A Tale of Two Cities* and star in popular genre films like *Fright Night* [1985], *The Princess Bride* [1987], *Child's Play* [1988], and *The Nightmare Before Christmas* [1993].) George Segal was considered for Tuskin; his casting would have reunited him onscreen with Richard Burton a decade after the two appeared together in *Who's Afraid of Virginia Woolf?* (1966). By the mid-1970s, Segal was at the commercial zenith of his career as a Hollywood leading man, and his salary was reportedly too high. Eventually, Boorman decided to make Tuskin female, believing the religion vs. science conflict between

68. Boorman, p. 229.

69. Boorman, p. 218.

Lamont and Tuskin be more interesting if contested between a man and a woman. Rospo Pallenberg suggested Jane Fonda or Ann-Margret for the role. (Fonda had been offered the role of Chris MacNeil in *The Exorcist* but turned it down on the grounds she didn't "believe in magic.") The part ultimately went to 41-year-old Louise Fletcher, who had won a Golden Globe *and* an Oscar for her portrayal of Nurse Ratched in Miloš Forman's *One Flew Over the Cuckoo's Nest* (1975). A veteran of episodic television, Fletcher had a strong supporting role in Robert Altman's *Thieves Like Us* (1974), before her falling-out with Altman led to the director replacing her with Lily Tomlin in his panoramic masterpiece *Nashville* (1975). Fletcher was a big name in Hollywood after *Cuckoo's Nest* and Boorman felt her no-nonsense practicality would contrast with Richard Burton: "She had an air of authority. She was tall and regal. Burton said to her, 'I'm a Welsh dwarf and it's always my fate to be cast with tall leading ladies.'" Boorman told Michel Ciment,

> We didn't manage to find a suitable male actor for the role; and I was stimulated by the decision to cast Louise Fletcher. Naturally, we revised the character, which considerably affected the film. All these changes meant that the film was very different from what had originally been planned and it's a pointless exercise speculating on whether it might otherwise have been better. It certainly wouldn't have been the same, which only goes to show how fallible and plastic a film is.[70]

On April 21, 1976, *The Lost Angeles Times* reported that Louise Fletcher had signed on to play the part of the psychiatrist—a role originally written for a man—in *The Heretic*. (In a *Hollywood Reporter* article published a fortnight later, Richard Lederer refuted claims the script had been re-written extensively to accommodate the Louise Fletcher's casting.) With Tuskin's gender-change, *The Heretic*'s main cast became predominantly female, and Boorman wanted the hair, make-up, and costume departments to give the characters distinctive looks to delineate their personalities (Tuskin: severity and sensuousness; Sharon: "an unwilling nun;" Regan: a simple teenager becoming gradually more luminous).

41-year-old American actor James Earl Jones was cast as the adult version of Kokumo, the Ethiopian exorcised as a boy by Father Merrin.

---

70. J Boorman, quoted in Ciment, p. 168.

Jones had begun his professional acting career in the 1950s, debuting on Broadway in 1957, and by the mid-1970s he had amassed numerous film and television credits in addition to his extensive career in the theater. In 1969 Jones won a Tony Award for his lead performance in Howard Sackler's play *The Great White Hope*; he later received Oscar and Golden Globe nominations for recreating the role in Martin Ritt's 1970 film version. (Jones also played Claudius in the 1972 New York production of *Hamlet* in which *The Exorcist*'s Kitty Winn played Ophelia.) Around the time he was cast in *The Heretic*, Jones was involved in the post-production of *Star Wars*, receiving $7,000.00 for giving his distinctive basso profondo voice to Darth Vader—a role the actor declined onscreen credit for because of *The Exorcist*: "When Linda Blair did the girl in *The Exorcist*, they hired Mercedes McCambridge to do the voice of the devil coming out of her. And there was controversy as to whether Mercedes should get credit. I was one who thought no, she was just special effects. So when it came to Darth Vader, I said, no, I'm just special effects."[71] (Incidentally, Max von Sydow and James Earl Jones both appeared in 1982's *Conan the Barbarian*—although, as was the case with *Exorcist II*, the two actors did not share any scenes.) Hired to play Kokumo as a boy was fifteen-year-old Los Angeles actor Joey Green, who was shaved bald for the role.

67-year-old Austrian actor/director Paul Henreid was cast as Cardinal Jaros, who tasks Lamont with investigating Merrin's death. Boorman claimed, "Henreid has those marvelous, dead, cold eyes—very good, indeed, for the part."[72] A stage actor who trained in Vienna's Dramatic Academy, Henreid transitioned to films in the 1930s. An avowed anti-Nazi, Henreid fled Germany for England before relocating to America in 1940. As a contract player for Warners, Henreid's best-known roles were opposite Bette Davis in *Now, Voyager* (1942) and as Victor Laszlo in *Casablanca* (1942). 35-year-old Ned Beatty was cast as "Ecumenical" Edwards, a religious goods salesman encountered by Lamont in Ethiopia. Perhaps the quintessential American "character actor" of the 1970s, Beatty made his film debut in Boorman's *Deliverance* before taking supporting roles in John Huston's *The Life and Times of Judge Roy Bean* (1972), Robert Altman's *Nashville* (1975), and Alan J. Pakula's *All the President's Men* (1976). For Sidney Lumet's *Network* (1976)—in which he delivered a riveting Paddy Chayefsky-penned monologue—Beatty earned an Oscar

---

71. JE Jones, quoted in "Fast Chat: James Earl Jones." *Newsday*, Mar. 16, 2008, http://www.newsday.com/entertainment/stage/ny-c5611250mar16,0,5264743.story.

72. J Boorman, quoted in Pallenberg, p. 136.

nomination for Best Supporting Actor. Beatty's then-wife Belinda Beatty (née Belinha Rowley), who had a minor role in *Deliverance*, was cast as Dr Tuskin's assistant, Liz. (Rowley is credited in both films as "Belinha Beatty.")

Rose Portillo, a 21-year-old Los Angeles actor, was cast as the "Girl Healer" who dies in the film's opening sequence. Portillo went on to play Della Barrios in the original 1978 L.A. production of Luis Valdez's *Zoot Suit*; she reprised the role in the play's 1979 Broadway run as well as its 1981 film adaptation. Cast in *The Heretic* as one of Dr Tuskin's children was Joey Lauren Adams (credited as "Joely Adams"), later to find fame in adulthood starring in the Kevin Smith films *Mallrats* (1995) and *Chasing Amy* (1997). Twelve-year-old Dana Plato was cast as Sandra, the autistic girl "healed" by Regan. Plato—who had auditioned for the role of Regan in *The Exorcist*—would later find fame on the small screen as Kimberly Drummond in the sitcom *Diff'rent Strokes* (1978-1986). Plato's highly publicized struggles with drug and alcohol abuse culminated in her death by suicide in 1999. Barbara Pallenberg recounted that Plato was the best of those who tested for the role of Sandra. One of the aspirants Plato won the part over was John Boorman's nine-year-old daughter Daisy, who was ruled out of contention after suffering a painful health scare, undergoing an operation to remove a tumor from her shinbone. Daisy's older sister Katrine—who appeared as an extra in *Zardoz* and would later portray Igrayne in her father's *Excalibur*—contributed the Aubrey Beardsley-esque drawings identified in the film as the work of Regan. Many years later, Katrine Boorman directed a documentary feature about her father, *Me and My Dad* (2013).

On April 21, 1976, *The New York Times* reported that *The Heretic* would net Richard Burton earnings "in the million-dollar range" and John Boorman's film—also starring Linda Blair—would begin shooting on May 17.[73]

---

73. "Richard Burton to Begin 'Heretic' Filming May 17." *The New York Times*, Apr. 21, 1976.

John Boorman prepares to film Regan's "sleepwalk" sequence on the roof of the Warner Building in New York City.

The sequence as it appears onscreen. The sleeping Regan (Linda Blair) is coaxed by the demon Pazuzu to the edge of the building.

4

On the Wings of a Demon: Filming *The Heretic*

"We were tackling huge aesthetic and technical problems, and doing experimental things on an epic stale, in the context of a big-budget studio picture. I knew how hard this would be to pull off. Yet again I was trying to do too much. The bigger a movie gets the less original it tends to become. My aesthetic theories and color codes seemed like indulgent whims to the crew of hardened cynical technicians. But we persisted. We were constantly obliged to rewrite as problems arose and new solutions were needed. Bill Fraker, the cameraman, was tested to his limits, having to light exterior scenes on indoor stages. And everything that could go wrong did go wrong, technically and professionally."

– John Boorman[74]

JOHN BOORMAN ASSEMBLED a predominantly Anglo-American production crew for *The Heretic*, retaining personnel from his earlier projects. Associate producer Charles Orme was an Englishman who had worked with Boorman on *Deliverance* and *Zardoz*; he was also the associate producer of *The Omen*, the hit 1976 horror film inspired by the success of *The Exorcist*. With locusts receiving more prominence in *The Her-*

---

74. Boorman, p. 219.

etic thanks to Boorman and Pallenberg's rewrites, Orme was entrusted with making contacts with two particular institutes: the Locust Research Centre in London (to provide research and advice regarding locusts) and Oxford Scientific Films (to provide advice as to how to integrate actual locusts into the film). In addition to the logistics of handling locusts, Boorman had to select a production designer up to the challenge of *The Heretic*'s unique requirements:

> It is very important to set the style with a designer at an early point, and to some extent, your circumstances determine what you can do. In *The Heretic*, we had scenes in primitive Africa and scenes and glass and steel New York, and bringing them all together was going to be what would give the film coherence. I got glazed looks and non-comprehension talking to most production designers about what I wanted.[75]

Boorman claimed the American production designers he spoke with were in favor of a naturalistic approach rather than the "visionary" look he had in mind. Englishman Richard Macdonald—a film industry veteran and an accomplished landscape painter—was therefore hired as production designer of *The Heretic*. A frequent collaborator of British-based American director Joseph Losey, Macdonald's credits included *Far from the Madding Crowd* (1967), *Jesus Christ Superstar* (1973), and, perhaps ominously, *The Day of the Locust* (1975). As *The Heretic*'s production designer, Macdonald was required to replicate Ethiopian villages and mountainous rock churches via carvings and paintings in the Warner Brothers soundstages. Boorman spoke approvingly of Macdonald's approach:

> He understood perfectly what I was aiming at and was very excited at the idea of having complete control in the studio. He was even more radical than I, and regarded any filming in exteriors—which is to say, nine days out of seventeen weeks!—as a kind of defeat. Thanks to the fact that we filmed in the studio, I was able to obtain a visual coherence, particularly where the colour was concerned.[76]

---

75. J Boorman, quoted in Pallenberg, p. 27.

76. J Boorman, quoted in Ciment, p. 169.

Boorman and Macdonald sought to imbue *The Heretic* with distinct visual motifs to underscore the hallucinatory, hypnotic quality of the story. Boorman, who made the Chattooga River foliage shot by Vilmos Zsigmond in *Deliverance* ominous by desaturating its colors, wanted *The Heretic* to have an unusual color palette: primarily amber, chestnut, red, and ochre, a contrast to the blue and grey of *The Exorcist*. Boorman believed these colors would make audiences sense unease and tension:

> I set up a colour palette for the film eliminating all blues and greens, the colours of comfort and hope. Their absence would make the audience uneasy, deprived, the way you feel in a city under grey skies where there are no trees. It externalised the notion of our world plunging into a technological nightmare of smog and desertification, and thus set up the desire for some kind of redemption.[77]

Another motif was the recurring presence of mirror panels and transparent glass instead of solid walls: glass and mirrors would convey a splintered, multi-faceted reality, and convey the illusion of other worlds. The most outlandish manifestation of the glass and mirrors motif was the set design of the Institute in which Dr Tuskin practices. Boorman described it as being "shaped like a hive with cells and glass partitions, further isolating characters who are already solitary creatures, capable of communicating only with the synchronizer. In addition, the theme of the mirror finds its correlative in the skyscraper which reflects Louise Fletcher and Kitty Winn, fragmenting their personalities and their universe."[78] Boorman also wanted "a giant nervous system" to be implied throughout the story's various locations, so snaking, confined, labyrinthine corridors (for the temple, the mud-city, the Vatican, the hotel, and the hospital) were built to connote radiating nerve-endings.

Veteran cinematographer Geoffrey Unsworth, who shot *Zardoz* for Boorman, was occupied with Richard Donner's *Superman*, and so William A. Fraker was hired as *The Heretic*'s director of photography. Fraker's film credits as cinematographer included *The President's Analyst* (1967), *Rosemary's Baby* (1968), *Bullitt* (1968), and *Paint Your Wagon* (1979); he also shot the documentary *Fritz Lang interviewed by William Friedkin* (1974) and directed two films, *Monte Walsh* (1970) and *A Reflec-*

---

77. Boorman, p. 219.

78. J Boorman, quoted in Ciment, p. 169.

tion of Fear (1971). Fraker said, "[Boorman]'s a fantastic man and really knows what he wants. He has exquisite taste and is very, very demanding of everyone—not just me, but everyone right down the line, including himself."[79] Of the film itself, Fraker later admitted, "It was a huge, huge picture and probably the toughest picture, physically, that I've ever done in my life. For example, recreating the Ethiopian desert on Stage 16 at the Burbank Studios—how do you do that?"[80] Fraker spoke positively of his collaboration with production designer Richard Macdonald, describing him as "a phenomenal man with a marvelous mind. He worked very closely with us. There were hours of discussions about how we were going to accomplish certain shots."[81] A decade later, Fraker and Macdonald reunited for the teen sci-fi movie *SpaceCamp* (1986).

34-year-old Californian Nick McLean was hired as a camera operator for *The Heretic*. Since 1969, McLean had worked as an assistant cameraman on many programs for Universal Television and had branched out into films such as Robert Altman's *McCabe & Mrs. Miller* (1973), Steven Spielberg's *The Sugarland Express* (1974), and John Schlesinger's *Marathon Man* (1975). McLean had most recently worked as a camera operator on Spielberg's *Close Encounters of the Third Kind* (1977). "The producers of *Exorcist II* asked me if I would come in for an interview after I finished the first unit work on *Close Encounters*, but Boorman wanted me to fly to New York for the interview," McLean recalled. "So I said, "Forget about it, I'm not flying all the way to New York from Los Angeles for an interview. If you want to hire me, then hire me!" So they hired me on the spot and I worked on the majority of the film."[82] McLean worked for three months on *The Heretic*, shooting interior scenes in Burbank and exterior scenes Arizona, but not the exterior scenes in New York City.

Matte artist Albert Whitlock, highly regarded for his years of collaboration with Alfred Hitchcock, was hired to provide *The Heretic's* special visual effects. Whitlock was reunited with Chuck Gaspar, *The Heretic's* head of special effects; both men had worked on Hitchcock's *The Birds* (1963). However, Whitlock's contributions to *The Heretic* were

79. WA Fraker, quoted in "The Photography of *Exorcist II: The Heretic*." *American Cinematographer* Vol. 58 no.8, Aug. 1977.

80. WA Fraker, quoted in "The Photography of *Exorcist II: The Heretic*."

81. WA Fraker, quoted in "The Photography of *Exorcist II: The Heretic*."

82. N McLean, quoted in W Byrne & N McLean, *Behind the Camera: The Life and Works of a Hollywood Cinematographer* (Jefferson: McFarland & Company, Inc., 2020), p. 49.

curtailed by Universal Pictures, where Whitlock was under contract. Another veteran hired for *The Heretic* was unit production manager John Coonan, who had been in the film industry since the 1930s; among his many film credits, Coonan was assistant director of George Stevens' classic western *Shane* (1953). Dick Smith, who earned plaudits for his ingenious make-up effects for *The Exorcist*—as well as for ageing Dustin Hoffman in *Little Big Man* (1970) and Marlon Brando in *The Godfather* (1972)—returned to provide his expertise for the sequel, albeit in a diminished capacity. Smith was unable to commit fully to *The Heretic* as he was already working on Michael Winner's demonic horror film *The Sentinel* (1977)—a film featuring Chris Sarandon and Christopher Walken, both considered for roles in *The Heretic*. In addition to providing demonic makeup for Linda Blair's double, Smith was to have created, for the demon's final manifestation, a grotesque Kabuki-like demon head that would disintegrate in the film's climax—an idea unrealized in the final version of the film.

About 200 people converged on Stage 1 of the Warners Studio in Burbank for *The Heretic*'s pre-production luncheon and press conference; by now, the film was known publicly as *The Heretic: Exorcist II*. The cast and crew broke from rehearsals to attend the lunch; also in attendance were Warners bigwigs Ted Ashley, David Geffen, Guy McElwaine, and Frank Wells. John Boorman, Richard Lederer, Linda Blair, Richard Burton, Louise Fletcher, and Max von Sydow fielded questions from the members of the press in attendance. (Barbara Pallenberg recounted a photographer from the French magazine *Cinematograph* wondering where William Friedkin was.) "Sequel" being something of a dirty word in the industry at the time, Boorman assured the press, "Not in any way can you consider [*The Heretic*] a sequel, just a continuation of the original, the same way *French Connection II* and *Godfather II* were continuations of the original."[83] Richard Lederer concurred, stating, "Each film has to make a connection with the audience which has already been achieved with *The Exorcist*... [*The Heretic*] is not a sequel, it is a continuation and we feel those people who went to see the original will flock to see this one."[84] Boorman further differentiated *The Heretic* from its predecessor, practically telegraphing the end of the film:

83. J Boorman, quoted in J Austin, "*The Heretic: Exorcist II*." *Photoplay Film Monthly*, Aug. 1976.

84. R Lederer, quoted in Austin.

In *The Exorcist*, Regan was possessed by an evil force which was trying to destroy her. In *The Heretic: Exorcist II* it is the forces of good and evil which are struggling for supremacy within her... If the force of good wins out, Regan will emerge as an extraordinary person who is herself capable of great healing powers and points the way to the future evolution of the human spirit.[85]

Richard Burton, who had recently arrived in California, told the audience, "The role of Father Philip Lamont is a very demanding, difficult role in this film and I only hope I'm up to it. I have done nothing but think about it and it has possessed me, you will pardon the expression, for several weeks."[86] The conference went well. Richard Burton was the star of the day, drawing the most applause and attention. According to Barbara Pallenberg, Richard Lederer was articulate and amusing but John Boorman's seriousness made those assembled uneasy. Boorman spoke at length about his theories on the existence and presence of evil, making references to Russian novelist/philosopher Aleksandr Solzhenitsyn.[87]

The Heretic finally began principal photography in Burbank on May 24, 1976. If the film's pre-production was fraught with difficulties—the schism between Boorman and Goodhart, the problems with casting—the actual shoot was even more problematic. "A well thought-out, well-crafted movie is naturally going to have more problems than a cheaply made quickie," Richard Lederer admitted to Barbara Pallenberg.[88] "*The Heretic*, all the way through, was a very difficult picture to do. Because we tried to do something that wasn't being done in Hollywood at the time; it had been done in Hollywood years ago," William Fraker recalled. "We were trying to bring back the old craft and the old art with the departments that used to do those things; they don't exist anymore. We had to rebuild whole studio departments in order to do certain things, like backings and set designs." Fraker remarked, "If the studio isn't set up for it, it costs a helluva lot of money. We'd shoot it, it wouldn't work, and we'd have to go back and do it again."[89] Shooting exteriors in a soundstage allowed Boorman to exercise

---

85. J Boorman, quoted in Austin.

86. R Burton, quoted in Austin.

87. Pallenberg, p. 58.

88. R Lederer, quoted in Pallenberg, p. 183.

89. WA Fraker, quoted in Dennis Schaefer & Larry Salvato, *Masters of Light:*

more stylistic control, but it also ate up time. Boorman said, "I want to light this picture in a very expressionistic way, lots of black shadows and lots of modelling. So we have to make pools of light where the main action of each scene is going on, and at the same time we have to keep the indirect lighting of the ceiling visible in the background. It all takes time."[90] William Fraker testified to the difficulty of lighting the film's African sequences:

> Probably the biggest [challenge] was trying to reproduce the Ethiopian desert exterior on an interior set. We were using one hundred and twenty arcs to give us that sunlight; I don't know how else to do it. I guess other people would have done it with ten arcs. I don't know how you simulate an exterior intensity without stopping down. So how do you stop down? You put the light in so you have to stop down. You sure as hell can't shoot an interior that looks like an exterior if you're open at $f1.4$. It doesn't work the same; the whole look is different. That was our philosophy and that's the way we went into it... That was extremely difficult—extremely difficult because, number one, when you're working with large crews, it's difficult to get the same people back day after day. You get somebody to work the way you want to work, the next day he's not there; then you've got to break in somebody else, so it takes that much more time. When you say, "Trim your arcs," one hundred and twenty arcs should go off but it would take ten minutes to turn them off and ten minutes to put them on. And when you want them back on, you have nothing but inexperienced people up there and they never put the arcs back in the same place. Therefore you have to rebalance the backing and the foreground again. The backing was eighty feet high by five hundred and fifty feet around. There were horrendous problems. For example, getting dust in the air and working with dust in the air with everybody complaining, moaning and groaning. Trying to out that whole act together is, logistically, as tough as running an army.[91]

Conversations with Contemporary Cinematographers (Berkeley and Los Angeles: University of California Press, 2013), p. 149.

90. J Boorman, quoted in Pallenberg, p. 64.

91. WA Fraker, quoted in Schaefer & Salvato, p. 148.

The expertise of Richard Macdonald and William Fraker was called upon to simulate Ethiopian rock church exteriors within the soundstage. "There's a sequence in which one of the Ethiopian monks, climbing in one of those rock churches 400 feet in the air, slips and falls all the way to the bottom. How do you do that on a stage?" Fraker mused later. "We set the rocks up sideways, using the whole length of the stage. Then we turned over the camera, wired the man on a pulley overhead and "flew" him through sideways, with a blue screen down at the bottom."[92]

The quality of footage proved to be extremely variable. "Some dailies looked terrific, and others made us feel like we wanted to commit suicide," Fraker revealed. "We did a lot of retakes. John Boorman was adamant about what it should look like, and if it didn't, he'd say, "Billy, reshoot." And I would, but it would be very expensive to do. It also involved a lot of persistence and a willingness to keep trying for a desired effect."[93] Camera operator Nick McLean recalled the difficulties incurred during the shooting of the film:

> I screwed up one shot really bad, I just didn't know how to get it right and Boorman was pissed off with me after he saw the dailies the next day. Garrett Brown was our Steadicam operator, he actually invented the Steadicam, so I brought him down to the set and showed him what they wanted me to do and he agreed that it was an impossible shot; they wanted me to go through these doors and down this flight of stairs and it was just a hard shot for me to get perfect. In the end, they got Garrett to do it and he nailed it. I was getting along great with Boorman in the beginning but then it started to turn sour near the end and I didn't know why until later on; it turned out we were rivals for the affections of the same girl.[94]

Boorman admitted the protracted filming process had an impact on the cast:

> The sheer scale of the picture slowed us down. Lighting ate up much of the day. Special effects held things up too. When there is a lot of waiting, momentum is lost. It is particularly hard

92. WA Fraker, quoted in "The Photography of *Exorcist II: The Heretic*."

93. WA Fraker, quoted in "The Photography of *Exorcist II: The Heretic*."

94. N McLean, quoted in Byrne & McLean, p. 49.

for actors to maintain concentration and energy. [Richard] Burton had a reputation for being difficult. On the contrary, I found him completely professional. The only demand made was that I should go personally to call him from his trailer when I was ready for him. He knew from experience that nervous assistant directors would tend to call actors early so as not to get caught out and earn the ire of the director.[95]

Time was also subject to the whims of Linda Blair. Although visual authenticity was the primary reason for Friedkin to film *The Exorcist* in New York and Washington rather than in Hollywood, it was also because California's child labor laws would have placed a greater limitation on Linda Blair's availability for daily filming—time further reduced by the application of the extensive demonic makeup required for Regan. Principal photography for *The Heretic* took place in California and, at 17 years of age, Blair was still legally a minor—therefore, she was only available at the studio for eight hours a day. This was reduced informally to six hours because of Blair's habitual lateness and her insistence on spending two hours in hair and make-up—and this was for the *non-demonic* Regan.

The screenplay of *The Heretic*, heavily rewritten in pre-production, underwent constant revisions by Rospo Pallenberg during production; the bones of Goodhart's story remained, but a more hallucinatory screenplay took shape around them. Father Lamont crosses paths with Regan MacNeil in New York City after being commissioned to investigate the circumstances surrounding the death of Father Merrin. Taking part in Regan's hypnotherapy sessions with Dr Tuskin and the experimental Synchronizer machine, Lamont sees visions of the demon Pazuzu, still dormant in Regan. Defying the orders of his superiors, Lamont travels to Ethiopia to find Kokumo, who was possessed by Pazuzu and successfully exorcised by Father Merrin in 1936. As Lamont travels deeper in his search, he risks falling under the persuasive power of the demon, especially as the Synchronizer has linked his mind with Regan (who hears demonic voices whilst sleepwalking). Boorman came up with the idea of Regan being a tap-dancer, believing it would serve as a metaphor for Regan becoming a "higher being," and Pallenberg wrote the scene in which Regan's tap-dance recital is juxtaposed with Lamont being pelted by stones in Ethiopia. Regan's seizure, occurring in tandem with Lamont's stoning, illustrates the psychic link between the characters. A

---

95. Boorman, p. 221.

copy of *The Heretic's* script found its way into the hands of William Peter Blatty: "A friend of mine pirated a copy of the script, and after my initial astonishment, I thought, 'This is some kind of sly send-up. They're trying to torment me. They're not really going to do this.'"[96] As principal photography of *The Heretic* continued, so too did production difficulties occur. Footage was over-saturated and necessitated reshoots; the miniature sets built at Burbank were unsatisfactory, reducing the number of usable shots (miniatures would eventually be built and filmed in Ireland); and the sequences involving locusts were extremely problematic.

"And there came out of the smoke locusts upon the earth: and unto them was given great power, as the scorpions of the earth have power. And the shapes of the locusts were like unto horses prepared unto battle..."

– Revelation 9: 3, 7

In *The Heretic*, locusts are a physical manifestation of the demon Pazuzu and a metaphorical representation of the demon's adverse effect on humankind. (In Mesopotamian and Babylonian mythology, Pazuzu is reputed to bring famine in dry seasons and locusts in rainy seasons.) Sean Morris and David Thompson of Oxford Scientific provided locust footage that would be integrated into the film via back projection, for scenes in which massive swarms appear overhead. The rewritten script also required a plague of locusts to descend upon Georgetown (pre-empting *The Swarm*, Irwin Allen's 1978 disaster movie about killer bees invading Texas, also filmed at the Warners lot in Burbank). Since live locusts were required to billow around actors and extras, 2,500 of the insects were shipped to California from England, only to die at a rate of 100 a day. It was also difficult to make the locusts fly: Boorman tried exposing the insects to bright lights, painting their eyes back, and even cutting their legs off, to keep them off the ground. Eventually, the crew resorted to supplementing airborne locusts with brown-painted Styrofoam pieces to simulate a billowing swarm.

The insect-free sequences were filmed more or less as they had been planned, but they still took time. The exorcism flashback during the first Synchronizer session, in which Father Merrin and the demonic Regan ap-

---

96. WP Blatty, quoted in DE Winter, *Faces of Fear: Encounters with Creators of Modern Horror* (New York: Berkley Books, 1985), p. 45.

pear to be visually superimposed over Dr Tuskin and teenage Regan, was not augmented by optical effects. Boorman opted to use a more vintage technique: "ghost-glass," a type of two-way mirror that allows the camera to record both the image beyond it and the reflected image. Boorman had used ghost-glass in his previous film, *Zardoz*. William Fraker explained the process by which the Georgetown exorcism was re-created in the "present time" set:

> It was shot through a transmission mirror, a fifty percent transmission mirror, which we call ghost glass... It's a piece of glass that has mirrors mixed in the glass, a special glass called transmission glass, which allows you to look through and reflect, at the same time, fifty percent of each scene— what you're seeing fifty percent and what you're reflecting fifty percent. Depending on which scene you gave more light to (with dimmers), you could bring one scene up and take the other one down. That's exactly what we did... What we did was we re-created the entire original exorcism scene of *The Exorcist* with Linda Blair and Max von Sydow and at the same time, we were shooting Linda Blair in present time. We had a double working on that scene with her back to us. We had no opticals on that at all; it worked on one piece of film. It took all of one day to do it but the scene covered six pages so we were way ahead.[97]

Unlike *The Exorcist*, which concentrated most of its special effects into its final act, *The Heretic* required such effects throughout almost its entire duration. Boorman remarked,

> The scale of it, the vaulting ambition, the succession of accidents and misfortunes, were always pushing us to the verge of disaster. Yet living on a knife's edge must be where— unconsciously, perhaps—I need to be. In the comfortable, protected world of the privileged there are few situations where we can test our mettle, discover our absolute potential, and even exceed our limitations.[98]

97. WA Fraker, quoted in Schaefer & Salvato, pp. 148-149

98. Boorman, p. 227.

Boorman's world was to become far less comfortable and protected—and far more dangerous—than he could have imagined. Just over a month into *The Heretic*'s shoot, his health took a turn for the worst:

> I began to suffer back pain and high fever. I dragged myself through each day's work. Nothing would shake the fever. It was coming up to the Fourth of July holiday. A rash broke out all over my body. At the end of that day, Friday night, I checked in to the UCLA medical centre. They got very excited when they saw that the rash covered the palms of my hands. They diagnosed syphilis. They told me that the law required me to write down all my sexual contacts for the last five years. They took blood tests and I went home and crawled into bed.[99]

The tests were negative for syphilis. Boorman had actually contracted Coccidioidomycosis, a mammalian fungal disease commonly known as "San Joaquin Valley Fever." The pathogenic fungus that causes the disease—potentially fatal, if it travels to the brain—is endemic to American desert regions and was in the sand brought into the studios for the African sequences. Far worse than the coral poisoning he suffered during the making of *Hell in the Pacific*, Boorman recalled being told "that the fever would persist until the body calcified the fungus in my lungs. I would then have to have a lumbar puncture to discover if the fungus had travelled."[100] From July 6 until August 3, 1976, Boorman was absent from production of *The Heretic*. According to Barbara Pallenberg, Warners did not hit the panic button:

> The studio is not considering hiring another director. Contractually, it could have done so by this time, but the film is so big and so complex that there are very few directors with the technical skill to pull it off. The chance that one of them be available, and willing, is almost nil. And even if one were to be found, his orientation would take as long as Boorman's recuperation.[101]

99. Boorman, pp. 221-223.

100. Boorman, p. 223.

101. Pallenberg, p. 117.

During Boorman's month-long absence, Rospo Pallenberg assumed some directorial duties; Linda Blair later claimed he directed much of the film. He definitely directed the tap-dance scene (choreographed by musical veteran Danny Giagni) and is credited as "2ⁿᵈ Unit Director" (for footage shot in Washington and Zululand). Uncertain about parts of the script, Pallenberg told his wife he had envisioned an ending more spectacular than the one written:

> I've been rereading the script, and I don't like it. I think it has a very weak ending, which John and I always had a bad feeling about, because it fails to satisfy all the elements of the story we are trying to tell. We have to have much more than the psychological story of Regan facing the evil within her. The movie has been leading up to a much broader, more epic, ending. A much greater battle between the forces of good and evil has to take place at the end. Pazuzu in the locust swarm has to confront Regan directly, to suppress her forever or be banished by her, and Lamont has to confront the face of evil directly, to finally overcome it and redeem himself, his failures.[102]

The ending as written involved Regan and Merrin converging spiritually before confronting the Regan/Demon "at its most inhuman stage of possession." Regan would then pull herself out of Merrin as if molting (thus continuing the locust motif) before viscerally dispatching her hideous, green-skinned doppelganger by snapping its head around and watching as the flesh melts off its bones, a special effects gross-out to be supervised by Dick Smith. Rospo Pallenberg had other ideas. Pallenberg conceived "a more alluring embodiment of Regan… supine, an arrogant object of desire." Louise Fletcher and Kitty Winn were reportedly unhappy with the revised ending, but Richard Burton apparently anticipated such changes when he agreed to star in the film in the first place: "I said to the chaps, 'Well, I'd be delighted to do it but you'll have to change the end, because I really don't understand what on earth is going on.'"[103]

Boorman was still weak when he returned to work on 3 August, and he would not regain his full strength until after the film's completion. Thanks to insurance coverage, Boorman's month-long absence did not lose the

---

102. R Pallenberg, quoted in Pallenberg, p. 116.

103. R Burton, quoted in J Maslin, "Burton: 'In Trouble All My Life." *The New York Times*, Oct. 5, 1977.

studio money, but it did affect the shoot's momentum. Linda Blair complained, "Movie-making takes so long and can be so boring. I thought the shooting of *Exorcist II* would never end."[104] Before *Exorcist II* had ceased shooting, Blair was shooting scenes in Burbank for another project—the hostage drama telemovie *Victory at Entebbe*, which would air on US television in December 1976, half a year before *Exorcist II* reached theatres. "The feeling was getting around that the picture was jinxed," Boorman recalled. "Louise Fletcher's husband fell seriously ill. She herself was rushed to hospital for a gall bladder operation. 'That's what happens when you play around with the occult,' a prop man told me."[105] Fletcher's husband, film producer Jerry Bick, underwent a coronary bypass operation while *The Heretic* was shooting—Richard Lederer underwent the same operation during pre-production—and Fletcher and Kitty Winn were both hospitalized with gall bladder infections. "Many weird things happened on the set… Nearly everyone involved with the film had some sort of mishap. It was a bit eerie," Lederer told *Circus* magazine. "This was my first stint as a producer on a film, after years as the head of international publicity for Warner Brothers. One week after I got the assignment, I was in the hospital having open heart surgery. I had no history of heart problems before!"[106] For any other film, stories like this would be unlikely to raise eyebrows— but for an *Exorcist* sequel, they played into the "cursed" hype that made fans more eager to view the finished product. There was tabloid intrigue of a more familiar kind when Richard Burton married British fashion model Suzy Hunt (née Miller) in Arlington, Virginia on August 21. Burton had left Elizabeth Taylor (whom he divorced, for the second time, in June 1976) for Hunt, 23 years Burton's junior and the ex-wife of British Formula One driver James Hunt. It was Burton's fourth marriage; John Boorman and his daughter Telsche attended the reception.

In mid-August, photography of *The Heretic* moved to the New York City metropolitan area for two weeks of location work. This caused further problems for Boorman, as union regulations forced him to use a local crew rather than his own personnel. Filming was permitted at Pennsylvania Station on August 24 for the scene in which Lamont and Regan take an Amtrak Train from New York to Washington. Boorman, Burton, Blair,

---

104. L Blair, quoted in S Mieses, "The Devil Made Her Do It (Again): A Grown-Up Linda Blair Talks about 'Exorcist II', Rock & Roll, and Her Life As A Teen Celeb." *Circus*, Jul. 7, 1977.

105. Boorman, p. 226.

106. R Lederer, quoted in Mieses.

and an assorted crewmembers, assistants, and extras filmed for nearly five hours; the event was reported the following day by newspapers like the *New York Daily News* and *The New York Times*. Elsewhere, Boorman had trouble acquiring locations to rent from private owners who were wary of the film's subject matter. For the apartment building in which Regan and Sharon lived, Boorman intended to film at The Galleria, a 55-story condominium located just off Park Avenue in Manhattan. However, the complex refused permission to shoot there, causing cost overruns for the production. It was decided that two buildings would be used to portray Regan and Sharon's apartment building. Exterior shots of the 39-story CBS Building on 51 West 52nd Street were combined with scenes filmed on the rooftop of the 41-story 666 Fifth Avenue Building which, at the time, housed Warners' New York offices. (This is where *The Exorcist* was edited, and where Friedkin screened the film's original 140-minute cut to Blatty. According to Revelation 13:18, 666 is "the Number of the Beast," and the number has satanic connotations in popular culture. Commentators have been quick to point out the synchronicity between the subject matter of *Exorcist II* and the address where it was partially filmed. Other works of fiction have utilized the same building for dramatic purposes: in William Hjortsberg's 1978 novel *Falling Angel*, the 666 Fifth Avenue Building is the place where doomed private detective Harry Angel meets the sinister Louis Cyphre.)

The Fifth Avenue rooftop—dressed by Richard Macdonald to suit a residential building—was where the sequence in which a nightgown-clad Regan, coaxed in her dream by Pazuzu, nearly wanders off the roof. This sequence climaxes with Regan teetering over the edge of the building, and we see a point-of-view shot above Regan's feet, suspended over Fifth Avenue, 41 stories below. These shots were achieved without stunt people or optical effects. For the shot in which Regan stumbles at the edge of the roof, Linda Blair was not at the actual edge of the building—she was on a platform one foot away—but the shoot still looked perilous enough to deter people who didn't need to be there to not watch it. To maintain suspense, the shot of Regan walking towards the edge of the roof was a continuous take, meaning safeguards like ropes or harnesses could not be used. Instead, two members of the crew stood on either side of the platform, ready to catch Blair if she fell. Richard Lederer assured *Circus* magazine that Blair "was really under no danger, and she handled it like a pro—but it gave her fits anyway, and I'm sure it's a scene she'll long remember."[107]

---

107. R Lederer, quoted in Mieses.

For the shot in which Regan's feet are seen over the edge of the building, production secretary Andrea Nachman stood in for Linda Blair; Boorman opted not to use Blair's "tiny [feet] with short pudgy toes".[108] Nachman lay flat on her back, positioned so her knees were raised and her toes were at the edge of the roof, and straddled by camera operator David Quaid, wearing a secure harness and Regan's nightgown. The nightgown was draped over Nachman's raised knees, and the camera was aimed down toward Fifth Avenue. Boorman later wrote about how this dangerous sequence served as symbolic of his profession:

> Driven by her demon, Regan sleepwalks to the edge of the roof garden and is on the point of falling. I wore a harness attached to a rope so that I could lean out safely and teeter on the edge as I lined up the shots with my viewfinder. At the end of the day I found that the other end of the rope had not been secured. Lee [Marvin] would have seen that as a metaphor for film-making itself—your invulnerability is illusory. The picture felt like a masterpiece, a breakthrough, but I was soon to plunge off the building.[109]

Boorman's sense of a masterpiece was not shared by Warners' upper echelons. Guy McElwaine told Boorman the movie's new ending was wrong. Boorman recalled McElwaine telling him "to remember that Regan is a movie star's daughter. That is, she is still a little girl and must go home again. Well, she *isn't* a little girl, she's a woman, and her mother was never around anyway. She is going off into the future, armed with a new spirituality."[110] (Fans of *The Exorcist* might take exception to Boorman impugning Chris MacNeil, the harrowed protagonist of Friedkin's film.) Going over McElwaine's head, John Boorman sent a copy of the rewritten script to Ted Ashley, later claiming, "Ashley agreed when I pointed out that during shooting the movie had gathered such force and power that the old ending seemed anticlimactic."[111] Indeed, Ashley was satisfied enough with the new ending—which he told John Calley was "terrific"—to approve the $600,000 and the extra week required to

---

108. Pallenberg, p. 146.

109. Boorman, p. 226.

110. J Boorman, quoted in Pallenberg, p. 127.

111. J Boorman, quoted in Pallenberg, p. 130.

film it. (Richard Burton reportedly received $250,000.00 for overtime.) The film would now climax with the MacNeils' house breaking apart, as Father Lamont kills Regan's doppelganger, and Regan herself defeats Pazuzu's locust plague by connecting spiritually with Kokumo; after the struggle ends, Lamont and Regan leave together. Boorman later explained to Michel Ciment that the house's collapse was storyboarded and executed intricately:

> [The house] was built entirely on a hydraulic system and each transformation had to be gauged exactly. [Richard] Macdonald is an amazing man who had a tough time contending with studio bureaucracy, since they really couldn't imagine anyone as imaginative as he is. He's a really hard worker, with an extraordinary power of concentration. I remember that, when he came to my home in the evening, I'd describe each shot to him and, with his eyes closed, he'd sketch it out like some practitioner of Zen.[112]

The destruction of the MacNeil house was written into the script after the filmmakers were told they could not film in Georgetown: Pallenberg reasoned that, as they had to build a replica of the house, they had the freedom to do destroy it. The lack of planning permission for the real house prompted Boorman to cancel principal photography in Washington D.C.; the Washington Airport, as seen in the film, is actually Hollywood-Burbank Airport, known today as Bob Hope Airport. It also served as a filming location for scenes in *Giant* (1956), *The Parallax View* (1974), and *Indiana Jones and the Last Crusade* (1989).

In the meantime, the disassembly of the "Hitchcock Steps" in Stage 16 allowed for completion of construction of the mud city of Jepti, which had progressed for several months. Father Lamont's encounter with Kokumo's doppelganger was filmed in this set of wire-mesh and plaster; also built in Stage 16 was the Locust Control Centre in which Lamont converses with the "real" Kokumo. For this sequence, James Earl Jones, playing Kokumo, had white streaks added to the hair on his brow to subtly connote the antennae of the locust head-dress worn by Kokumo in Lamont's trance. In the Control Centre set, Jones was uneasy handling live locusts and so he wore an arm brace—unseen by the camera—to steady his involuntary shaking whilst holding an insect aloft and extolling the virtues of

---

112. J Boorman, quoted in Ciment, p. 172.

"the Good Locust." Joey Green, the teenager playing the young Kokumo in other scenes, was also perturbed by the locusts, which had been placed on his face and body during the possession scenes.

With Warners insisting upon the shooting of *The Heretic* to wrap, Boorman and his crew filmed the violent destruction of the MacNeil house, the centerpiece of the film's rewritten ending. Key to this ending was the concept of "The Void," a black hole-like pit that opens up under the house. The house would be sucked into this otherworldly dimension, conveying the notion that the rest of the world would be sucked into the pit unless Pazuzu is defeated. This idea was scaled down for budgetary and scheduling reasons—Richard Burton's availability was limited—and so, as filmed, the house merely collapses into a heap of rubble, rather than being sucked into a supernatural vortex. (*The Heretic* reprises the dénouement of Boorman's *Leo the Last*, which ends with Leo's mansion, located at the end of a Notting Hill *cul-de-sac*, going up in flames and collapsing into rubble.) "The Void," at least in the form Boorman and Pallenberg envisioned, does not appear in the finished film at all. A climax remarkably close to what Boorman and Pallenberg intended—a suburban house being sucked into another dimension—would be realized successfully in the Steven Spielberg/Tobe Hooper ghost movie extravaganza *Poltergeist* (1982). (1986's less-successful *Poltergeist II: The Other Side* seems to have drawn inspiration from *Exorcist II*, or at least utilized similar tropes. In its attempt to provide an explanation for the supernatural events of the first film, *Poltergeist II* draws upon elements of "exotic" mysticism—Native American, rather than Ethiopian—and suggests Carol Ann Freeling's benign clairvoyance attracts malevolent psychic turbulence.)

"They must've shot ten different ends and I didn't understand one of them," Richard Burton told *The New York Times*. "I'd become so beaten down by California sunshine and California smog that I said, 'I'll do any ending, I'm sure you gentlemen with your exquisite taste will choose the right one... [I remember] being in a house on a bed with Linda Blair, and suddenly the roof falls in and the bed collapses and we slide into an abyss and I can't tell you what it was like."[113] In the revised climax of the film, the demon Pazuzu would be defeated by both Lamont and Regan: after Lamont physically defeats Regan's doppelganger, Regan herself would banish Pazuzu by ritually dispelling the locust swarm conjured by the demon. Despite trepidation from the crew, Burton proved to be cooperative

---

113. R Burton, quoted in J Maslin, "Burton: 'In Trouble All My Life.'" *The New York Times*, Oct. 5, 1977.

Regan MacNeil (Linda Blair) finds herself caught between Father Lamont (Richard Burton) and Dr. Tuskin (Louise Fletcher).

Locust madness: the insect motif as it appears throughout *Exorcist II*.

for the scenes in which Lamont is slumped against the walls with locusts on his face; a stuntman doubled for Burton for the more arduous scenes in which Lamont is thrown around. Linda Blair was doubled for the scene in which Regan's demonic counterpart slides down the house's falling floor;

"The flames!" The fire motif as it appears throughout *Exorcist II*.

however, the young star did not manage to avoid physical harm during photography of the film's climactic scenes. According to Barbara Pallenberg, a tear-stricken Blair fled the set after enduring half a day in which she was slammed against a wall by Burton playing the possessed Lamont. Boorman ran after Blair and calmed her down; when Blair reported for work the next day her back and upper arms were bruised.

The collapse of the house took days to film, following which John Boorman finished shooting *The Heretic*'s climactic scenes in the Prospect Street set in Stage 4/11. With these scenes completed, Linda Blair returned home for rest and relaxation while John Boorman, Richard Burton, and the film crew travelled to Page, Arizona, to shoot further scenes. It was in Arizona that canyon footage would be filmed and composited with matte paintings to simulate the African terrain; it was also where Lamont's meeting with "Ecumenical" Edwards (Ned Beatty) and Lamont's near-perilous stoning by misunderstanding Ethiopians were filmed. After completing his scenes for the film, Richard Burton travelled to Ontario to begin filming *Equus* under Sidney Lumet's direction.

By the time principal photography for *The Heretic* ended on November 5, 1976, John Calley had returned to the post he had occupied when he gave the film the green light. Despite the beleaguered nature of the five-and-a-half-month shoot and Boorman's month-long absence from the set, principal photography finished, quite remarkably, only one week over schedule. (By comparison, *The Exorcist*'s planned 85-day shoot had lasted 224 days.) *The Heretic* now entered its post-production phase; it would be almost half a year before release of the completed film.

Warner Music's 2001 CD re-release of the *Exorcist II: The Heretic*
soundtrack album. Music by Ennio Morricone.

5

Fat-Free:
Post-Production of
The Heretic

"The work you're doing is incredible. Miraculous!"

– From *Exorcist II: The Heretic* (1977)
by William Goodhart

Upon completion of principal photography of *The Heretic*, John Boorman returned to Ireland to shoot the African village shots he had previously attempted at Burbank. Miniatures were set up in the soundstages of south-west Ireland's Ardmore Studios, where Boorman had completed post-production of *Leo the Last* and filmed the interior scenes of *Zardoz*. 34-year-old Garrett Brown had used the camera mount he invented, the Steadicam, in the full-scale village set in Burbank; he was now required to glide across the miniatures in Ardmore, serving as the point of view of the demon Pazuzu flying over the village. Brown's stabilizing camera mount—comprising a system of balances and gyros strapped to the operator's waist—was an innovation in cinematography, superior to cumbersome wheeled dollies and hand-held cameras by way of its ability to film smooth tracking shots with no jostling. Introduced in 1975, the Steadicam had been used in the filming of several high-profile films released in 1976—*Marathon Man*, *Rocky*, and *Bound for Glory*—and would go on to become standard equipment in the industry; Brown won his first Academy Award in 1978 for inventing it. Boorman told Michel Ciment the Steadicam is "half muscle, half machine, and has a floating,

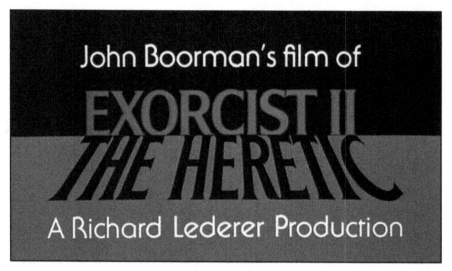

Title still from Warners' *Exorcist II* teaser trailer.

drifting quality which I wanted for the flight across Africa... It enabled me to suggest the point of view of Pazuzu."[114] Boorman claimed Garrett Brown's involvement in *The Heretic* led to infiltration from the film equipment company Panavision:

> [Brown] had taken his invention to Panavision, but they rejected it before going to develop a version of their own. He was lining up his device on Stage 16 when he saw Robert Gottschalk, the president of Panavision, taking pictures of the Steadicam from the shadows—a little industrial espionage. Garrett had just strapped on the camera. He shouted at Gottschalk, who scampered off the stage. We all enjoyed the next day's rushes of Gottschalk running for the car.[115]

Two years later, Garrett Brown brought his Steadicam expertise to another big-budget horror film from Warners, with more memorable results: Stanley Kubrick's *The Shining* (1980).

The Heretic was scheduled to be edited in Los Angeles by John Merritt, editor of Boorman's *Zardoz*, before homesickness prompted him to

---

114. J Boorman, quoted in Ciment, p. 172.

115. Boorman, pp. 227-228.

quit the film and return to London. His replacement was Tom Priestley, who had worked with Boorman on *Leo the Last* and *Deliverance*, earning an Oscar nomination for editing the latter. Ironically, *The Heretic* was edited closer to John Merritt's home. Unable to obtain a permit to cut the film at Burbank, Priestley edited *The Heretic* under Boorman's supervision in Ireland. "John loves visual interest generally at the expense of the narrative, and my job is to preserve narrative in his films," Priestley told Barbara Pallenberg. "One tries with cuts to release the energy in a film."[116] The time spent editing in Ireland also served as a period of convalescence for Boorman, still weak from his recent illness and hospitalization:

> The family gathered back together, and we got back our strength in the healing hills, and took comfort from the trees and flow of the river. Then, all too soon, I was back to Burbank for the track laying and sound mix. The mixers all complained about a young director who preceded me in the dubbing theatre. He constantly changed his mind and insisted on re-cutting the picture during the mix, confusing everybody. I ran into him. He was small and softly spoken. He was about to turn the movie business on its head. George Lucas was fretting over *Star Wars* as I struggled to shape *The Heretic*.[117]

Aware that Boorman was working with less freedom than in his earlier films, Priestley lamented that "the studio was clogged up with television work, so there was a shortage of skilled people and facilities. Getting it finished in time to meet the almost impossible deadline became a nightmare: administrative problems overshadowed creative problems."[118] The rough cut of *The Heretic* was 132 minutes long—relatively short for a film at that stage of editing. Boorman noted with pride to Barbara Pallenberg, "When you consider how much we worked, how many months, how many shots, you realize that there is not an ounce of fat in the rough assembly—it is only two hours, twenty minutes long—after eighteen weeks of shooting, not an ounce of fat."[119] Boorman was putting a positive spin

---

116. T Priestley, quoted in Pallenberg, p. 204.

117. Boorman, p. 228.

118. T Priestley, quoted in Ciment, p. 243.

119. J Boorman, quoted in Pallenberg, p. 204.

on the fact there was not enough usable footage to assemble a rough cut of the usual size. Priestley admitted, "Because of the complexity of many of the scenes—elaborate sets and difficult camera moves, never mind the enormous set-piece stunts—there was less cover than on the earlier films, and therefore less opportunity to use the editing creatively, and never enough time."[120] Boorman and Priestley subsequently trimmed the film down to 118 minutes for its final cut.

Italian composer Ennio Morricone, best known for scoring Sergio Leone's "Spaghetti Westerns" in the 1960s, was commissioned to provide original music for *The Heretic*—further distancing the film from *The Exorcist*, which had a score of source music by various artists. (Lalo Schifrin, who scored Boorman's *Hell in the Pacific*, was hired to score *The Exorcist* only for Friedkin to deem his work unsatisfactory and discard it in favor of a selection of pre-existing pieces by various composers.) One of the most influential and versatile composers of the 20th century, Morricone in the mid-1970s was yet to make a dent in American films although he was extremely prolific, writing ten to fifteen scores a year for (mostly European) films. "He is a tremendous enthusiast and he loves films," Boorman recalled. "What he's doing with music is responding like an audience."[121]

Morricone was approached when *The Heretic* went into production but was unable to commit to the film due to scheduling issues. By the time principal photography had ended, Morricone agreed to score *The Heretic* and duly provided a soundtrack encompassing a wide range of elements: ominous strings; African, Latin, and Middle Eastern melodies; tribal chants and percussion; female vocalizations; and guitars and drums. (Morricone applied a similar approach a decade later to his score for *The Mission* [1986], which also reflected competing cultures in its blending of liturgical chorales and European and non-European music.) *The Heretic* came at a pivotal time in Morricone's career; it was one of his earliest forays into American film; indeed, the composer recalled the first time he visited the United States was to record *The Heretic's* score after meeting with Boorman: "I remember the first time we met was in Dublin, where Boorman was shooting, and we watched the film together. He allowed me a considerable amount of freedom; I took some initiative and scored everything before going to Los Angeles to record the soundtrack."[122] The re-

---

120. T Priestley, quoted in Ciment, p. 243.

121. J Boorman, quoted in A De Rosa, *Ennio Morricone In His Own Words* (New York: Oxford University Press, 2019), p. 108.

122. E Morricone, quoted in De Rosa, p. 107.

cording of the score was one of the few elements of *The Heretic*'s production to proceed smoothly, and it was a pleasant experience for Morricone:

> Based on my experience thus far, I was very anxious that the recording with the American choir would turn out good. I arrived in Los Angeles a week ahead of schedule, because I was so stressed about it and I wanted to attend the choir's rehearsal. The first thing I did after I landed was rush into the studio where they were rehearsing. As I walked through the door and approached the rehearsal room, I could hear those voices gradually becoming more intense—they were rehearsing the "Little Afro-Flemish Mass." They were incredibly talented and extraordinarily committed. "Holy cow," I gulped, and almost broke out in tears of joy. They had already studied everything. When I entered, they stopped, and I applauded. I was moved. "Bravissimi," I exclaimed with great emotion. Thinking about it still gives me goosebumps. Suddenly one of them approached me and told me, "You should listen to how well our choir conductor sings." The conductor was a black woman, like nearly all of them, with a head full of hair. I remember her well. "Madam, I was told you sing beautifully, why don't you join in the choir?" I asked her. She accepted and went to the microphone. Her voice was so profound that it sounded like it came from a baritone, and she knew all the parts by heart.[123]

Morricone's inventive score contained sound collages of melodic and harmonic fragments. Influenced by Anton Webern and working from a handbook of combinable music modules, Morricone explained the process by which he recorded the "swarming, dissonant sonorities" of the score: "In the recording room, I would assign to the orchestra the free dissonant structures that I had previously prepared; while a group of instruments would play parts 1 and 2, I would give the attack for part 3 to another group."[124] Engaging with *The Heretic*'s intercontinental story and sense of the hallucinatory, Morricone gave Boorman's film an aural accompaniment that provided some sense of stylistic cohesion to the narrative and imagery. The composer spoke positively of its recording and Boorman's use of it:

123. E Morricone, quoted in De Rosa, p. 108.

124. E Morricone, quoted in De Rosa, p. 169.

Everything worked out for the best. You know, at the time Los Angeles had the reputation of being a place where one could make six recordings with six different orchestras and compare them all, only to realize that they were all equally extraordinary. There was a lot of competition and many excellent musicians to work with. For that film I wrote pieces like "Little Afro-Flemish Mass" for a multiple chorus formed by six or seven solo singers, percussion, and other instruments, and "Night Flight," for which I used the same multiple chorus but with nontraditional vocal techniques. In both pieces, each part was thought out to be independent; it could play or remain silent depending on my arbitrary decision to give soloists the signal. The procedure engendered a free counterpoint, an agglomerated texture where the harmonic relations were no longer decisive and where each resulting combination could be different every time. I remember that [Boorman] employed both the pieces in a very clever way—he used "Night Flight" in the moment in which Father Philip Lamont, the exorcist, meets the demon Pazuzu shortly before climbing on his wings; in that context, one of the chorus's voices becomes precisely that of the demon.[125]

Continuing his penchant for identifying characters with signature themes, Morricone crafted his score around two main leitmotifs—one theme for Pazuzu in several iterations, and another for Regan, reminiscent of Krzysztof Komeda's lullaby theme for *Rosemary's Baby*. "Regan's Theme," however, lacks Komeda's sinister undertone, being a benign piece for acoustic guitar, a small string section, and wordless female vocals. Many years later, "Regan's Theme" was repurposed in Quentin Tarantino's Morricone-scored, ultra-violent western *The Hateful Eight* (2015).

The film's sound mix was completed in Burbank in early June 1977, but its title was subject to further revision. Beginning as *The Heretic* before being renamed *The Heretic: Exorcist II* at the outset of production, Warners finally settled upon *Exorcist II: The Heretic*, foregrounding the film's link to the studio's biggest success. It is also likely Warners sought to avoid confusion with *The Heretic: The Strange Odyssey of Bishop Pike*, a film project about the life and death of the controversial Episcopalian bishop James

125. E Morricone, quoted in De Rosa, p. 108.

Pike. (The screenplay, by Irving S. White and Harold Lieberman, circulated in the 1970s but was never filmed.) Television's *Saturday Night Live* had actually beaten Warners to the title of *Exorcist II*, which was the name of a sketch aired during the seventh episode of *SNL*'s first season, on December 13, 1975. (Written by Michael O'Donoghue, the sketch starred guest host Richard Pryor as Father Karras, guest star Thalmus Rusalala as Father Merrin, and *SNL* regular Laraine Newman as Regan.) A *Daily Variety* article on September 8, 1976 was one of the earliest publications to cite the release title of *Exorcist II: The Heretic.* Pointedly, Boorman refers to the film only as *The Heretic* in his books *Adventures of a Suburban Boy* (2003) and *Conclusions* (2020); Michel Ciment's *Boorman: Un visionnaire en son temps* (1985) does likewise. Onscreen, although *Exorcist II* appears above *The Heretic,* the latter's typeface is larger. (Title Designer Dan Perri replicated the dour, red-on-black Weiss typeface he had provided for *The Exorcist.*) In lieu of "A John Boorman Film," or "John Boorman's *Exorcist II: The Heretic,*" the film and its trailers display a Richard Attenborough-style possessory: "John Boorman's Film of *Exorcist II: The Heretic.*" William Peter Blatty received no onscreen credit for the use of his characters.

The production of *Exorcist II: The Heretic* cost Warner Brothers $14 million—$1½ million higher than its scheduled budget, and $3½ million more than the budget of *The Exorcist.* Warners reportedly spent $4 million on the *Exorcist II* advertising campaign.

> *"In 1974, a motion picture shocked the world. It has become one of the most acclaimed and successful films in history. The* Exorcist *is a classic in its own time. And now, Warner Bros. takes you a step beyond—*Exorcist II: The Heretic. *Starring Linda Blair, Richard Burton, Louise Fletcher, Max von Sydow, James Earl Jones. Their minds locked together with the most terrifying vision of all..."*

> – Narration from the *Exorcist II: The Heretic* teaser

Employing conceptual artwork, photographic stills, ominous stock music, and a portentous voiceover, the 75-second *Exorcist II* teaser manages to make the film look reasonably scary. Then Warners released the full two-minute trailer which, like the teaser, begins with stills from *The Exorcist,* accompanied by a grave voiceover. The brief narration ("*Four years ago,* The Exorcist *shocked the world. Now, the struggle between good and evil goes on...*") precedes a fast-cut montage of *Exorcist II* scenes spanning practically every major scene of the entire film, backed by a bass-driven musical cue by Morricone featuring electric guitars, whip-lash-like sounds, and choral wailing. Audiences in 1977 might have been intrigued or baffled by the trippy freak-out the trailer promised; viewed today, there's a sense of camp about the trailer but it does convey a pace and sense excitement that the film itself does not match up to. Neverthe-less, Warners' *Exorcist II* press kit described the teaser as "chilling" and the trailer as "surefire." The trailer was truncated into a thirty-second TV spot, featuring a different introduction (*"Regan MacNeil. Once she was brushed by the wings of evil. It is four years later. What does she remember? Where will it lead her?"*). The teaser, trailer, and TV spot do not contain any spoken dialogue from the film itself.

Exorcist II's printed advertising campaign began with posters for the film (advertised uniquely as *Exorcist 2: The Heretic*) featuring Linda Blair and Richard Burton's portraits united by an eye motif, with the ta-gline *"Their minds joined together—with the most terrifying vision of all."* (This artwork also appeared in the teaser.) The campaign subsequently unleashed by Warners echoed the minimalist design employed so ef-fectively by *The Exorcist* and concentrated almost solely on Linda Blair. Bill Gold, the veteran graphic artist who designed *The Exorcist's* instantly iconic theatrical release poster (as well as the domestic and international posters for Boorman's *Deliverance*), was tasked with *The Heretic's* artwork. The central image of *Exorcist II* advertisements was a stylized, black-and-white photograph, replacing *The Exorcist's* shot of Father Merrin outside the MacNeil house with a backlit portrait of a rather befuddled-looking Linda Blair. This image was used for *Exorcist II* posters, day-bills, and newspaper and magazine advertisements (and for later VHS and DVD releases). Leading up to the release of *Exorcist II*, a huge billboard of Blair's portrait loomed over New York City's Times Square. Most versions of the *Exorcist II* poster featured the tagline *"It's four years later... What does she remember?"* and a disaster-movie-style horizontal line of boxes depicting the faces of Blair, Richard Burton, Louise Fletcher, Max von Sydow, Paul Henreid, and James Earl Jones. (Kitty Winn was not featured, despite her billing above Henreid and Jones.)

William Peter Blatty's novel of *The Exorcist* was re-issued in paper-back with a new tagline emblazoned across the front cover: "This electri-fying experience in fiction inspires a great new motion picture, *Exorcist II: The Heretic.*" Motion picture novelizations were a large industry in the 1970s, but no such adaptation of *Exorcist II* was released. William Peter

Blatty turned down a sizable financial offer to novelize the film and reportedly filed an injunction to prevent anyone else from writing it, lest people think the novelization was his work. (In hindsight, it is unfortunate that *Exorcist II* was never novelized. Film novelizations often adapt earlier versions of the script, and an *Exorcist II* novel written concurrently with the film's production might well have been intriguingly different from the finished film—perhaps closer to William Goodhart's conception than John Boorman and Rospo Pallenberg's.) Warner Books did, however, publish Barbara Pallenberg's *The Making of Exorcist II: The Heretic* as a promotional item. Pallenberg's book was published in August 1977 and her account ends at the beginning of *Exorcist II*'s post-production phase, just before Christmas 1976. The front of Pallenberg's book and the sleeve of Ennio Morricone's soundtrack album bore the ubiquitous Linda Blair deer-in-the-headlights portrait. (The 2001 CD edition of the album features a different sleeve.) Warners' music division also released a 7-inch single containing Morricone's themes for Regan and Pazuzu.

During filming of *Exorcist II*, Warners engaged the production company Robbins Nest to create a featurette on the making of the film. The seven-and-a-half-minute short features behind-the-scenes footage as well as interviews with Boorman, psychiatrist Dr. William Baumann and professional hypnotist Henry Prokop (uncredited consultants for *Exorcist II*), and Jesuit priest Father John J. Nicola (technical advisor for *The Exorcist*.) "Why is it that we like to be frightened and horrified by a movie? I think it releases something—our deepest fears, our most horrible nightmares are exorcized by the process of watching it—be tortured, really, perhaps by a film," Boorman explained in the featurette. "But I think what we've done is something more because out of this horror and tension and fear and terror emerges the possibility of the human race rising to something better."[126]

With his work on *Exorcist II* seemingly at an end, John Boorman urged Warners to hold a test-screening of the film and suggested Tucson, Arizona as the location. However, the studio refused to hold a preview screening—a decision that would prove to be fateful—and duly scheduled *Exorcist II*'s general release date for Friday, June 17, 1977. Cinemas booked the film under the "Blind Bidding" policy, the practice of film distributors requiring theatre owners to bid for and book movies without actually seeing them. This was standard procedure at the time for the

---

126. J Boorman, quoted in *Exorcist II: The Heretic* production featurette. A Professional Films/Robbins Nest Production, 1977.

licensing of first-run film engagements; given the massive success of *The Exorcist*, it is not surprising that cinema owners figured similar grosses for *Exorcist II* would be a foregone conclusion. Without seeing the film, exhibitors signed a contract guaranteeing Warners a hefty advance and a sizeable percentage of *Exorcist II* ticket sales. The contract stipulated theatres had to screen *Exorcist II* for a minimum of twelve weeks.

On May 25, 1977, a month before *Exorcist II* premiered, Twentieth Century-Fox released George Lucas' science-fiction fantasy *Star Wars*. Breaking box office records to become the highest-grossing film in motion picture history, *Star Wars* became an unprecedented cultural and filmmaking phenomenon, changing the way movies were made and marketed, and heralding a new era of special-effects-driven summer blockbusters. (It also instantly dated and all but obliterated the trend of dreary sci-fi films depicting people in silly costumes roaming around dehumanized futures, of which Boorman's *Zardoz* was a prime example.) Not anticipating the staggering success it would soon have on its hands, Twentieth Century-Fox initially released *Star Wars* to relatively few theatres in the United States before expediting its nationwide release.

John Boorman did not stay in the United States for the premiere of *Exorcist II*. On Sunday, June 12, 1977, he returned home to Ireland to resume work on his King Arthur screenplay, *Merlin* (later titled *Knights*, and finally *Excalibur*). On Friday, June 17, 1977—thirteen months after it began filming, and over seven months since filming had ceased—*Exorcist II: The Heretic* was released to over 700 theaters across North America.

The onscreen title of *Exorcist II: The Heretic*. Title design by Dan Perri.

6

Exorcist II:
The Synopsis

"I'm sorry. I understand now. But the world won't."

– From *Exorcist II: The Heretic* (1977)
by William Goodhart

Ted *"Theodore" Logan* (Keanu Reeves): *I hope this works.*
Bill S. Preston, Esquire (Alex Winter): *It worked in* The Exorcist, One *and* Three!

– From *Bill & Ted's Bogus Journey* (1991)
by Chris Matheson & Ed Solomon

FOUR YEARS AFTER THE EVENTS of *The Exorcist*, a middle-aged Jesuit priest, Father Philip Lamont, attempts to perform an exorcism on a possessed woman in a small hillside chapel on the outskirts of a South American city. The woman momentarily breaks free from the demon's control, asking Lamont, "Why me? Why me? I heal the sick!" The demon regains control and Lamont is unable to prevent the woman from then setting herself on fire and burning to death. Recalled to Rome, Lamont is assigned by his superior, Cardinal Jaros, to investigate the circumstances surrounding the death of Father Lankester Merrin, who died in Georgetown, Washington D.C., whilst attempting to exorcise the 12-year-old Regan MacNeil. Jaros informs Lamont the Church has indicted Merrin

A hypnotherapy session goes awry. Engaged with the mind of Regan (Linda Blair) using the Synchronizer, Dr. Gene Tuskin (Louise Fletcher) is imperiled when the recall of Regan's exorcism by Father Lankester Merrin (Max von Sydow) unleashes the demon Pazuzu.

posthumously on charges of heresy and impounded his controversial writings. Jaros and Lamont are both former pupils of Merrin, and Jaros hopes that Lamont's investigation will restore Merrin's reputation and dispel notions he was a Satanist. Lamont, who is struggling with his faith because of the evil he sees in the world, claims he is unworthy. Jaros insists he is suitable, since he knew Merrin, was exposed to his teachings, and is an experienced exorcist.

Regan MacNeil, now sixteen years old, is living in a New York City penthouse apartment while her actor mother, Chris MacNeil, is working on location. Regan lives with Sharon Spencer (formerly Chris' live-in secretary) and is regularly attending therapy sessions at a psychiatric institute, where her therapist is Dr Gene Tuskin. Tuskin believes Regan has repressed her memories regarding what happened to her in Washington; Regan only remembers being sick and having bad dreams and insists there is nothing wrong with her. She feels she is only attending therapy for her mother's sake.

Father Lamont visits the Institute, intent on asking Regan questions about the night Father Merrin died. Tuskin, who believes the exorcism did more harm than good to Regan, disapproves of Lamont's approach and rebuffs his attempts to question Regan although she allows him to stay on as an observer in the session. Tuskin introduces Regan to an experimental biofeedback device, "the Synchronizer," which allows two subjects to synchronize their brainwaves and share memories. Tuskin believes the Synchronizer is the key to unlocking Regan's repressed memories of the exorcism.

Tuskin and Regan undergo a mental link through the Synchronizer. Regan recalls her memories of Father Merrin's fatal heart attack on the night of the exorcism, and through the Synchronizer, Tuskin telepathically witnesses the event. Tuskin is attacked by the Assyrian demon Pazuzu (the entity that possessed Regan), and almost has a heart attack, in telepathic unison with Merrin's fatal heart attack. Regan is unlinked from the Synchronizer; Lamont uses the Synchronizer himself to rescue Tuskin. Lamont tells Tuskin he saw something "evil;" Tuskin replies what he saw could have been "a dream, a fantasy, a hallucination—not a memory at all." Regan gives Lamont a picture she has drawn, which Lamont interprets as a premonition of a fire in the hospital, which comes to pass. That night, Regan is haunted by strange dreams, in which strange voices tell her "We're going flying," and she sees an African village being attacked by a swarm of locusts. In tandem with the climax of the dream, a sleepwalking Regan very nearly walks off the roof of her apartment building.

Lamont is met in Georgetown by Sharon, who lets him into the Mac-Neil house at the request of Chris MacNeil. Sharon tells Lamont she left the MacNeils for two years before returning to them. She feels she is never at peace unless she remains near Regan, which confuses her. Lamont asks Sharon questions about the exorcism. He enters Regan's bedroom, where the exorcism took place: there is a locust in the room. Upon returning to New York, Lamont is coupled with Regan for another session with the Synchronizer. They both see an event that took place forty years ago: Father Merrin exorcising Pazuzu from a boy in Africa.

Merrin explains in a voiceover that the boy, Kokumo, had powers that kept away Pazuzu (the demon being manifested in the form of a locust swarm), but he believes these very powers could be what drew Pazuzu to the village in the first place. Pazuzu begins speaking through Regan to Lamont; Lamont accepts Pazuzu's offer of a demonstration of power. Pazuzu telepathically transports Lamont across Africa; at the climax of the journey, Lamont sees Kokumo, now a middle-aged man. After being brought out of the Synchronizer-induced trance state, Lamont tells Tuskin that Kokumo has power over evil. He also believes that research such as that practiced by Tuskin with the Synchronizer can accelerate mankind's spiritual evolution. Lamont is convinced that finding Kokumo would prove the validity of Merrin's exorcisms, but he is forbidden by Jaros from going to Africa. Frustrated that his investigation is being stonewalled, Lamont defies the Cardinal's orders and flies to Africa.

In the Institute, Regan inadvertently demonstrates a mysterious healing ability when she reaches into the mind of an autistic girl and cures her. As Lamont journeys through Africa in search of Kokumo, he sees places he telepathically encountered through the Synchronizer. Lamont visits the towering church in which Merrin exorcised Kokumo. Now sharing a mental link with Lamont, Regan, during a tap-dance recital, suffers a seizure in tandem with Lamont being assaulted with stones after he mentions seeing Pazuzu in a trance, and is mistaken by the locals for a devil-worshipper. In hospital, a sedated Regan is able to communicate with Lamont telepathically, even though neither of them is connected to the Synchronizer. Pazuzu speaks through Regan; Lamont calls upon Pazuzu to help him find Kokumo. Lamont finds Kokumo—or a doppelganger of him—outfitted in an insect costume. Kokumo accuses Lamont of having lost faith in God, as the priest called upon Pazuzu to find him. To prove his faith, Lamont must walk barefoot across a moat of upright nails. At first step, the nails pierce Lamont's foot; he pitches forward onto the nails and awakens in a laboratory in an equatorial station: his experience in the village was a hallucination, and now Lamont converses with the "real" Kokumo, who is working as a scientist, studying locusts and methods of preventing them from destroying native crops. Kokumo tells Lamont when the locusts breed in large numbers, their wings brushing against each other causes agitation, and the locusts become a marauding swarm. However, a female locust will break the swarm mentality. This "Good Locust" has been bred to "resist the brushing of the wings" and will dissuade the others from their destructive path.

Lamont returns to New York and is reunited with Regan, who has taken the Synchronizer and run away from the hospital. In a motel, Lamont and Regan use the Synchronizer, and in the course of their shared vision, the disembodied voice of Father Merrin informs them that Kokumo, and other people (including Regan and the South American woman Lamont failed to exorcise), have developed a psychic healing ability, and Satan has sent Pazuzu to destroy them via possession. Father Merrin believes these psychic powers are a spiritual gift which will one day be shared by all humanity in a kind of global consciousness; people like Kokumo and Regan foreshadow this new type of humanity. Merrin entrusts Regan to

Lamont and asks him to watch over her. Lamont emerges from the session in a strange, silent state, affected by Pazuzu. He leaves the motel and Regan follows; the pair travel by train and bus to Georgetown. Tuskin and Sharon are concerned for Regan, and they trail her and Lamont by plane. During their flight, Tuskin and Sharon's plane is buffeted by turbulence caused by Pazuzu via Lamont, but this ends when Regan is able to draw Lamont's attention. Tuskin and Sharon arrive in Washington and take a taxi cab to the MacNeil house.

At Prospect Street in Georgetown, Lamont and Regan enter the MacNeil house. When he opens the door of Regan's old bedroom, Lamont is attacked by a swarm of locusts—at the same time, the taxi Sharon and Tuskin are riding in loses control and crashes into the fencing in front of the MacNeil house. The taxi driver is killed. Sharon and Tuskin extract themselves from the cab, but Sharon begins to act strangely: she refuses to let Tuskin into the house, and forces Tuskin to name Pazuzu, acknowledging the demon's existence. Regan finds Lamont slumped outside the bedroom. He silently points to the room. When Regan enters the room, she sees a demonic Regan doppelganger. She reacts with horror, and Lamont, in a trance state, enters the room and grabs Regan menacingly, only stopping when Regan invokes the name of Father Merrin. The demon says to Lamont that "Pazuzu's Regan is the only Regan," and transmogrifies into a tarted-up, yellow-eyed Regan in a slinky nightgown, whom Lamont embraces at her invitation. The demon tells Lamont to kill Regan. Lamont begins shoving the real Regan violently against the wall.

Outside, Sharon deliberately breaks one of the taxi's headlights over an open fuel line, immolating herself in the conflagration. Tuskin shouts around the neighborhood for help, but nobody responds. Inside the house, Lamont halts his attempt to kill Regan when the near-unconscious girl begins speaking in unison with the disembodied voice of Kokumo: "We like to call her the good locust. She was evolved to resist the brushing of the wings." The demon says to Lamont, "Once the wings have brushed you, you're mine forever!" to which Regan/Kokumo reply, "She will break the chain reaction." After Regan echoes the words of the girl Lamont failed to exorcise at the beginning of the film ("Why me? Why me? *¿Por qué? ¿Por qué?*"), Lamont embraces Regan and Regan/Kokumo instruct him, "You must tear out her evil heart." Lamont straddles the demon, who struggles against him. The demon calls upon Pazuzu. The house begins to break apart amid a maelstrom of locusts, the physical manifestation of Pazuzu. Lamont rips out the demon's heart.

Regan and Lamont manage to escape from the house as it crumbles to its foundations. Regan waves her arm around in the air, enacting the young Kokumo employing a sling against the locust plague. The dead locusts pile up around Regan's feet and disappear, Pazuzu apparently having been killed or banished. Lamont approaches Tuskin, who is holding onto a dying and repentant Sharon. Lamont administers the last rites to Sharon, who dies, and proclaims that Pazuzu has been subdued. A tearful Tuskin apologizes to Regan and says she "understands now… but the

"Pazuzu's Regan is the *only* Regan." The demon transmogrifies into a double of Regan (Linda Blair).

A selection of *Exorcist II* lobby cards by Warner Bros. (1977).

world won't." Lamont embraces Tuskin, who tells Regan and Lamont they have to go. "Take care of her," Tuskin says to Lamont. Lamont and Regan walk off into the distance, their arms clasped around each other. A cluster of onlookers and some policemen suddenly arrive. One of the policemen asks Tuskin questions, but she silently and tearfully gazes into the distance.

Note: This is a synopsis of the original theatrical version of *Exorcist II.* Other cuts of the film feature largely the same plot but a different ending.

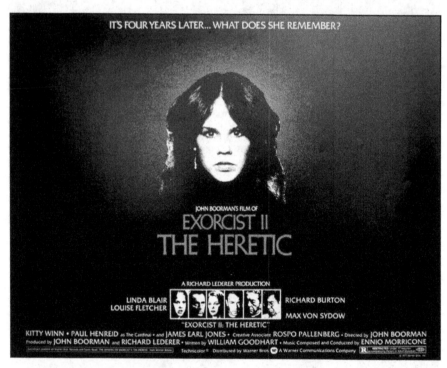

Exorcist II: The Heretic theatrical release poster by Warner Bros. (1977).

7

Exorcist II: Release, Recut, and Reception

"My life was threatened Saturday night following a screening of Exorcist II: The Heretic *at the downtown Oriental Theater.*

At approximately 11:55 p.m. on Saturday, an unidentified black male—approximately 6 feet tall, weighing 200 pounds, and 40 years old—walked up to me and yelled, "If you say one nice thing about that lousy movie, I'm going to burn your paper, kick in my television set, and then I'm coming after you!" He was kidding, and his embarrassed wife smiled weakly and said, "Don't mind him; he's just upset."

He should be. Exorcist II *is the worse major motion picture I've seen in almost eight years on the job."*

– Gene Siskel[127]

THE FOLLOWING THINGS HAPPENED in 1977: Apple Computers became a corporation. Jimmy Carter was sworn in as US President. *Roots* premiered on television. Optical fiber carried live telephone traffic for the first time. Right-wing forces in Turkey killed at least 34 leftist demonstrators in Istanbul's Taksim Square massacre. Studio 54 opened in New York City. Queen Elizabeth II celebrated her Silver Jubilee. David Frost interviewed

---

127. G Siskel, "'Exorcist II' haunted by howlingly awful special effects and script." *Chicago Tribune*, Jun. 20, 1977.

'Heretic' Is Bedeviled 'Exorcist II' Confusing Claptrap

'Exorcist II' *'Exorcist II' haunted by howlingly* The Devil made
can go away *awful special effects and script* them do it?

Whatever **'Heretic' a sorry** 'Exorcist II' goes on
in the fight against

possessed **sequel to 'Exorcist'** evil—a locust

them? Exorcist II: Silliest sequel Mumbo-Jumbo
mixture brought
a few shivers

New 'Exorcist' evokes 'Exorcist II' Devilishly Bad Film
not terror but laughter *UPROARIOUS UNREALITY* **Did Devil win**

'Exorcist II' Defies Belief **'Exorcist II': Heresy of Horror** **this time?**

Cinematic heresy 'The Heretic' Is No 'Exorcist'

The reviews were not good. A selection of headlines in response
to *Exorcist II*'s cinematic run.

Richard Nixon. The Supremes disbanded. Serial killer David Berkowitz
was arrested. Interpol prohibited motion picture videocassette piracy. Anti-
apartheid activist Steve Biko was beaten to death by South African police.
Personal computers began selling to the public. The world's first profes-
sionally managed video rental store opened. The US Department of Energy
was formed. Andreas Baader, Jan-Carl Raspe, and Gudrun Ensslin of West
Germany's Red Army Faction died in prison. Three members of Lynryd
Skynyrd were killed in a plane crash. Smallpox was eradicated. The Nobel
Peace Prize was awarded to Amnesty International. The Sex Pistols, The
Clash, Talking Heads, and Elvis Costello released their debut albums; Kate
Bush and Devo recorded theirs. David Bowie released *Low* and *"Heroes"*
and produced Iggy Pop's *The Idiot* and *Lust for Life*. Roger Waters conceived
The Wall while touring Pink Floyd's *Animals*. J.R.R. Tolkien's *The Silmaril-
lion*, P.G. Wodehouse's *Sunset at Blandings*, and T.H. White's *The Book of
Merlyn* were published posthumously. Peter Finch, Anaïs Nin, Roberto
Rossellini, Vladimir Nabokov, Elvis Presley, Groucho Marx, Marc Bolan,
Bing Crosby, Charles Chaplin, and Howard Hawks died.

1977 was a decisive and divisive year for film. Received wisdom has it
that *Star Wars* ended American cinema's *auteur*-driven "New Hollywood"
period and ushered in the era of audience-pleasing blockbusters, but the writ-

ing was on the wall before George Lucas' space opera upended the industry. In March 1977, the feel-good hit *Rocky*—written by and starring Sylvester Stallone—beat Alan J. Pakula's *All the President's Men*, Hal Ashby's *Bound for Glory*, Sidney Lumet's *Network*, and Martin Scorsese's *Taxi Driver* to win the Academy Award for Best Picture. Yet the decade was not done with darker films from New Hollywood's chief exponents: after a grueling year-long shoot in the Philippines, principal photography of Francis Ford Coppola's *Apocalypse Now* ended in May 1977. By then, *Annie Hall*, *Star Wars*, and *Smokey and the Bandit* had been released; still to come that year were *Close Encounters of the Third Kind*, *Saturday Night Fever*... and *Exorcist II: The Heretic*.

Public expectations for *Exorcist II* were high. Not only was it the sequel to one of the most successful films in history, but it was the third most expensive film production of 1977 (after *Close Encounters of the Third Kind* and *The Spy Who Loved Me*) as well as Warners' most expensive production to date. (1974's *The Towering Inferno* had a higher budget but it was a Warners/Twentieth Century-Fox co-production.) *The Exorcist* was re-released to cinemas in 1976, earning a further $10 million and whetting the public's appetite for the sequel. For many people, *The Exorcist* was an assault on the senses and seeing the movie was an endurance test. They expected the same from *Exorcist II*. "It will be a terrifying, frightening experience, almost unbearable," John Boorman assured the *Los Angeles Times*.[128] Conversely, Linda Blair told *Circus* magazine that *Exorcist II* was "tamer than the original, not so much the shocker."[129] Richard Lederer also downplayed *Exorcist II*'s horror factor:

> It's a shocker, too, but it's not as concentrated in its intensity as the first movie was. It's more of a search movie, a suspense movie... It's not a rip-off movie. It doesn't attempt to top the shocks of the first film—it's a different kind of film, a thriller, and a very effective one.[130]

Warner Brothers' expectations for *Exorcist II* were guarded. If William Peter Blatty is to be believed, Warners—in the person of vice-chairman Frank Wells—had doubts about the film:

128. J Boorman, quoted in P Talbot, "The Unmaking of *Exorcist II: The Heretic*." *Video Watchdog* #171, Nov.-Dec. 2012, p. p. 23.

129. L Blair, quoted in Mieses.

130. R Lederer, quoted in Mieses.

> A couple of weeks before it was to open, I called Frank Wells
> at Warners... He said "We'll be glad to set up a screening
> for you, Bill, but please give your word—a handshake
> agreement—if you don't like it, you won't go on television
> or to the press." I said "Hell, Frank, I can't do that. If it's
> really bad, don't show it to me." He said "I'll get back to
> you." He didn't. So I paid my three, four dollars, went down
> to see it—unbelievable. Amazingly bad. Extraordinarily
> bad, if I remember... My favourite bit was when the cab
> driver gets out and runs over to Kitty Winn, and she's an
> ember, she's charred, her car has been burned to a crisp
> and she has also, and he says "Are you alright?" I couldn't
> believe it.[131]

(Blatty's recollection is inaccurate: the cab driver dies before Sharon does, and a *policeman* later says "Lady, are you okay?", not unreasonably, to the non-charred *Dr Tuskin*.)

Wary of hostile advance publicity, Warners pre-screened *Exorcist II* for critics in selected venues—most notably in Los Angeles and New York City—on Thursday, June 16, 1977, the night before the film went into general release. The late slot ensured critics would not have time to have their reviews published in Friday's newspapers and would have to wait until Saturday or the following Friday. Gary Arnold of *The Washington Post* was one of the critics who saw *Exorcist II* before the film's general release, attending a press-only preview screening of the film in Maryland's Bethesda KB Theatre on 16 June. In his review printed two days later, Arnold reported, "I've never heard an audience reject a movie as vocally and resoundingly as the packed house at the Bethesda Thursday night."[132] Like Blatty, Arnold testified to the effect of *Exorcist II*'s unwitting comedy, describing an audience "unified in its ridicule" of an "endless parade of inexplicable, hysterical or unintentionally funny spectacles that the effect was almost the same as being at a good comedy with a receptive audience."[133] Arnold foretold a negative reception of seismic proportions when the film went public:

---

131. WP Blatty, quoted in McCabe, p. 163.

132. G Arnold, "'Exorcist II': Giving the Devil His Due." *The Washington Post*, Jun. 18, 1977.

133. Arnold.

The local theater owners who had agreed six months ago to pay cash advances for the privilege of showing *Exorcist II: The Heretic* when summer rolled around looked shellshocked Thursday night. So would anyone who had invested sums ranging from $50,000 to $200,000 in a product revealed on the eve of its opening to be a fiasco of stunning, mortifying proportions, likely to bomb out after a single weekend of public exposure and perhaps cause a major scandal in the movie business. "We're going to need two cashiers," cracked an exhibitor still capable of gallows humor. "One to sell tickets and another to hand out refunds."

Arnold recognized the dubiousness of *Exorcist II*'s narrative links to *The Exorcist*, invoking Mel Brooks' comedic fictional restaging of the Third Reich in *The Producers* (1968):

> Someone at Warners ought to have trembled at Goodhart's premise for the sequel, which begins from the nest-fouling idea that the exorcist played by Max von Sydow failed in his act of self-sacrifice that appeared to save Regan... Far from taking a new approach, the sequel merely undermines the original. In the lobby afterwards people resembled the first-nighters at "Springtime for Hitler" in *The Producers*. Perhaps Warners should change the title to "Springtime for Regan" and hope that the movie public also decides to misconstrue it as a put-on."[134]

There were also reports of members of the press snickering during the *Exorcist II* screening at the Academy of Motion Picture Arts and Sciences Theatre in Beverly Hills. In any case, Warners' tactical delay with the press screenings worked: *Exorcist II* reportedly made $6.7 million in its opening weekend. Warners was keen to exploit the fact it was the studio's biggest ever two-day opening, with *Variety* running a full-page ad announcing "The Biggest Grossing Week-End in Warner Bros. History!" *Exorcist II* was New York City and LA's top-grossing film in its first week; nationwide, it was #2 (after Peter Hyams' *The Deep* and just ahead of *Star Wars*, which at the time was running in only forty theatres and yet to go into wide release). The backlash, however, was inevitable. Advertising and brand recognition made

134. Arnold.

audiences aware of *Exorcist II* and created interest in seeing it, but Warners selling an *Exorcist* sequel that didn't deliver the expected scares resulted in bad word of mouth. Reports indicated *Exorcist II* was drawing less-than-favorable responses from audiences. William Peter Blatty recalled, "I saw it with a paying audience in Washington D.C., where I was living at the time. I must say, I was the first to giggle, breaking the respectful silence, and that broke the dam for everyone in the audience. We roared from that point on—you'd think we were watching *The Producers*."[135] Blatty also claimed,

> I called the producer Dick Lederer the next day and I said, "Dick, I beg you, take the film out of release. Give it to me and, without touching a frame of the film, I will create an entirely new plot, new dialogue. It'll all be in subtitles or we'll dub it and pretend it's a foreign film, but it will be a comedy." And I was dead serious.[136]

In another version of the anecdote, Blatty said, "I called the producer and suggested that they retitle it *Son of Exorcist*, that they give me the film and allow me to write some additional funny dialogue and dub it in and well, you know, go with it. Make them think we intended it should be camp. He hung up the phone on me."[137] Although Blatty's *What's Up, Tiger Lily?*-style offer to retool *Exorcist II* was not taken up, Warners realized *something* had to be done, as the film's box office receipts dropped by 60% after the film's first week in general release.[138] *The Wall Street Journal* reported, "Word-of-mouth about the film was so derisive that in the second week its drawing power waned disastrously... Rarely, if ever, have box office receipts declined so drastically."[139] A week after the film's premiere, *Variety* reported,

> [*Exorcist II*] was laughed at frequently during the first L.A. area screening last Thursday night at the Academy of Motion Picture Arts and Sciences, and on the opening day, Friday, patrons at the Hollywood Pacific Theatre actually threw

135. WP Blatty, quoted in S Biodrowski, "Self-Possessed." *Fear* #19, Jun. 1990.

136. WP Blatty, quoted in McCabe, p. 163.

137. WP Blatty, quoted in Winter, p. 46.

138. L Bouzereau, *The Cutting Room Floor* (New York: Carol Publishing Group, 1994), p. 119.

139. S Grocer, *The Wall Street Journal*, June 1977.

things at the screen. Much the same response, laughter and booing, has been reported around the country, where the pic is playing in almost 800 theatres.[140]

At Los Angeles' 1400-seat Westwood Village Theater, audiences pelted *Exorcist II* with popcorn and soda cups, causing the manager to complain, "It was really getting out of hand—I stopped wearing my tuxedo because I thought I was going to get lynched."[141] Blatty claimed audiences rioted at *Exorcist II* screenings in Westwood: "They ripped the box office out of the ground; they tore the place apart. And Boorman, according to the reports, looked around and said, "Well, the film is obviously too good for them.""[142] Such a reaction from paying audiences is difficult to gloss over. While the incidents reported were not as dangerous as the riots that greeted Alejandro Jodorowsky's *Fando y Lis* (1968) in Mexico City or South American cinemagoers lobbing Molotov cocktails at the campy Che Guevara biopic *Che!* (1969)—to give two examples—it was still extreme behavior.

Rospo Pallenberg attended *Exorcist II*'s opening night in Los Angeles. The next morning, he phoned Boorman in Ireland to deliver the grim news about audiences' reactions. The same morning, Boorman received a similar phone call from Tommy Culla, his personal assistant during the film shoot, who was in New York City. (Also in New York was Linda Blair, who attended a premiere screening of *Exorcist II* in Manhattan.) Boorman recalled,

> There were lines around the block waiting for the film to open. *The Exorcist* had been a phenomenon. They had screamed, passed out, vomited on the seats. They were ready for more. What they saw outraged them. They threw things at the screen. There were mass walkouts. They found the ending particularly offensive.[143]

About the ending, Pallenberg told Boorman audiences laughed at Father Lamont emerging unharmed from the house's crumbled second floor and throughout the ensuing dialogue.

140. J McBride, "Boorman Shoulders Responsibility for *Heretic*, Which He's Recutting." *Daily Variety*, Jun. 24, 1977.

141. Talbot, p. 23.

142. WP Blatty, quoted in McCabe, p. 163.

143. Boorman, p. 228.

After its disastrous opening night, *Exorcist II* was recut by John Boorman, who stated, "I cut [the film] by telephone from 6,000 miles' distance. I had a print at home. I worked on it, and I called them with the frame numbers for the cut."[144] The edited print made the Westwood Village's 5:40 PM screening, twenty-four hours after the first-night show. Boorman flew to Los Angeles to make more extensive changes to the film, but these revisions (examined in depth in the next chapter) failed to prevent *Exorcist II* from disappointing at the box office. *Variety* reported, "The new ending is not a happy ending as this one plummets fast."[145] Responding to catastrophic reviews, Boorman defended his film to *The Wall Street Journal* and called out the unruly behavior of the crowds:

> It's a fairy story, not a scary story. Audiences were laughing at all the wrong things, and they created a kind of hostility… I basically made the wrong movie. I misjudged what audiences were bringing to the film based on *The Exorcist*. They loved [*The Exorcist*] for its raw sensation… They felt cheated by [*Exorcist II*].[146]

Recalling *Exorcist II*'s near-unanimous critical drubbing, Boorman remarked, "The press hounded me. How did I feel about making such a disaster? Rospo, Barbara and I watched as the ambitious work we had labored over was torn to pieces by the mob and ridiculed by the critics."[147] If Boorman felt critics were trying to outdo each other's professional scorn, he might have been right: the opprobrium heaped on *Exorcist II* was arguably unrivalled until Michael Cimino's *Heaven's Gate* hit theaters in 1980. It was the reaction Warners had most feared: *Exorcist II* was floundering and, smelling blood, the critics piled on. The film was pilloried in reviews from coast to coast and subjected to withering headlines like "*Exorcist II*: They Couldn't Get the Bugs Out," "*Exorcist II*: Heresy of Horror," and "*Exorcist II* should be repossessed." *People* magazine's otherwise laudatory Linda Blair cover story referred to *Exorcist II* as a "debacle" and in the context of *The Exorcist*'s numer-

---

144. J Boorman, quoted in Talbot, pp. 23-24.

145. Talbot, p. 25.

146. J Boorman, quoted in Talbot, p. 24.

147. Boorman, p. 228.

ous imitations, Rob Edelman of *Films in Review* announced, "We now have the ultimate *Exorcist* rip-off—*Exorcist II: The Heretic*. While there are first-rate production values and actors/characters from the original, the film is cinematic claptrap."[148] Singling out the film's lack of scares, F.C. Westley of *The Spectator* noted *Exorcist II* "has less gore and gutter language than the original, but also less nasty power."[149] A similar observation from other reviewers. "*Exorcist II: The Heretic* is not just a sequel, it's a travesty," complained George Anderson of the *Pittsburgh Post-Gazette*. "The new Warner Bros. release should be repossessed for nonpayment of thrills."[150] *Variety* also declared *Exorcist II*'s inferiority to its predecessor:

> Since any title containing Roman numerals invites comparison, the answer is: No, *Exorcist II* is not as good as *The Exorcist*. It isn't even close. Gone now is the simple clash between Good and Evil, replaced by some goofy transcendental spiritualism. Linda Blair is back as Regan, four years older and still suffering the residual effects of her demonic possession. For the most part, however, she's cheerful and good, seemingly no more bothered by her lingering devil than a chronic zit that keeps popping out on prom night.[151]

Exorcist II was "about as scary as a June wedding" according to Dean Johnson of Orlando's *Sentinel Star*.[152] "When Linda Blair's head turned fully around on its axis in *The Exorcist*, strong men were known to leave the theater," wrote *The Miami Herald*'s Candice Russell. "The sequel, *Exorcist II: The Heretic*, may also propel crowds to the exits, but with a difference. Anyone who tries to puzzle through the mystical claptrap of good, evil, Catholicism and locusts may bolt for the door in sheer confusion."[153] Elbert Marshall of North Carolina's *The Daily Times-News* wrote, "Whereas *The Exorcist* was a terror-filled, believable movie, its se-

---

148. R Edelman, *Films in Review* vol. 28 (1977).

149. F.C. Westley, *The Spectator* vol. 239, 1977.

150. G Anderson, "'The Heretic' Is No 'Exorcist.'" *Pittsburgh Post-Gazette*, Jun. 22, 1977.

151. *Variety*, 1977. Reprinted in *Variety Portable Movie Guide*, Penguin (2000), p. 393.

152. D Johnson, "The Devil made them do it?" *Sentinel Star*, Jun. 22, 1977.

153. C Russell, "'Exorcist II' Confusing Claptrap." *The Miami Herald*, Jun. 18, 1977.

quel, *Exorcist II: The Heretic*, escapes the realm of credibility, bogs down and becomes just another movie trying to draw audiences on the basis of its predecessor."[154] Tim Yagle of *The Michigan Daily* observed, "The film is unbelievably poorly put together; there is absolutely no natural dramatic flow of events, rather it is more a case of ideas being thrown in almost randomly," adding, "Director John Boorman seems to have no idea of how long a sequence should be sustained."[155] Kevin Thomas of the *Los Angeles Times* wrote,

> Minutes into *Exorcist II: The Heretic*, it gets perfectly clear why Warners held back press screenings of the film until the day before it opened to the public. All the considerable talent, time and money poured into this picture, and all its vast scope and rich production values serve only to underline the frequent unintended and therefore devastating humor in William Goodhart's solemn and bizarre script.[156]

Unintentional humor and audience reactions to same were recurring themes in reviews of *Exorcist II*. "A recent preview screening of *Exorcist II: The Heretic* may stand as some sort of show-business landmark," commented Christine Nieland for New York's *Press & Sun-Bulletin*. "The giggles began about a third of the way into the movie, when Richard Burton, as part of a hypnotic experiment, momentarily rolled his eyeballs back into his skull, as Linda Blair and Louise Fletcher had previously done. By the time the movie was over, audience members were bowling their disapproval, hissing, booing and roaring with laughter."[157] Dave Zurawik of the *Detroit Free Press* wrote,

> *Exorcist II: The Heretic* may be one of the funniest films of the year… When the film premiered in Detroit, there was a house full of *Exorcist* viewers waiting to be scared. Ten minutes into the sequel, the first subdued giggles came. By the end of the picture, they were rolling in the aisles… If this were a parody

---

154. E Marshall, "Exorcist Sequel Disappointing." *The Daily Times-News*, Jul. 18, 1977.

155. T Yagle, "Cinematic Heresy." *The Michigan Daily*, Jul. 8, 1977.

156. K Thomas, "'Exorcist II' Puts On Straight Face." *Los Angeles Times*, Jun. 18, 1977.

157. C Nieland, "'Exorcist' is just silly," *Press & Sun-Bulletin*, Jul. 3, 1977.

of *The Exorcist* it would be great stuff.[158]

Zurawik criticized specifically the film's ending, noting, "The sense of campy unreality is incredible." George McKinnon of *The Boston Globe* wrote,

> A special preview audience quickly discovered the only way to accept this movie botch was to treat it as a comedy... They greeted the atrocious dialogue and the cliché film techniques with derisive sniggers and all but dissolved into laughter and hisses at what amounts to a stereotyped off-into-the-sunset happy end.[159]

Gene Siskel, film critic of the *Chicago Tribune* and co-host (with Roger Ebert) of television's *Sneak Previews*, reported an audience that was half "dumbstruck" and half "hooting the screen" at Chicago's Oriental Theater:

> While the house is being splintered by the locusts, and the taxi is set aflame by naughty Kitty, not a single neighbor is stirring. Why not? Is this a comment on urban man's unwillingness to get involved in his neighbor's problems? No. I'm afraid the answer is even more pedestrian than that. *Exorcist II* was made cheaply on Warner Bros. sound stages; the background homes are just a cheap painting. When the neighbors and police finally did arrive a wee bit late, the audience howled with laughter... What isn't funny about *Exorcist II* is that it will sucker in audiences who enjoyed the original picture as I did. The new film is a ripoff from start-to-finish, which was totally unnecessary because the original made Warners a pile of money. The sequel should bomb once the word gets out, thereby killing the exorcism egg for Warners.[160]

Joel Baltake of the *Philadelphia Daily News* described *Exorcist II* as "either the biggest disaster ever recorded on celluloid or else the wildest, most radical spoof ever made by a major director," adding it "can't be

---

158. D Zurawik, "'Exorcist II': Heresy of Horror." *Detroit Free Press*, Jun. 19, 1977.

159. G McKinnon, "'Exorcist II' is cursed." *The Boston Globe*, Jun. 18, 1977.

160. G Siskel, "'Exorcist II' haunted by howlingly awful special effects and script." *Chicago Tribune*, Jun. 20, 1977.

denied that it's wildly creative and funny and it has a strange vitality that miraculously holds it together."[161] Christopher Porterfield of *Time* magazine was less charitable: "Most sequels offer more of the same," he wrote. "This one offers less of the same," going on to write,

> William Friedkin's original was well enough made to be offensive. Here we are spared many of Friedkin's cheap shocks— the mutilations, the vomiting, the bestiality. But what remains is twaddle. The supernatural antics are dressed up with a notion vandalized from Teilhard de Chardin: the film suggests that Blair's character is one of a vanguard of human mutations evolving toward a synthesis of man and God, and thus is a target to be headed off by Pazuzu. In truth, the only synthesis in the film is between the ludicrous and the unintentionally comic.[162]

Rudy Purificato of Texas' *Fort Hood Sentinel* noted, "Other than magnificent photography, special effects and makeup techniques, [*Exorcist II*] lacks a cohesive plot structure and an intelligently conceived 'believable' script."[163] In another Texan publication—the *Austin-American Statesman*—Patrick Taggart wrote,

> No doubt about it, *Exorcist II: The Heretic* is about as lousy as movie as is likely to be found among today's big budget films... Boorman, who flashed so brightly in the pan with 1972's *Deliverance*, just doesn't know a thing about making a horror movie. He is a master with a camera, delighting in color experiments and camera movement. But at storytelling he's a lightweight, and it's our loss... About 10 minutes into a Friday showing audience members let loose with catcalls and Bronx cheers.[164]

Writing for New York's *Daily News*, Katleen Carroll noted that Richard Burton and Louise Fletcher "appear to be acting in an advanced state of catatonia as if they were silently praying for some kind of miraculous re-

161. J Baltake, "Exorcist II—The Heretic." *Philadelphia Daily News*, Jun. 20, 1977.

162. C Porterfield, "Cinema: Pazuzu Rides Again." *Time*, Jul. 4, 1977.

163. R Purificato, "Sounds & Scenes." Fort Hood Sentinel, Jul. 7, 1977.

164. P Taggart, " 'Heretic a sorry sequel to 'Exorcist.'" *Austin-American Statesman*, Jun. 20, 1977.

lease from their contracts."[165] Will Jones of Minneapolis' *Star Tribune* also singled out Fletcher for criticism, noting she was "still speaking in the same ominous butter-wouldn't-melt institutional *Cuckoo's Nest* tones."[166] Malcolm L. Johnson of Connecticut's *The Hartford Courant* criticized *Exorcist II* for having taken "a popular horror film and sought to rationalize its mysteries with bargain-basement theology." Johnson also lambasted Pazuzu's corporeal form—"the sight of an oversized grasshopper is more ridiculous than frightening"—and the gimmick of the Synchronizer, which "soon becomes a little absurd through overexposure, along with the locust." Hartford was still more diplomatic than most other critics, singling out positively William Fraker and Richard Macdonald's contributions positively and venturing praise for Linda Blair, stating *Exorcist II* "contains proof that Linda Blair has matured into a young actress who is capable of persuading us of much of Regan's turmoil, despite the pretentiousness of what is going on around her… Ms. Blair's ability to suggest both goodness and the memory of possession is the strongest performance in the film."[167]

The reviews north of the US border were no better. Urjo Kareda of the Canadian magazine *Maclean's* announced,

> *The Heretic* is a sequel to *The Exorcist*, the devil-possession, here's-bile-in-your-eye shocker which had audiences shrieking and retching in the aisles in 1973. This *Exorcist II* is quite a howler, too, but the release is through laughter. It is an exceptionally terrible film compounded of the greed that is its only visible motive, the pretentiousness that allows it to invoke the Jesuit palaeontologist Teilhard de Chardin as a resident thinker, and the sheer silliness of a director (John Boorman) who seems not to know which end is up.[168]

Noel Taylor of the *Ottawa Citizen* named *Exorcist II* "the strongest contender at this stage for the silliest-film-of-the-year award. Anyone who sits through its two hours of supernatural hokum and pseudo-psychology

165. K Carroll, "'Heretic Is Bedeviled." *Daily News*, Jun. 18, 1977.

166. W Jones, "'Exorcist II' goes on in the fight against evil—a locust." *Star Tribune*, Jun. 21, 1977.

167. ML Johnson, "'Exorcist II' Defies Belief." *The Hartford Courant*, Jun. 22, 1977.

168. U Kareda, "The Devil must have made them do it. There's no other explanation." *Maclean's*, Jul. 11, 1977.

without so much as a snigger may well be badly in need of an exorcism." Taylor described Linda Blair as an actress who "shows her limitations" and the film's depiction of Africa as "a Warner Bros studio-lot village fashioned in Styrofoam, which director John Boorman films in a peach-colored glow as though it were perpetual evening."[169] Perhaps the most scathing contemporary review of *Exorcist II* came from John Simon, *New York* magazine's film and theater critic:

> Whereas it is impossible to designate even approximately the worst film one has ever seen, there is a very strong possibility that *Exorcist II* is the stupidest major movie ever made. I hate to sound that categorical, because it may send collectors of imbecilities scurrying off in droves to see this execrable product; but then, collectors of imbecilities are the fitting audience of this film, and they deserve each other… In this quasi-sequel, there is no plot, but all kinds of disparate plot fragments churning around chaotically; and there is decidedly no point of view, except the determination to exploit everything that is exploitable, from zoom lenses to religion, from boutique décor carried to absurd heights to aerial photography sinking to new depths of eye-blasting pretentiousness. I shall not insult you and myself by trying to summarize the plot, which is incomprehensible anyway, though not nearly as incomprehensible as what motives besides greed could have led a director like John Boorman, who in some of his earlier films, showed a certain intelligence as well as some craftsmanship, to concoct this foul-smelling witch's brew of meaningless turbulence, this storm not exactly in a teapot, but in a vessel of a somewhat similar sort.[170]

Notorious for focusing obsessively on the physical appearances of actors, Simon sneered misogynistically, "Linda Blair, not a very talented or pre-possessing youngster [in *The Exorcist*], is even less interesting now, though considerably more bovine; I doubt whether a post-pubertal acting style can be made out of mere chubbiness."[171] Unfortunately but unsurprising-

---

169. N Taylor, "Exorcist II: Silliest Sequel." *Ottawa Citizen*, Jun. 22, 1977.

170. J Simon, "Flaws." *New York*, July 4, 1977.

171. Simon.

ly, Linda Blair's physicality was lascivious fodder for the predominantly male critics of the day, many of whom had no compunction about making weight-based remarks and/or sexualizing the teenage star (who was 18 years old by the time *Exorcist II* was released but a legal minor when her scenes were actually filmed). Mike Petryni of *The Arizona Republic* saw fit to refer to "sweet little Miss Blair... still wrapped in an abundance of baby fat" and "chubby little Miss Blair" in his *Exorcist II* review.[172] To the *Ottawa Citizen*'s Noel Taylor, Blair was "a chubbyish plastic doll of an actress" who had "put on four years quite becomingly."[173] Alexander Keneas of Long Island's *Newsday* described Regan as having "blossomed into a babyfat-cute nymphet,"[174] Allen Oren of *The Charlotte Observer* referred to the "well-developed Linda Blair,"[175] and Bob Ross of the *St. Petersburg Times* noted, "Regan has changed a bit... The tormented adolescent has become a voluptuous nymph, with luscious pouty lips and a plush figure."[176] To the *Fort Worth Star-Telegram*'s Perry Stewart, Linda Blair had "grown enticingly nubile"[177] and under the subheading "Linda blossoms out," R.H. Gardner of the *Baltimore Sun* used his *Exorcist II* review to note that "in the four years since she qualified as the little girl you would least like to be caught in the upstairs bedroom with, [Blair] has blossomed out like a *Playboy* bunny. I mean that kid has undergone a lot of spiritual development!"[178]

As for the film itself, the *New Times* asked who was to blame for putting up the "$10 million" for it, remarking that "you may begin to feel some stirring of sympathy, or even pity, for the craftsmen involved in making these expensive bowwows. After all, you were trapped in the movie for only a couple of hours; the filmmakers were there for months, maybe years."[179] *The New West* bemoaned that "*Exorcist II: The Heretic* is an embarrassment, particularly depressing because it involves talent-

172. M Petyrini, "'Exorcist II' - - Did Devil win this time?" *The Arizona Republic*, Jun. 23, 1977.

173. Taylor.

174. A Keneas, "Movie Review: More exorcism." *Newsday*, Jun. 18, 1977.

175. A Oren, "'Exorcist II' Devilishly Bad Film." *The Charlotte Observer*, Jun. 20, 1977.

176. B Ross, "'Exorcist II': Hollywood's encore for the devil." *St. Petersburg Times*, Jun. 20, 1977.

177. P Stewart, "'Exorcist II' can go away." *Fort Worth Star-Telegram*, Jun. 21, 1977.

178. RH Gardner, "New 'Exorcist' evokes not terror but laughter." *Baltimore Sun*, Jun. 19, 1977.

179. *New Times*, Volume 9, Number 9, Jul. 22, 1977.

ed people like Richard Burton, Louise Fletcher and director John Boorman. The first *Exorcist* was crudely exploitative on a visceral level. The sequel subordinates horror to spiritual blather."[180] *The Bulletin* alluded to the film's floundering box office, noting that "even the dependability of the shock-horror market is failing to keep afloat *Exorcist II: The Heretic*. The original kitsch has been obscured by some very cloudy mysticism."[181] Film and TV critic Steven H. Scheuer was vitriolic:

> This may just well be the worst sequel in the history of films—a stupefying, boring, vapid and NON-SCARY follow-up to the box office champ of 1973... *Exorcist II* is a disaster on every level—a sophomoric script, terrible editing, worst direction by John Boorman, inevitably coupled with silly acting. In one scene that typifies this lamentable sci-fi horror pic, [Richard] Burton and [James Earl] Jones, two splendid actors, are spouting inane dialogue while Jones is outfitted like a witch doctor.[182]

Exorcist II was not the only film in 1977 to suffer from expectations raised by *The Exorcist*. Essentially, two direct follow-ups to *The Exorcist* played in theaters simultaneously: Boorman's *Exorcist II* and the new film from William Friedkin, his first since directing *The Exorcist*. Friedkin's *Sorcerer*, distributed domestically by two major studios (Universal Pictures and Paramount Pictures), opened on June 24, 1977, one week after *Exorcist II*'s premiere. Starring Roy Scheider, *Sorcerer* retold *The Wages of Fear*'s tale of four fugitives undertaking the white-knuckle mission to truck volatile, explosive cargo across 200 miles of perilous terrain (including a wooden suspension bridge in the midst of a violent thunderstorm). Whereas *Exorcist II* replicated New York, Washington, Rome, and Ethiopia on Californian soundstages, *Sorcerer* was filmed on location in the Dominican Republic, the USA, Mexico, France, and Israel, the film's budget ballooning from $15 million to $22 million throughout its troubled shoot. *Sorcerer*'s title and its promotional campaign (linking the film to *The Exorcist*, Friedkin's previous film) misled audiences into expecting a film about the supernatural. Rex Reed reviewed *Sorcerer* and *Exorcist II*

---

180. *New West*, Volume 2, 1977.

181. S Hall, *The Bulletin*, 1977.

182. SH Scheuer, *Movies on TV* (New York: Bantam Books, 1977), p. 224.

together for New York's *Daily News* and was one of the relatively few high-profile reviewers to praise Friedkin's film; although he questioned the validity of remaking the "perfect" *Wages of Fear*, Reed described *Sorcerer* as "extremely well-made, filled with tension, suspense, steamy atmosphere and first-rate acting and production values."[183] Going on to discuss *Exorcist II*, Reed blasted, "This is a movie for morons, a total cheesy ripoff that makes not one minute of coherent sense. The script, direction, camera work and sets are the work of cretins."[184] Of the two films, it was Boorman's that made more money: *Sorcerer* was a very expensive flop, earning less than half its budget. Although it failed to recoup its costs and ended William Friedkin's critical and commercial hot streak, *Sorcerer*'s esteem has grown over the years; the film is now considered by many film critics and aficionados to be an overlooked masterpiece of 1970s cinema, and Friedkin considers it to be his best film. Interest in *Sorcerer* was renewed upon the film's restoration in 2013 and its screening at the 2016 Cannes Film Festival. Friedkin's post-*Sorcerer* career has been frustratingly uneven, although his neo-noir crime film *To Live and Die in L.A.* (1985) ranks among his best work, and his Tracy Letts adaptations *Bug* (2006) and *Killer Joe* (2012) are rightfully acclaimed.

By mid July 1977, Warners paired *Exorcist II* in some venues as part of a double bill with *It's Alive*, Larry Cohen's 1974 shocker about a vicious mutant baby. On July 20—a month into its initial run—*Exorcist II* was listed by *Variety* as the twentieth highest-grossing film in the country. By the end of the month, Boorman's film had dropped off the *Variety* chart completely and Warners allowed some of the larger theaters to stop screening the film, in spite of contracts mandating a minimum three-month run. The box office failure of *Exorcist II* and contemporaneous flops like Stanley Donen's *Lucky Lady* (1975), Jack Smight's *Midway* (1976), and Peter Bogdanovich's *Nickelodeon* (1976) led to the end of the "Blind Bidding" policy in some US states, where laws were passed requiring studios to view films before having to bid for the right to screen them. *Exorcist II*'s middling box office meant that Linda Blair—who had a profit participation clause in her contact—missed out on a potential $1 million on top of her $750,000.00 salary.

Exorcist II's controversial legacy, born of widespread cultural derision upon its first release, gave rise to perception of the film as a "flop," but like Steven Spielberg's comedy misfire *1941* (1979) and Sylvester

---

183. R Reed, "The second time around: one hit, one error." *Daily News*, Jul. 1, 1977.

184. Reed.

Stallone's junky *Saturday Night Fever* sequel *Staying Alive* (1983) *Exorcist II* was a flop by reputation, not by numbers. If a "flop" is defined as a film that earns less than what it cost to make, *Exorcist II* does not qualify. *Sorcerer* was a flop; *Exorcist II* was not. "A lot of films fail and lose millions of dollars and pass unnoticed, but some movies like *Heaven's Gate, Cleopatra* and *The Heretic* become infamous, notorious failures," Boorman recalled. "In fact, Warners did not lose money on *The Heretic*. They were covered by advances from theatre chains."[185] *Exorcist II* did not lose money—its $30 million US domestic intake more than doubled its $14 million budget—but it was a massive commercial disappointment in relation to *The Exorcist* (which cost $10 million to make and hauled $89 million in American grosses alone) and to Warners' commercial expectations. In this respect, *Exorcist II* is comparable to Stanley Kubrick's *Barry Lyndon* (1975). Arguably the best film produced by Warners in the 1970s (and often cited today as one of the greatest films ever made), *Barry Lyndon* made a profit during its original theatrical run but fell short of the commercial success Warners had hoped for. The fact is, *Exorcist II* was guaranteed to make money from theaters keen to exhibit another *Exorcist* film and audiences keen to see it—tellingly, *Exorcist II*'s opening weekend made up 20% of its eventual domestic haul. In this respect, *Exorcist II*'s quality (or lack thereof) was immaterial, but the film could only ride on its predecessor's coattails so far. The money *Exorcist II* made was due to *The Exorcist*; the money *Exorcist II* did *not* make was due to *Exorcist II*.

On July 16, 1977, *Exorcist II* was released in Japan. On September 15, 1977—roughly three months after its American release—the film was loosed upon Boorman's native Britain, to mainly negative reviews. The weekly magazine *New Society* opined, "There is nothing in *The Heretic* that grabs you in quite the same way that Mercedes McCambridge's superb demon voice did in *The Exorcist*, nothing that has you chewing your nails with tension as did the early scenes of the original movie, nothing to make you recoil with horror."[186] Ian Christie of *The Daily Express* wrote, "Richard Burton is attacked by a swarm of locusts. He deserves all he gets, believe me."[187] Jack Lewis of *The Daily Mirror* claimed the film is "all too

---

185. Boorman, p. 231.

186. *New Society* vols.41-42, 1977

187. I Christie, quoted in C Tookey, *Named and Shamed: The World's Worst and Wittiest Movie Reviews from Affleck to Zeta-Jones* (Leicester: Troubador Publishing Limited, 2010), p. 47.

ludicrous to frighten, and the only time you're likely to hide your head will be in shame for watching it."[188] "Writing for the *Evening Standard*, Alexander Walker complained, "Frankly, it's not much fun watching two people with bands around their heads talking to each other through a count-down to Hell, even when Max von Sydow appears, making what I guess you'd call a "ghost appearance" rather than a "guest" one."[189] Tim Radford of *The Guardian* found *Exorcist II* to be "swiftly paced entertaining mumbo-jumbo" in which "Richard Burton potters through... with a look of weary distaste, or even nausea... The film was apparently re-edited after a disappointing opening in the United States; but it is hard to imagine that it is a better or worse film for that. Hard to take seriously at all, in fact."[190]

September 15 was also the date of *Exorcist II*'s Australian premiere. The following day, Helen Frizell of *The Sydney Morning Herald* reported a "mumbo-jumbo mixture" that "was engrossing at times with its special effects, its music, and with William A. Fraker's direction of photography." Admitting the film "did bring a few uncontrollable shivers to the spine," Frizzell was especially receptive to its visuals: "There were some brilliant scenes of Coptic churches on clifftops in Ethiopia, of mud-walled African villages (all shot in earthy colors) and of the American hospital and its mirrored, schizophrenic architecture."[191] Romola Constantino of Sydney's *The Sun-Herald* was less complimentary, dismissing *Exorcist II* as "nasty drivel."[192] *Exorcist II* was distributed throughout the European, South American, and Asian markets between September 1977 and April 1978.

Some perspective is required. It *is* true that *The Exorcist* was not unanimously praised upon its release and had, in fact, polarized critics. (Its media circus status probably made professional reviews a fleeting consideration for most of the cinema-going public.) High-profile reviewers like Vincent Canby, Andrew Sarris, and Pauline Kael reviewed *The Exorcist* negatively. On the other hand, the film drew praise from Charles Champlin, Roger Ebert, Stanley Kauffmann, Rex Reed, and Gene Sis-

188. J Lewis, quoted in A Frank, *The Horror Film Handbook* (Totowa: Barnes & Noble Books, 1982), p. 56.

189. A Walker, "Whatever possessed them?" *Evening Standard*, Sep. 22, 1977.

190. T Radford, "Bad patches beneath the brilliantine." *The Guardian*, Sep. 15, 1977.

191. H Frizell, "Mumbo-Jumbo mixture brought a few shivers." *The Sydney Morning Herald*, Sep. 16, 1977.

192. R Constantino, "Sight-N-Sound: Films with Romola Constantino." *The Sun-Herald*, Sep. 18, 1977.

kel. Relatively few critics in 1977 were willing to bestow glowing reviews upon *Exorcist II*, and even those who didn't care for *The Exorcist* couldn't recommend the sequel wholeheartedly. Robert C. Cumbow of Seattle's *Movietone News* claimed that *Exorcist II* was "infinitely more spirited, adventurous, and visually exciting than *The Exorcist*," but still regarded it as "undeniably one of the most monumentally dumb movies of all time."[193] Vincent Canby of *The New York Times* did not like *The Exorcist* but claimed *The Heretic* was worse:

> Linda Blair may be the least fleet-footed actress Hollywood has produced since the incomparable Joan Crawford attempted to keep up with Fred Astaire in *Dancing Lady*. Seen tap-dancing, as she is on two occasions in *Exorcist II: The Heretic*, the chubby-kneed Miss Blair appears to be stomping on live cigar stubs. The rest of the movie is even heavier and more lugubrious. Given the huge box office success of *The Exorcist*, there had to be a sequel, but did it have to be this desperate concoction, the main thrust of which is that original exorcism wasn't all it was cracked up to be? It's one thing to carry a story further along, but it's another to deny the original, no matter what you thought of it... [*Exorcist II*] is of such spectacular fatuousness that it makes the first seem virtually an axiom of screen art... *Exorcist II* begins by looking foolish and slowly becomes a straightfaced film of the absurd... [Boorman's strength] is not in his narrative or in his handling of actors, all of whom (especially Miss Blair and Miss Fletcher) look extremely ill at ease. It's in his sets and décor... Everything else, including two immolations, is cold mashed potatoes.[194]

The most noted film critic of her day—Pauline Kael of *The New Yorker*—didn't care for *The Exorcist*, claiming "a viewer can become glumly anesthetized by the brackish color and the senseless ugliness of the conception" and—rather ludicrously—that neither Blatty nor Friedkin "shows any feeling for the little girl's helplessness and suffering, or for

---

193. RC Cumbow, *Movietone News* #55, Sep. 1977.

194. V Canby, "Film: 'Exorcist II: The Heretic' is Heavy Stuff." *The New York Times*, Jun. 18, 1977.

her mother's."[195] In the wake of *The Exorcist*'s success, Kael complained, "A critic can't fight [the film], because it functions below the conscious level"[196] and concluded her review with a parting shot at the mothers who allowed their daughters to audition for the role of Regan. This set the stage for one of the more amusingly acerbic grudges in the *Exorcist* story. "Pauline Kael needs an enema," William Peter Blatty declared wryly when he guest-starred on television's *The Tonight Show starring Johnny Carson* on January 17, 1974. Blatty proceeded to tell Carson that Kael brought "personal poison" to her reviews and accused her of being a neurotic elitist, caged in her own ego. Kael, for her part, preferred *Exorcist II* to *The Exorcist*, but her assessment of Boorman's film, printed over a year after the film's release, was not the ringing endorsement selected excerpts have made it seem. Rather, Kael described the film as a curate's egg:

> The pressing against the bounds of the medium doesn't necessarily result in a good movie (John Boorman's debauch *Exorcist II: The Heretic* is proof of that), but it generally results in a live one—a movie there's some reason to see— and it's the only way great movies get made. Even the madness of *Exorcist II* is of a special sort: the picture has a visionary crazy grandeur... Some of its telepathic sequences are golden-toned and lyrical, and the film has a swirling, hallucinogenic, apocalyptic quality; it might have been a horror classic if it had had a simpler, less ritzy script. But, along with flying demons and theology inspired by Teilhard de Chardin, the movie has Richard Burton, with his precise diction, helplessly and inevitably turning his lines into camp, just as the cultivated, stage-trained actors in early-30s horror films did. Like them, Burton has no conviction in what he's doing, so he can't get beyond staginess and artificial phrasing. The film is too cadenced and exotic and too deliriously complicated to succeed with most audiences (and when it opened, there were accounts of people in theatres who threw things at the screen). But it's winged camp—a horror fairy tale gone wild, another in the long history of moviemakers' king-size follies. There's enough visual magic in it for a dozen

---

195. P Kael, *5001 Nights at the Movies*, Arrow Books (1987), p. 174

196. P Kael, "Back to the Ouija Board." *The New Yorker*, Jan. 7, 1974. Reprinted in *Reeling* (New York: Warner Books, 1976), p. 441.

good movies; what it lacks is judgement—the first casualty of the moviemaking obsession.[197]

Reviewing *Excalibur* in 1981, Kael made reference to Boorman's previous two films:

> . . . we might have considered [*Zardoz* and *Exorcist II: The Heretic*] classics if we hadn't known English. If we'd been able to imagine that the words were as lyrical and hallucinogenic as the images, we might have acclaimed Boorman instead of falling on the floor laughing (as a friend assures me he did when he saw *Zardoz*) or throwing things at the screen (which happened at some theatres showing *The Heretic*)... In *The Heretic*, the dialogue and how it was directed were ruinous; Richard Burton's recitatives were theological gibberish... I loved watching *The Heretic*, but I couldn't recommend it to anyone without starting to grin shamefacedly.[198]

Molly Haskell of *The Village Voice* claimed *Exorcist II* was "hardly the unqualified disaster that critics and word-of-mouth have made it out to be" but she did not argue it was a misunderstood masterpiece: "It may be that the film's thematic point is precisely the character's isolation from one another and the lack of integration of conscious and unconscious states of mind. If this is so, if disconnectedness is the evil for which Boorman's plague is the metaphor, then Boorman is, alas, more its victim than its prophet."[199]

In spite of the fact horror films rarely attract mainstream film awards, in 1974 *The Exorcist* won two Oscars and four Golden Globes from ten and five nominations respectively. Brian De Palma's Stephen King adaptation *Carrie* (1976) also bucked the trend, with stars Sissy Spacek and Piper Laurie earning Oscar nominations—Spacek for the title role and Laurie for her portrayal of Carrie's deranged mother (a role Louise Fletcher had been considered for). *Exorcist II*, on the other hand, was all but absent from Hollywood's awards season. (Fortunately for *Exorcist II*, the Golden Raspberry Awards were four years away from being founded.) However, in

---

197. P Kael, "Fear of Movies." *The New Yorker*, Sep. 25, 1978. Reprinted in *When the Lights Go Down* (London: Marion Boyars Publishers Ltd, 2009), p. 429.

198. P Kael, "Boorman's Plunge." *The New Yorker*, Apr. 20, 1981. Reprinted in *Taking It All In* (London: Arrow Books, 1987), p. 184.

199. M Haskell, "Boorman Finds the Devil in Africa," *The Village Voice*, Aug. 1, 1977.

the lead-up to the 1978 Academy Awards, William Fraker was among the preliminary ten nominees for Best Cinematography, for two films—*Exorcist II: The Heretic* and Richard Brooks' *Looking for Mr. Goodbar*. (The final ten also included two other films Fraker was involved with—*Islands in the Stream*, for which Fraker did second unit work, and *Close Encounters of the Third Kind*, for which Fraker provided additional cinematography.) *Exorcist II* did not make the final five nominations. At the 1978 Saturn Awards, the Academy of Science Fiction, Fantasy and Horror Films nominated Albert Whitlock and Chuck Gaspar for Best Special Effects in recognition of their work on *Exorcist II*. (They lost to John Dykstra for *Star Wars*.)

In light of *Exorcist II*'s critical drubbing and lackluster commercial performance, John Boorman took stock of the film and his own career:

> After the completion of the film, I was absolutely furious at having subjected myself to such an ordeal. I'd inflicted all that suffering on myself. No one had forced me to make the film. Also, instead of taking the easy way out, I had decided to set myself a number of challenges so that I might overcome them... *The Heretic*, and the reception it was given was a traumatic experience for me. It forced me to question my relations with the public and with my own films; it forced me to question myself on the future. [200]

---

200. Ciment, p. 177.

The closing chaos of *Exorcist II* as the demon Pazuzu tears apart the MacNeil house while Father Lamont struggles with Regan's doppelganger.

L: Dr. Gene Tuskin (Louise Fletcher) in the closing shot of the original version of *Exorcist II*. R: Regan MacNeil (Linda Blair) in the closing shot of the revised version of *Exorcist II*.

8

"A retreat? Why not an advance?" The Revision of *Exorcist II*

"At the time, I remember John Boorman saying "I've redubbed everything. I've improved the performances one hundred percent." I thought the performances were appalling. And that dialogue and that situation—"I've flown this route before, on the wings of a locust"—Jesus!"

– William Peter Blatty[201]

"I think the exorcism made the problem worse!"

– From *Exorcist II: The Heretic* (1977)
by William Goodhart

INEXTRICABLE FROM THE CONTROVERSY surrounding *Exorcist II*'s release is the fact John Boorman re-edited the film hastily during its first-run engagement, leading to *four* different cuts of the film playing in various theatres in 1977. Shortly after its premiere, Boorman recut *Exorcist II* in response to poor audience reactions. (Had the film been previewed before a test-audience, it almost certainly would have been recut *before* it went into general release. In Boorman's defense, he *had* lobbied

---

201. WP Blatty, quoted in McCabe, p. 163.

Warners to hold a test-screening, to no avail.) This was far more drastic than the abrupt, explosive ending imposed by the studio against Boorman's wishes on *Hell in the Pacific*. Boorman supervised from Ireland the first re-edit of *Exorcist II*, telling Warners by phone which frame-numbers to cut: "I made a hasty attempt to re-cut the last reel, and we pulled the prints and changed them overnight."[202] This truncated version of *Exorcist II* had a run time of 114 minutes, compared to the version that premiered at 118. With exhibitors displeased by the film's dismal reception, Warners decided to make Boorman's new edit the official ending of all cuts of the film. On the morning of Tuesday, June 21, Warners' distribution department contacted the 707 theatres screening *Exorcist II*, informing them that new reels of the film, with a modified ending, were being printed and transported immediately. By the end of that day, fifteen new reels had been flown to the biggest cinemas in New York City. The remaining cinemas received their copies of the print in time for the following weekend. (Projectionists were instructed to return or destroy the now-obsolete reels of the original version of the film. This instruction was not followed to the letter and, inevitably, a number of *Exorcist II* prints ended up in private collections.) John Wilson, founder of the Golden Raspberry Awards, recalled:

> [The original ending] went over so poorly with audiences that by the 8 p.m. showing the second night, many theatres were emergency-shipped a new final reel that simply jump-cut from Blair on the collapsing stairway with a locust on her lip to the end titles, a change so ineptly executed that a ten-year-old child asked the theatre manager in Westwood, "Was this recut!?!?" I know, because *I* was that theatre manager.[203]

This was only the beginning of the strange story of *Exorcist II*'s myriad versions. Although he makes no mention of it in his 2003 memoirs, Boorman returned from Ireland to California to supervise more re-edits of *Exorcist II*. At first, he decided to personally supervise a new cut that would be less sloppy than the studio rush-job trimming the film's final reel via instructions by phone. On Tuesday, June 21, Boorman arrived in Los Angeles and attended a screening of *Exorcist II* with an audience to gauge

---

202. Boorman, p. 228.

203. J Wilson, *The Official Razzies Movie Guide: Enjoying the Best of Hollywood's Worst* (New York: Warner Books, 2005), pp. 307-308.

which scenes and dialogue prompted the most laughter. He then returned to Burbank to re-edit the film, later telling *Variety*,

> To some extent, I'm allowing the audience to recut it. I'm considering our openings to be like 800 sneak previews, hopefully without damaging the integrity of my original concept. People think of cutting and recutting as defeat, but it's not... We're victims of audience expectations based on the first picture. The sin I committed was not giving them what they wanted in terms of horror. There's this wild beast out there, which is the audience, and I just didn't throw enough Christians to it. I was terribly shocked and hurt by all this... I thought I'd produced a film which was thoughtful and beautiful and involving.[204]

The second re-edit of *Exorcist II* had some scenes removed, but Boorman also added some shots of the possessed Regan from *The Exorcist* and some outtake footage of the bleeding cab driver after Tuskin and Sharon's taxi crash. These additions constituted an attempt to make the film more palatable for the horror film audience. On Sunday, June 26, ten days into *Exorcist II*'s theatrical run, the second re-edit played for an audience of 500 at the Westwood Village Theater. A *Daily Variety* article on June 28 reported a positive reaction at this screening which, according to Boorman, was a qualified success:

> [The audience was] far more appreciative. We showed them the new version...and the response was entirely different. This time, they came to laugh. But instead they got absorbed in the new version, and they calmed down. There was also mild laughter at the screening and one patron was especially boisterous. In one seat was Warner executive Ted Ashley, who said afterwards, "One thing I learned, I'll never ever put a picture out again without previewing it."[205]

Boorman wasn't finished with the film, however. Believing the second re-edit was only a temporary measure—"an experiment"—Boorman announced he was working on yet another cut of the film, stating, "I'm not

204. J Boorman, quoted in Talbot, p. 24.

205. J Boorman, quoted in Talbot, p. 24.

just recutting it... I'm refashioning it. [The film originally] ended on a note of unequivocal goodness. Evil was defeated. But, in the world we live in, that's an unpopular notion. It's also unrealistic." Boorman added that in the new version, "the girl triumphs over evil. But now it's a personal victory, not a victory for mankind."[206] In the third and most thorough re-edit of *Exorcist II* since its premiere, Boorman made some 130 changes from the theatrical cut, trimming and re-ordering scenes, deleting some lines of dialogue and adding others, and altering some musical cues, most noticeably over the opening and closing titles. (Elaborations of the changes Boorman made were published in the October 1977 issue of *The British Monthly Film Bulletin* and in Todd McCarthy's "The Exorcism of The Heretic" article in the September-October 1977 issue of *Film Comment*.) The film's plot, however, was not changed significantly by the alterations, except for Father Lamont meeting a different fate. John Wilson recounted the premiere of Boorman's re-edit:

> Three weeks [after *Exorcist II* opened] Boorman's complete re-edit was finally ready, and the Westwood theatre where I worked was chosen as the venue where *Exorcist Three* (as wags had dubbed it) would "premiere." When a nattily dressed gentleman came up to me that afternoon and asked for my opinion of the film, I told him that Warners was in such a panic that an "all-new version" would be showing that evening. He asked if there was anything I thought could be done to salvage the movie, and I snidely replied, "The only one thing that could help it is if Warners could convince Mel Brooks to put his name on it." The man turned out to be the chairman of the board of Warner Bros.—and the recut played even worse than the tap-dancing, Hypno-Syncing, walk-into-the-sunrise original version.[207]

Since it would have been too expensive for Warners to recall *all* of the prints of that had already been allocated to cinemas, multiple versions of *Exorcist II* played in American theatres. Boorman, in fact, had asked Warners to deliver his final cut to US theatres but the studio adjudged the $75,000.00 cost too risky a venture for a film already in commercial freefall. In fact, *The New York Times*' Vincent Canby, who had already

---

206. J Boorman, quoted in Talbot, pp. 24-25.

207. Wilson, p. 308.

panned *Exorcist II* upon its first release, threw up his hands at the news of the film's post-production tinkering:

> I suppose there's nothing unethical about this sort of fiddling with a film after it has opened and been reviewed—if a film can be improved upon at any point, so much the better. Yet how is a member of the public to know whether he's seeing 'an early edition' *Exorcist II*, a partially reedited version, or a completely reedited version? Who edited the version that was reviewed? Are these directors admitting that the original versions were no damn good, or are they simply trying to cater to critics and the public to make a buck? What does this have to say about the artistic authenticity of directors?[208]

On July 1, 1977, *Daily Variety* reported that Warners would distribute Boorman's "extensively recut" version of *Exorcist II* in overseas territories. The 110-minute version of *Exorcist II* was released theatrically in Europe, Asia, and Australia; it was the version of the film released by Warner Home Video in 1981; and it was the only version of the movie available on VHS until the original, 118-minute cut was released on video in the early 1990s. (The only version of *Exorcist II* released on DVD is the 118-minute cut. Prior to Shout! Factory's *Exorcist II* Blu-ray release in 2018, the 110-minute version was available only on out-of-print VHS and laserdisc.)

Today, the public is swamped with multiple versions of innumerable motion pictures, and although there *can* be valid artistic reasons for "director's cuts" and "special editions," often they are mere sales ploys. The multiple versions of *Exorcist II* came about when alternate versions of films were relatively rare, and the differences between the two major versions of the film warrant discussion. For brevity's sake the 118-minute version will be referred to hereafter as the "Original Version," and the 110-minute cut will be referred to as the "Revised Version." The major differences in the Revised Version are as follows:

The title music playing over the opening credits is different. The Original Version begins with a slow-paced theme; the Revised Version begins with the same melody, but faster paced with tribal percussion. Both pieces are on the *Exorcist II* soundtrack album: the theme that opens the Original Version is titled "Seduction and Magic" and the theme that

---

opens the Revised Version is titled either "Pazuzu (Theme from *Exorcist II*)" or "Magic and Ecstasy" depending which edition of the album you have. (Most editions list it as "Pazuzu (Theme from *Exorcist II*).") Although the title music differs between the two versions of the film, both feature identical vocal chanting and shrieking in the mix. The change to the title music is puzzling, given the original track is more ominous and its replacement is overwrought and somewhat zany.

After the credits, the Revised Version begins with narration by Lamont over stills from *The Exorcist* and *Exorcist II*, recapping the first film and setting up the second. This dialogue (derived from an opening screen caption that appeared in the July 1976 draft of the screenplay) was recorded by Burton during production:

> *"Father Lankester Merrin died in Georgetown near Washington, D.C., while attempting to exorcise a twelve-year-old girl, Regan MacNeil. The name of the spirit that possessed her was Pazuzu, an Assyrian demon traditionally known as the King of the Evil Spirits of the Air. Father Merrin had first encountered the demon in Ethiopia forty years earlier, when it possessed a young African boy. Father Merrin believed the human spirit was on the threshold of a great leap forward, either into goodness, or evil. His teachings inspired many disciples, of which I was one, and his death dispirited us deeply. So it was that four years later, I climbed a hill in South America with a heavy heart, for it had fallen to me to carry on Father Merrin's struggle."*

A shot of Lamont climbing the steps to the chapel in the opening exorcism scene is added. (In the Original Version, the film begins with Lamont already inside the chapel.) The opening sequence (minus titles) is an extra feature, titled "alternate opening," on the *Exorcist II* DVD. The film benefits from the introductory narration: although the freeze-frames and Lamont's potted summary of the first movie are shoddy, they give Lamont a better entrance. If nothing else, viewers get to hear Richard Burton utter the name "Pazuzu" ten seconds after the opening credits end.

In the chapel, Lamont's prayer to Father Merrin, as he touches a picture of the late priest, is cut out—one of the deletions that minimizes Merrin's presence in the film.

Regan practicing her tap-dancing routine is cut out. In the Original Version, this is the first time we see Regan in the film; in the Revised Version, we don't see Regan until the first scene in the Institute. The Revised Version thus deprives viewers of the sight of Regan bouncing to a baritone sax rendition of "Lullaby of Broadway."

The order of opening scenes in the Original Version is the South American exorcism; the tap-dance practice; Lamont's meeting with Jaros; and the first Institute scene. The order of opening scenes in the Revised Version is the introductory narration; the South American exorcism; Lamont's meeting with Jaros; and the first Institute scene.

Almost all of the first conversation between Lamont and Cardinal Jaros is cut out; only the beginning and the end are retained. Thus, Paul Henreid's screen time in the Revised Version is significantly shortened; the personal friendship between Lamont and Jaros is not revealed; and the title *The Heretic* makes less sense, as the dialogue alluding to Father Merrin being accused of heresy is deleted. Boorman either felt the addition of Lamont's opening narration made much of the dialogue between Lamont and the Cardinal superfluous or he wanted to move to the action, so to speak, as soon as possible (which is presumably why he also did away with Regan's tap-dancing practice). Nevertheless, the deletion does a great disservice to Paul Henreid.

In the hypnosis sequences, shots of the characters with their eyes rolling and crossing are trimmed or deleted entirely, making the scenes less authentic and less amusing.

Tuskin's "Don't you ever need a woman, Father?" exchange with Lamont is gone. Boorman said, "It was one of my favorite things in the picture. But the fact is that the audience knows that [Burton]'s this terrible womanizer and they laugh."[209] The Revised Version has dialogue confirming Lamont is a psychologist. Boorman claimed this gave the character more authority, but Lamont barely comes across as a person with psychological training, contrasting poorly with *The Exorcist*'s Damien Karras.

During the hypnosis scene, Lamont's "I know where she is" line about Tuskin is deleted (sensibly, as the next thing Lamont says is "Help me to find her…").

The Revised Version downplays Lamont's fascination with the demon Pazuzu. His line "horrible… and fascinating" is cut to just "horrible," and in a later conversation, Tuskin's line "How about adulation?" as she storms away is replaced with "You're obsessed with the idea!" Considering that Lamont falling under the sway of Pazuzu figures prominently in

---

209. J Boorman, quoted in Talbot, pp. 26-27.

the climax of the film, it's puzzling as to why Boorman did away with the moments that presage Lamont's temptation.

Lamont's reference to Teilhard de Chardin is deleted, although the film's onscreen reference to spoon-bending "psychic" Uri Geller remains. (This is almost a metatextual reference: Geller's celebrity status was, like *Exorcist II*, a cultural expression of public interest in psychic powers.) Since Merrin is, essentially, the Teilhard de Chardin of the (fictional) *Exorcist* universe, perhaps Boorman felt it made no sense for the film to explicitly acknowledge the existence of Teilhard himself.

More demonic voiceovers are added to Regan's dream about Africa as she wanders to the edge of the penthouse roof.

Some lines are edited out of the scene in which Regan talks with the autistic girl and the girl's mother walks into the room. In particular, the mother's baffling reaction ("You're talking! She's talking! Oh, God, her father would never forgive me if he didn't hear her. I've got to take her home!") is gone. Paring the scene down by a few lines achieves nothing: the entire scene should have been junked. However, Boorman had to retain it as Regan's interaction with the autistic girl is the only explicit demonstration of her healing powers, even if the scene's remaining legacy is Regan's chirpy "I was possessed by a demon... Oh, it's okay, he's gone!" line.

The second scene between Lamont and Jaros has been edited. The Cardinal's "I've asked you to investigate the exorcisms of Father Merrin, not to step into his shoes! You are in dire need of prayer. I suggest you make a retreat!" and Lamont's rejoinder, "A retreat? Why not an advance?!" have been removed, but Boorman reinstated a speech from Lamont that had been unfortunately removed from the theatrical cut: "Merrin looked evil in the face and recognized it. Everywhere. And named it. And fought against it desperately to the end. Alone. And we deny him. And why? Because he was trying to show us the way to the Kingdom of Christ upon earth? And that's something that deep in our hearts we've given up hope on. What you really believe is that the word is incurably sick, lost. And that's a denial of our sacred mission!"

The Communion scene in the mountaintop church is almost entirely cut out, as is part of Lamont's subsequent explanation for knowing the location of the missing body.

Moments cut from the film's home stretch to speed up the story include Tuskin playing with her children in the bathtub; Sharon uttering "Stupid bitch" under her breath; Lamont telling the train conductor "Leave her alone! She belongs to me!" in reference to Regan; Tuskin comforting a nervous plane passenger; Sharon and Tuskin stopping to help a man injured in a car crash; Sharon telling the cab driver "Someone is dying;" and Lamont telling the bus driver to hurry as Regan has to get home. It's a shame Sharon's "stupid bitch" line was removed: it foreshadows Sharon's defection to Pazuzu and is one of the film's few genuinely shocking moments.

In the hallway of the MacNeil house, Regan's "Let me reach you" line to Lamont is dubbed out.

A single close-up shot of the dead cab driver, bleeding on the dashboard, is added (presumably as an attempt to appease the gore-minded horror-film crowd).

Two redubbed shots of Linda Blair from *The Exorcist*, in demon make-up, are spliced in as Regan enters her old bedroom (originally, after Regan recoils from what she sees, the film cuts to Tuskin and Sharon outside the house). Rehashing footage from *The Exorcist* is an obvious capitulation to the audience (and it probably chagrined Boorman to use scenes from Friedkin's film), although in the context of the narrative, it makes sense as an illusion conjured by Pazuzu or a flashback in Regan's mind.

The Evil Regan's "Be joined with us, Father," and Lamont's carnal embrace of the doppelganger, are cut out and replaced with the line "Kill her." The grunting-Lamont-necking-Evil-Regan sequence reportedly gained the film its biggest unintentional laugh, and its deletion undermined further the sexual element of the story. Needless to say, the "Kill her" dub doesn't synchronize with the movements of Blair's mouth.

The Revised Version's faster-paced title music plays over the scene of Sharon immolating herself and Regan struggling against Lamont.

The scene in which Tuskin tries to get Sharon out of the fire, and the scene in which Tuskin runs around in the street yelling for help, are both deleted. Audiences had responded with derisive laughter to Tuskin's futile attempts to rouse the neighborhood, hence the scene's deletion.

A significant change near the end: Lamont does *not* survive his struggle with Pazuzu. His yelling of Regan's name is dubbed over the shot of the roof falling in and only Regan emerges from the destroyed house. (A change not dissimilar to Hugh Hudson's war film *Revolution*: Nastassja Kinski survives in the final reel of the 1985 theatrical version but apparently dies in the 2009 Director's Cut.) Aware of how audiences laughed at Lamont emerging unscathed from the house rubble, Boorman probably banked on them responding more favorably to a denouement that aped the end of *The Exorcist* (i.e. a hitherto-faithless priest achieves redemption by sacrificing his life for Regan). Boorman might have always had this in mind as a possible ending for the film, as he began principal photography feeling uncertain about how the story should conclude. Michel Ciment felt that "If [Lamont's death] is more faithful to the conventions of the genre... it might nevertheless be defended as in keeping with the personality and performance of Burton, who strikes one, while he seeks the truth, as crushed by the weight of his own failure."[210] Viewers, though, might wonder how Regan would feel about a *third* priest dying for her sake, since Tuskin had alluded to Regan's guilt complex over the deaths connected to her exorcism.

With Lamont no longer surviving, the entire last scene is removed in which Sharon dies after receiving absolution from Lamont, Regan weeps over Sharon, and Tuskin apologizes to Regan before saying goodbye to Regan and Lamont, both of whom walk off together. Instead, after the locusts disappear, we see a shot of Regan walking out of the rubble, a shot of Tuskin standing amid a crowd of onlookers (the last shot of the Original Version), a close-up of Regan, and a white fade to the credits. This ending features no new footage; it was created by jettisoning scenes. As to which ending is better, the Original Version has the edge. It's a terrible finale—albeit one in keeping with the two hours of lunacy that preceded it—but the truncated ending of the Revised Version is too abrupt and denies viewers Father Lamont's hilarious victory speech: "The time has come. Now we are saved and made strong. The enemy of the human race has been subdued!" If anything, the pessimistic shorter ending negates Boorman's intention to make a film about "goodness"—with Lamont buried under rubble, Sharon dying without receiving forgiveness, Tuskin confused and weeping, and Regan's future uncertain, how does this serve as "an antidote" to *The Exorcist*?

The Original Version plays "Regan's Theme" throughout the entire end credits. Halfway through the Revised Version's end credits, "Regan's Theme" is replaced with a fast-paced rock music cue (used prominently in the film's theatrical trailer) titled "Magic and Ecstasy" in some editions of the soundtrack album and "Pazuzu (Theme from *Exorcist II*)" in others (although "Magic and Ecstasy" is more common). The change in music has the connotation of the demon returning; the track itself has a psychedelic, fuzz-bass, satanic prog-rock vibe not far removed from the then-contemporaneous work of Germany's musical outfit Goblin (as heard in the *giallo* films of Dario Argento) and was covered by late

---

210. Ciment, p.159.

British guitarist Snakefinger (Philip Charles Lithman) in his 1979 album *Chewing Hides the Sound.*

There is no real consensus as to which of the two major versions of *Exorcist II* is superior, although cases have been made for both. Writing for *Video Watchdog* in 2012, Paul Talbot claims, "The truncated version clunks along and plays like the hastily-altered rush job that it is" and compares it unfavorably to the "superior, original cut."[211] The Original Version has a marginally stronger plot (by virtue of retaining the lengthier expository scene between Lamont and Jaros, and the story's longer ending), while the Revised Version is more surreal and perhaps easier to appreciate on a camp level, as it uses the energetic cues from Ennio Morricone's score more prominently. ("Magic and Ecstasy" isn't heard in the original version at all.) Most of the revisions were made for the purposes of expediency: shortening the film's length should, in theory, have tightened the pace and made the plot more accessible, but a difference of 8 minutes didn't make *Exorcist II* less meandering. Since the film's plot isn't significantly different between the two cuts—if anything, the shorter version makes *less* sense—the re-edit was an exercise in futility, and an expensive one at that. Boorman probably knew the revisions were pointless, but he had to be seen doing *something* to try to save the picture; speaking to *Film Comment*, he alluded to the desperation and futility of the re-edit:

> I don't think it's a better picture, particularly, this new version, but I think it's a picture that would satisfy audiences better. Play better, maybe... When I think that I was having screaming fits because there was one shot, really a minor shot, where the lab broke the negative and we had to lose a frame, I was out of my mind! I was down at Technicolor tearing my hair out and screaming at everybody, and here I am, three weeks later, chopping great chunks out of it... In hindsight, I think there are two different pictures one could have made. One could have gone for straight horror, flat out. The other approach would have been to do a kind of send-up, a picture that audiences could laugh at... I felt, misguidedly, that you could take a kind of captive audience and characters that they knew about and had some concern about and lead them into a movie that was adventurous in a way that you couldn't if you were starting from scratch. I felt, in this case,

---

211. Talbot, p. 29.

we have such a tremendous captive audience that one could take them into a kind of spiritual adventure that would be a tremendous opportunity to take these ideas and themes to an enormous audience. And, of course, that was obviously a mistake.[212]

The character who suffers the most in re-editing is Lamont. The minimization of the character in the Revised Version was deliberate on Boorman's part, who felt the middle-aged and British Richard Burton was not connecting with American audiences and lacked onscreen chemistry with co-star Linda Blair:

> We had a 17-year-old star [Blair] and with Chris Walken, for instance, we would have had someone young enough to carry the feelings of the moviegoing audience, which we all know is very young... At a very dumb level, when you go down and look at this, [America] is a very insular country, really. You go into these black audiences, and you see that Richard Burton, he's like a Martian! He's not just a foreigner. He's so far away from their experience, the way he talks and everything, they have no feeling for him at all. They just don't give a shit about him.[213]

Unfortunately, *Exorcist II's* problems are so deep-rooted that one suspects nothing short of a new director re-filming it from scratch could have saved it. (That expensive course of action was not implemented with an *Exorcist* film until the prequel debacle nearly thirty years later.) One of the biggest problems with *Exorcist II* in *any* incarnation is the fact that Boorman's skills were unable to live up to his ambition—a similar problem plagued *Zardoz*—resulting in a confused story and characters spouting awkward, pretentious dialogue. How could re-shuffling scenes and some minor deletions rectify *that?* Furthermore, retooling the film probably did more harm than good, as news of the studio pulling and re-editing the film was an admission of the film's deficiency. "It's to openly acknowledge that one of the goals of this belated repair work is to eliminate the most explosive outbursts of laughter provoked by the original, unexpurgated fiasco," reported Gary Arnold of *The Washington Post*. "Ironically, the sagging box

212. J Boorman, quoted in Talbot, p. 26.

213. J Boorman, quoted in Talbot, p. 26.

office returns for the film will probably sag even further now that the studio is trying to lock the barn door after allowing the horses to escape in the first place."[214] *The Wall Street Journal*'s Stephen Grocer announced, "In what is possibly the most expensive surgery ever performed in a movie after it has gone into release, director and producer John Boorman is "refashioning" his latest movie." This sort of thing didn't usually happen in the 1970s. Boorman biographer Michel Ciment, admitting the cuts Boorman made in the Revised Version are "regrettable," envisions the "ideal" version of *The Heretic* as one containing all the material from both versions. (Reportedly, another version of the film *does* exist, although it is not Ciment's ideal amalgam. Released in parts of Europe, this cut—shorter than the Revised Version but ending with Father Lamont surviving—is the most obscure version of *Exorcist II* and has never received an official home media release.)

On Wednesday, February 13, 1980, *Exorcist II*, via the Revised Version, made its American network television debut, on CBS the night after *The Exorcist*'s TV premiere. "THE DEVIL STILL LIVES WITHIN HER!" thundered printed advertisements for the premiere. "A CHILD IN THE GRIP OF EVIL. A PRIEST WITHOUT GOD. TOGETHER, THEY FIGHT THE FORCES OF DARKNESS." (*Exorcist II* actually made its television debut before *The Exorcist* did, premiering on America's cable channel HBO on Sunday, July 16, 1978. Warners likely would not have sought TV profits quite so quickly had the film enjoyed a successful theatrical run the previous year.) In September 1980, *The Exorcist* and *Exorcist II* were re-released as a theatrical double-bill in the UK, advertised as "TWO STORIES STRAIGHT FROM HELL." *The Exorcist* and *Exorcist II* were among the earliest releases Warner Home Video made available for the burgeoning home video market at the dawn of the 1980s. Existing largely on decades-old VHS, the Revised Version of *Exorcist II* eventually fell into relative obscurity: it was not included in Warners' 2006 DVD set *The Exorcist Complete Anthology* (even though that collection includes the 1973 and 2000 cuts of *The Exorcist* and both versions of the *Exorcist* prequel). Both cuts were finally released together in a "Collector's Edition" *Exorcist II* Blu-ray from Shout! Factory in September 2018, in which the Revised Version was described as the "Original Home Video Cut."

Michel Ciment claims there was nothing scandalous about Boorman re-editing *Exorcist II*, pointing to Kubrick's revisions of *2001: A*

214. G Arnold, "Exorcising the Laughs from a 'Heretic' Fiasco." *The Washington Post*, Jun. 29, 1977.

Space Odyssey after premiere screenings as a precedent. This is not an apt comparison. Kubrick merely trimmed some scenes—he did not alter the film's ending; he was not asked by the studio to change anything; and *2001* did not cause *riots* in its original form. In his book *The Cinema of John Boorman*, Brian Hoyle criticizes the Revised Version of *Exorcist II* for truncating the story's theological and philosophical ideas, noting "these omissions rob the film of complexity without turning it into a noticeably more satisfying horror film."[215] The existence of multiple versions of *Exorcist II* has led to some misconceptions that persist to this day. One is that the studio took creative control away from the director and recut the film against his "vision," an overused cliché that is not true in this case, as Boorman had personally supervised the various cuts of *Exorcist II*. (Also, *Exorcist II* was not released in a compromised state to meet a release deadline, as Steven Spielberg's *Close Encounters of the Third Kind* and Francis Ford Coppola's *Apocalypse Now*, to give two examples, were.) Furthermore, the relative unavailability of the Revised Version for many years fostered a sense of mystique—namely that it is a vast improvement over the version of *Exorcist II* that was more readily available. Some alternate versions *do* offer a fascinating glimpse of looking at a film in a different way. This is not the case with the Revised Version of *Exorcist II*. It is an interesting comparison to the original cut, but it is not an improvement (a point Boorman conceded when recording his audio commentary for the *Exorcist II* Blu-ray). In hindsight, the revision of *Exorcist II* was little more than an attempt to patch up bullet-holes with band-aids.

---

215. Hoyle, p. 108.

Part Two

Regan (Linda Blair) "heals" Dr. Tuskin's autistic patient Sandra (Dana Plato).

9

"I flew with Pazuzu in a trance!"
The Screenplay of
Exorcist II

"...it was a really good script at first. Then after everybody signed on they rewrote it five times and it ended up nothing like the same movie. That was one of the big disappointments of my career."

– Linda Blair[216]

LIKE *DELIVERANCE, EXCALIBUR,* and *The Emerald Forest, Exorcist II: The Heretic* is a John Boorman fable about the need to redress the balance between humanity and nature. Its story has a philosophy that could be considered alchemical. Symbols and objects are interchangeable, and action of one affects the other; Pazuzu is symbolically *and* corporeally a plague of locusts, and *physical* action against the swarm diffuses the demon's power. With this philosophical underpinning, the locusts aren't there to "gross out" audiences *a la* the cockroaches in George A. Romero's *Creepshow* (1982). *Exorcist II* attempts to fuse spiritualism and science to create something hip for everyone—but the film's muddled ideas and approach pleased few people, in spite of Boorman's ambition to "remain personal within the context of a big-budget, mass-audience Hollywood

---

216. M Kermode, "My Blair Lady," *The Dark Side: The Magazine of the Macabre and Fantastic*, Nov. 1991.

movie."[217] Reviews of *Exorcist II* singled out William Goodhart for criticism—Steven H. Scheuer described his screenplay as "abominable"—and Goodhart *is* the film's sole credited writer. However, the film's script was massively retooled by John Boorman (who liked the ideas in Goodhart's script, but not the script itself) and Rospo Pallenberg. *The Heretic* entered production in May 1976 with Pallenberg's revised draft, which underwent further revisions on July 26, August 2, August 9, and September 21. (Not receiving screenwriting credit proved to be a blessing in disguise for Pallenberg, who escaped the wrath of the critics.)

With *Exorcist II*'s script in a massive state of flux during principal photography, the actors had difficulty bringing conviction to what they were required to say. At the outset of filming, Boorman told his cast, "Your responsibility is to thoroughly know your characters, so whatever happens, if I were suddenly to improvise a scene, you would know exactly what to say, you could invent lines."[218] This leeway was not helpful: little in *Exorcist II* approaches the naturalistic dialogue of *The Exorcist*, and overwritten, implausible lines constitute one of the film's biggest shortcomings. Film cultists have derived amusement from the following verbal atrocities:

> *Lamont:* You realise what you're up against, don't you?...
> *Evil!!!*

> *Merrin:* Get thee hence!
> *Pazuzu:* No! She's *mine* always!

> *Lamont: Evil* is gaining... Father Merrin was killed!
> *Tuskin:*... by Regan?
> *Lamont: She* didn't! *It* did! That wasn't the mind of a child.
> It was horrible... Utterly horrible... and fascinating.
> *Tuskin:* Look, we don't know all that much about
> synchronized hypnosis yet. What you saw could just as
> easily been a dream, a fantasy, an hallucination... not a
> memory at all.
> *Lamont:* Names. Just names! Better to see the face than to
> hear the names!

---

217. J Boorman, quoted in Ciment, p. 177.

218. J Boorman, quoted in Pallenberg, p. 56.

Lamont: The flames! Flames! Doctor! Doctor, the flames! They're getting bigger! We've got to put the fire out!
Tuskin: Take it easy! It's probably some post-flashing. It's an after-effect of the hypnosis.
Lamont: No, no, no! You've got to help me. We may be too late, we may be too late!
Tuskin: Where are you going?
Lamont: You've got to help me! Regan's picture... !
Tuskin: Come on, Father. Give me a break...
Lamont: No, there's *fire!* There's a *fire* somewhere!!!

Lamont: I was face to face with the evil that's inside her. Your machine has proved *scientifically* that there's an ancient demon locked within her!

Sharon: I couldn't bear to be near her after... Two years I stayed away. Two haunted years, going out of my mind. And all the time I longed to see her. Finally, I came back and found that... when I'm with her is the only time I'm at peace. Why would that be? I can't understand. It frightens me.
Lamont: Have you tried a psychiatrist or a priest?
Sharon: I'm talking to one now, aren't I?
Lamont: I'm not here for you.

Tuskin: It's hard to live alone. Don't you ever need a woman, Father?
Lamont: Yes.

Regan/Pazuzu: Fly by the teeth of the wind! Share my wings!

Lamont: A leopard. It jumped right at me! The boy's still alive!

Tuskin: Let's stick to science.
Lamont: Don't hide behind science! You're better than that!

Lamont: You've got to fight that demon that's inside her! It's preventing her from reaching full spiritual power!

Lamont: I'm not obsessed! I'm not!

Regan: Father, do priests believe in E.S.P.?
Lamont: Some do. In fact a French priest, Teilhard de Chardin, thought we'd all come together eventually in some sort of mental telepathy. A kind of world-mind in which everybody would share.
Regan: When's that supposed to happen?
Lamont: I don't know. Father Merrin himself believed that with modern scientific research, it could happen quite soon. I mean the kind of research Dr Tuskin is doing. But if it happens before we're ready, we may find ourselves pointing in the wrong direction. Towards Satan!

Jaros: I've asked you to *investigate* the exorcisms of Father Merrin, not to step into his shoes! You are in dire need of prayer. I suggest you make a retreat!
Lamont: A retreat? Why not an advance?!

Lamont: I flew with Pazuzu in a trance! It's difficult to explain... I was under hypnosis!

Regan/Pazuzu: Call me by my dream name. Call me!

Lamont: I've flown this route before... It was on the wings of a demon!

Lamont: Pazuzu, king of the evil spirits of the air, help me to find Kokumo!

Kokumo: If Pazuzu comes for you I will spit a leopard!

Lamont: Were you ever... ?
Kokumo:... possessed by Pazuzu? That's what my mother used to tell me!

Kokumo: The key factor is the brushing of the wings. When it is dry, the grasshoppers go their own way, happy individuals. When a heavy rain hatches them in large numbers, they

crowd together. Their wings brush against each other. The agitation transforms them... The brushing of the wings changes their personality. They become a destructive, voracious, marauding swarm, with a single mind. A locust mind, if you will. The evil swarm sweeps over the earth, possessing all that it touches. Evil breeding evil by contact.
Lamont: Is there no hope once the wings have brushed you?
Kokumo: We try, with the help of science! Look at this young female. She has been evolved to resist the brushing of the wings. At least, that is our hope. We like to call her "the Good Locust." Her children will be our agents in the swarm, breaking the chain reaction. Remaining forever happy-go-lucky grasshoppers. Let us pray it succeeds.
Lamont: The... Good Locust?

Lamont: The power... it's getting nearer. Can't you feel it? The power is immense. It fills me. I can do anything!

Pazuzu: He's mine! He's chosen *me!* Pazuzu's Regan is the *only* Regan!

Lamont: The wings are brushing me!!! The wings are brushing me!!!

Tuskin: At least help Regan!
Sharon: To do what?
Tuskin: To fight this thing!
Sharon: Name it.
Tuskin: Pazuzu!

Lamont: REEEEEGAAAAAN!!!!!
Pazuzu: PAZUUUUUZUUUUU!!!!!

The *worst* dialogue occurs during the meeting between Regan and Sandra, the autistic girl:

Regan: What's the matter with you?
Sandra: I'm autistic.
Regan: How do you mean?

> *Sandra:* I'm withdrawn. I can't talk.
> *Regan:* But you're talking now... Yes, you are! I can hear you!
> *Sandra:* You can hear me?
> *Regan:* Sure!
> *Sandra:* What's the matter with you?
> *Regan:* I was possessed by a demon... Oh, it's okay, he's gone!

Equally clumsy (if less memorable) dialogue occurs when Lamont and Sharon visit the MacNeil house, and Sharon's answers don't fit with Lamont's questions:

> *Lamont:* When Father Merrin arrived, how did he prepare himself? Did he pray?
> *Sharon:* They couldn't explain it—the police—could they?

> *Lamont:* Was... was Father Merrin afraid?
> *Sharon:* You'd better see where it happened.

The conversational discordance between Lamont and Sharon rears its head near the end of the film. At death's door, an incinerated Sharon repents, "I... chose... evil," to which Lamont replies, "No, Sharon. Your hunger for belief was your truth!" (What does that *mean?*)

Exorcist II bears the worst indications of a script hastily rewritten: the questionable lines; artless expository dialogue; fraying connective tissue between the story's set-pieces; and events expediting the plot without conviction. The constant revision of the script during filming is probably the reason why the characters act erratically and their behavior is wildly contradictory: anything to move the plot from A to B. (In some ways, *Exorcist II* follows the pattern of formulaic James Bond films: An opening scene only mildly related to the rest of the story; the lead male protagonist being given plot exposition and assigned to a mission by his grumpy superior; and a story which amounts to a lot of time travelling between continents.) *Exorcist II* is an example of an "idiot movie"—for the story to work (so to speak), characters are required to say and do idiotic things. Situations that *could* be more readily resolved if people talked sensibly are allowed to escalate to ridiculous proportions. (To put it another way—the characters behave in seemingly insane ways and the plot is ludicrous, and it's practically impossible for audiences to not notice this.) There is also no sense of pace. *The Exorcist* maintains and intensifies a sense of dread up to and throughout the exorcism sequence, but *Exorcist II* lurches around murkily, prior to its nonsensical ending. Not just inconsistent with the events of *The Exorcist*, the plot of *Exorcist II* is baffling on its own terms. Aside from the film's woeful grasp of science (namely, the Synchronizer and its Vulcan-mind-meld-style attributes), consider the following:

How did Lamont know where to find Regan? How did he know Regan was seeing a psychiatrist, and how did he know which psychiatrist it was? (Was he stalking Regan?) If Chris MacNeil told Lamont where Regan was, why didn't she contact Regan about him, and why didn't Tuskin or Sharon contact her? How was Lamont permitted to see Tuskin? When Tuskin answers Lamont's questions about Regan, isn't she violating doctor/patient confidentiality? Why does Tuskin allow Lamont to observe Regan's initial hypnotherapy session, when a) she shouldn't be letting an outsider into this session; b) she doesn't know what exactly Lamont wants of Regan at this point; and c) after she tells Lamont that his line of questioning might be harmful to Regan, Lamont responds by babbling on about "evil" being "alive and living, perverting its way insidiously in the very fabric of life"? (Would any reasonable medical practitioner allow this man to stay around a traumatized patient?) Why does Tuskin tell Lamont that the shock of memory recall could be harmful to Regan, when Tuskin is intent on making Regan recall those memories via the Synchronizer anyway? (When Lamont tells Tuskin that he wants to question Regan over Merrin's death, Tuskin becomes defensive, claiming that any attempt to get to the bottom of the exorcism will result in severe feelings of trauma and guilt in Regan, which could ultimately lead to suicide. Yet earlier in the film, Tuskin was pressuring Regan into recalling all of what happened—offering the use of an untested and potentially dangerous machine! The machine Tuskin tries so hard to push onto Regan turns out to be so dangerous it nearly *kills* Tuskin during the first session. Tuskin later admits to Lamont, "We don't know all that much about synchronized hypnosis yet...") Given its revolutionary properties, would the Synchronizer really be on standby for use on citizens in a private clinic, rather than in a government lab? During the first Synchronizer session, after Tuskin starts breathing erratically and is clearly ill, why does Liz the nurse—who concludes that Tuskin's heart is fibrillating—not perform CPR or call an ambulance? (Lamont jumps in to save the day, saying he "knows where she is," and engages with the Synchronizer so he can bring Tuskin down like the pilot of a stricken airplane. But with Lamont replacing Regan, why are *Regan's memories* still being played back, since the girl is disengaged and only Tuskin and Lamont are in sync?) Why does the flashback to Merrin's death conclude with the elderly priest collapsing onto the floor when, in *The Exorcist*, Karras found Merrin slumped across Regan's bed, and why is Regan wearing a white nightgown rather than the blue one she wore in *The Exorcist*? Why does Regan's stylized drawing convince Lamont there is a fire somewhere in the Institute? Why does Lamont attempt to extinguish the fire by beating it with a wooden crutch? Why is Sharon coy about her reasons for going to Washington, not telling Regan that it's anything to do with the exorcism, when Regan *already knows* there is a priest investigating the whole thing? Why is Lamont deliberately rude to the obviously-suffering Sharon? ("I'm not here for you!") Why does Pazuzu aid Lamont and Regan in their quest to find Kokumo, which ultimately leads to the demon's own destruction? (Pazuzu helps Lamont find Kokumo, and *Kokumo instructs Lamont specifically on how to kill Pazuzu.* If it wasn't for Pazuzu letting Lamont fly with him in an earlier vision, *Lamont wouldn't even know that Kokumo exists!* It's as if the screenwriters couldn't think for Lamont to solve the problem, so they let Pazuzu give him the answer for no reason.) When Regan "heals" the autistic girl Sandra, why does the girl's mother respond by rushing to the receptionist rather than to her own daughter? Without the Church's consent, how did Lamont afford the flight to Ethiopia? In *forty years* of searching, why did the Ethiopians never find the body of the dead monk, when the corpse turns out to be not significantly far from where they had been looking all that time? Why is Lamont incapable of keeping his mouth shut when almost everything he says gets him into trouble? (Talking about demons to Tuskin gets him barred from speaking with Regan; talking about demons to Jaros gets him thrown off the Merrin investigation; talking about demons to the Ethiopians gets him assaulted with stones.) If Lamont actually, *physically* travelled to the mud city of Jepti, taken there by Edwards, how did he get to the laboratory? (At the climactic moment of his encounter with Kokumo in the hut, when Lamont has to prove his faith, he awakens with the "real" Kokumo in a research lab in equatorial Africa—so was Jepti an elaborate hallucination? Was Edwards a figment of Lamont's imagination? How and when did Lamont travel to the lab? Was he really, *actually,* in the mud city before being *magically teleported* to the lab? The lab couldn't have been a hallucination, otherwise Lamont would have *really* maimed himself on the nail-moat.) Why does Liz the nurse let Regan leave the clinic when the girl is supposed to be under sedation? Isn't the Synchronizer's importance undermined by the fact Lamont and Regan can link minds *without* use of the machine when they are *separated by two different continents?* Given the status of the Synchronizer as a ground-breaking (and therefore presumably very expensive) piece of technology, why does Tuskin leave it in *an unlocked drawer* (in a facility full of *disturbed children*), and why is Tuskin nonplussed when Regan reveals she left it in a hotel room? ("Listen, that doesn't matter. Where are you?")

Furthermore, viewers of *Exorcist II* would be justified in asking exactly *what* is going on in the last half-hour of the film. Why does Lamont take Regan to the MacNeils' old house in Georgetown? Since Pazuzu clearly wants Regan to be done away with, why doesn't the demon just have Lamont kill Regan in New York? Would Pazuzu's plan have been ruined had Regan *refused* to accompany Lamont to Georgetown? Pazuzu possessed Kokumo and would have killed him had it not been for Merrin, an expert exorcist. Pazuzu succeeded in killing the South American girl, because Lamont is an incompetent exorcist. If Pazuzu wants Regan out of the way, why does the demon not possess Regan and impel her to kill herself? It's not as if Lamont could offer much resistance. (He's ineffectual even when he's *not* under the influence of the demon.) The trip to Washington makes more sense as a sop to audiences—returning the "action" (so to speak) to the house of the first film. If Pazuzu's *modus operandi* is to destroy victims via possession (hence the earlier possessions of Kokumo, Regan, and the South American healer), how and why does the demon create the corporeal form of an *entirely separate* Regan? Why doesn't Pazuzu just possess the real Regan, or possess Lamont (the demon had leapt into Karras' body with ease) and use *him* to kill Regan, rather than merely *commanding* Lamont to do it, which proves to be an ineffectual course of action? Since Tuskin *knows precisely where Regan and Lamont are heading*, if she believes Regan is in genuine danger, why doesn't she warn anyone in Washington (the police? Mental health authorities?) rather than try to race Regan and Lamont there? Isn't it a huge coincidence that the taxicab crashes into the front of *the very house* Tuskin and Sharon want to get to? Why does Sharon suddenly become an acolyte of Pazuzu? Why does Tuskin suddenly elect to believe in Pazuzu's existence just because the taxi crashed and Sharon is acting strangely? Why are the Georgetown streets quiet and deserted when a taxi crashes into a fence, a plague of locusts descend, a woman sets herself on fire, and an *entire house loudly breaks apart and collapses,* but then a throng of people suddenly spring up behind Tuskin after Regan and Lamont leave? (Does the final confrontation with

Pazuzu take place in some sort of spatial/temporal zone in which the laws of time are suspended, barring anyone besides Regan, Lamont, Tuskin, and Sharon from witnessing, and partaking in, it? Boorman told Michel Ciment that the frontiers of time and space no longer apply when one is synchronized, so does this mean Regan, Lamont, Tuskin, and Sharon are all synchronized, and the taxi crash, Sharon's death, the locust plague, and the collapse of the house took place in the blink of an eye for everybody *besides* those four characters?) Is Tuskin going to tell Chris MacNeil that her old house is a pile of rubble, Sharon is a burnt corpse, and her teenage daughter has run off with a middle-aged priest? (Maybe those tears streaming down her face indicate the dread of making that phone call.)

Exorcist II presumes to end upon a note indicating some sort of redemption for humankind, but since the threat had been dealt with in the abstract, and since its portrayal of humanity (in the persons of Regan, Lamont, and Tuskin) is scarcely credible, the story's attempt at catharsis, and progress, falls flat. *The Exorcist*—in its original 1973 incarnation at least—ends on a note of uncertainty, one that can be read as pessimistic or optimistic depending on the viewer. (Blatty wanted *The Exorcist* to end on an invitation to embrace Christianity. In the novel and first-draft script, Father Karras' friend, Father Joe Dyer, suggests to Chris MacNeil that believing in the existence of the Devil because of the evil in the world means accepting God as an explanation for the good. Chris then decides to keep Karras' St Joseph medal, the symbol of faith. Friedkin did away with this in the film: Dyer doesn't deliver the "religious commercial" and Chris gives the medal back to him. In the film's very last moment, Dyer walks away sadly after gazing at the site where Karras died. Although this understated moment is a respite after the onslaught of the exorcism sequence, it's hard to disagree with Blatty's complaint that Friedkin made the film "a downer.")

One gets the impression that John Boorman labored to make *Exorcist II* "hallucinatory" and "dreamlike" to disguise the baffling plot holes in the narrative schemata and he attempted profundity to disguise bad dialogue. A film is, of course, under no obligation to spell everything out— many great films are deliberately ambiguous—but *Exorcist II*'s inscrutability comes from weak writing. How could audiences have responded to the story when none of its characters behave in a realistic manner? Regan does not act like a person who is experiencing psychic terror. Tuskin does not act like the professional scientist we are supposed to take her for (and she ceases to have any real influence on the story after Lamont's return from Ethiopia). Jaros is required to be friendly with Lamont for the sake of exposition, only to become stodgy and combative to create dramatic conflict. And Lamont himself is thoroughly baffling. Compare him to Father Karras, the character in the first film he is roughly analogous to, inasmuch as both characters are brooding, self-doubting priests. (Indicative of the notion that Lamont is a combination of Karras and Merrin is that his surname begins with L—between K and M.) In *The Exorcist*, Karras' crisis of faith was understandable, stemming from self-doubt over his profession; guilt for not being able to provide for his aged mother (and his absence when she died); and from the despair and poverty surrounding him. We are to accept Lamont's feelings of "unworthiness" as a given, with no real explanation besides vague references to the "evil" he sees in the world around him, and, presumably, the disillusioned weariness that comes from age. The character of Lamont, and by extension the narrative drive of the story, were altered significantly when Richard Burton was cast over Christopher Walken. As Boorman explained,

> Burton, to be sure, was a very persuasive, very powerful actor—he was totally credible. But the choice immediately posed new problems, since a middle-aged man would behave in a quite different fashion [to a young man]. As a result, we had to make changes both to the character and to the scenes in which appeared… [We] gradually changed Lamont from a passionate, impulsive priest to the disillusioned Jesuit he is in the film.[219]

Boorman clarified to Michel Ciment the motivations of Lamont in the story:

> What Lamont is going through is the kind of crisis which many priests today experience. He feels spiritually 'blocked'. He's afraid that God might be dead. He's looking for alternative paths to transcendental experience, and he believes he's found one in science. It's perhaps a difficult idea to convey in a 'thriller' like *The Heretic*, but what we have is a priest who, by the intervention of a psychiatrist, attempts to establish spiritual contact with the young heroine.[220]

---

219. J Boorman, quoted in Ciment, p. 168.

220. J Boorman, quoted in Ciment, p. 173.

As Boorman himself noted, the idea central to Lamont's dramatic function in *Exorcist II* is conveyed with difficulty. In fact, Lamont's gullibility and stilted personality undermine the story: whereas Karras investigated Regan with an appropriate air of skepticism—not wanting to believe in the authenticity of the possession and only changing his mind when it became clear that possession was the *only* explanation—Lamont yammers on about evil and demons from the start. (Lamont annoys almost everyone he meets in the film: Tuskin, Jaros, various Ethiopians, and Sharon. If he fails to annoy Regan it is only because Regan is incapable of responding to anything or anyone in a credible manner.) Lamont's impulsive behavior would perhaps be more understandable coming from the younger character originally envisaged; it's much more incongruous coming from the persona onscreen. In his overview of *The Heretic*, Ewen Millar takes the character of Lamont to task:

> Whether it be the fault of the actor Richard Burton's general demeanour, or simply the fault of the hammy dialogue and overearnest direction he received, the character of Father Lamont comes across not as the sort of priest one would want to have looking after anyone's spiritual care, with his constant, droning invective about evil, his jet-setting to the African "Highlands" at the drop of a hat, and his willingness to ask favours from the "demon" that he believes he is supposed to be protecting the young Regan from: Lamont comes across as an individual who seems to oscillate between being unhealthily obsessed and completely off his trolley.[221]

Dr Tuskin is problematic in another way: somewhat contradictorily, the story positions her as a therapeutic specialist dispensing scientific rigmarole *and* an audience identification figure. "Louise Fletcher as the psychiatrist is confronted in the film by a form of precognition. She represents the rational human being who, like the audience, has the same kind of problems about dealing with these phenomena," Boorman explained. "Through her we associate with the problem of facing this supernatural phenomenon. Now, it's very difficult for her as a scientist to accept this, accept the evidence that's before her and this causes tremendous conflict in her character."[222]

---

221. E Millar, "On Otherness and Illusion in *Exorcist II: The Heretic.*" *Studies in the Horror Film: The Exorcist* (ed: D Olson, Lakewood: Centipede Press, 2011), p. 394.

222. J Boorman, quoted in *Exorcist II: The Heretic* production featurette.

The characters in *The Exorcist* have depth; the characters in *Exorcist II: The Heretic* are flimsy, programmatic constructs: products of lazy writing, contributing to the film's implausibility. This contrasts with its predecessor: Since *The Exorcist* concerns the supernatural invading a *normal* world, Friedkin grounded the film in realism, to allow those who regarded the subject matter as fantasy to suspend their disbelief. John Landis, director of the horror classic *An American Werewolf in London* (1981), was receptive to this approach:

> The best horror film ever is probably Bill Friedkin's *The Exorcist*, the first release, not after he went back and fucked it up. The first cut of *The Exorcist* is just incredible. Really in terms of suspension of disbelief—and I'm a total atheist—I was sitting there for the length of that movie. I was perfectly willing to accept the concept of Satan. The Vatican should be kissing Friedkin's ass because that is the most blatant commercial for the Church and the power of Christ ever made. I saw that movie with Jim O'Rourke and George Folsey, both had been Catholic altar boys, and both had fallen away from the Church. We loved it. We went out afterward, all excited talking about it. I went home, went right to sleep. George and Jim had nightmares for weeks because they had had that fear instilled into them as children. The movie is really shocking. It's still shocking![223]

David Cronenberg—also an atheist—told Landis of the ambience key to the film's success: "*The Exorcist* felt absolutely real and it drew you in slowly, slowly, before it started to hit you over the head."[224] Film critic Roger Ebert also lauded this aspect of the film:

> I've revisited *The Exorcist* over the years and found it effective every time. Because it's founded on characters, details and a realistic milieu, the shocks don't date; they still seem to grow from the material. In the early 1990s I joined Owen Roizman, the film's cinematographer, in a shot-by-shot analysis of

---

223. J Landis, quoted in G D'Agnolo Vallan, *John Landis* (Milwaukie: Milwaukie Press, 2008) pp. 51-52.

224. D Cronenberg, quoted in J Landis, *Monsters in the Movies: 100 Years of Cinematic Nightmares* (New York: DK Publishing, 2011), p. 88.

the film over four days at the Hawaii Film Festival. As we dissected it, I gained an appreciation of the craft of the film -- how it embeds the sensational material in an everyday world of misty nights, boozy parties and housekeeping details, chats in a laundry room and the personal lives of the priests. The movie is more horrifying because it does not seem to want to be. The horror creeps into the lives of characters preoccupied with their lives: Father Karras with his mother and his faith, Father Merrin with his work and health, Chris MacNeil with her career and marriage... *The Exorcist* was and is a brilliant horror film, one with an archetypal ability to reach and disturb us. It will survive as long as people care about well-made movies. [225]

There is no "everyday world" in *Exorcist II*. Like *Zardoz*, *Exorcist II* is Boorman's exploration of a hallucinatory realm, but the dream world in both films is ineffective because audiences are not given an identifiable character, someone who behaves in a *credible* manner, to journey with. (*Exorcist II* repeats other sins of *Zardoz*: characters reacting with po-faced seriousness to pretentious lunacy, clumsy direction of extras, and ambitious visuals failing to mask Boorman's deficiencies as a storyteller.) *Deliverance* takes place in a nightmarish world, but it is a world that is recognizably *real*, and the characters are so well-established at the outset of the film that we can understand the ways in which they react to the events they subsequently experience. (Like *The Exorcist*, the basis of *Deliverance* was a strong novel.) Although dreams play a prominent part in *Exorcist II*, the first movie trumps it on that front, via Father Karras' dream sequence. In this elegiac moment, Karras dreams he catches sight of his recently deceased mother across a crowded NYC street. Not hearing her son's calls, Karras' mother descends into a subway. This entirely silent scene is beautiful, sad, and unsettling—it's almost peripheral to the story, but it gives more depth to Karras, illustrating his self-admonishment and presaging the demon's psychological attacks on him (the demon talks cruelly about Karras' mother, speaks in her voice, and even *appears* as her). The shot of Karras' St Joseph medal falling to the ground symbolizes Karras' crisis of faith, and the stairway descent is an eerie portent of Karras' own death. (There are also near-subliminal flashes of the demon, played by Linda Blair's stand-in, Eileen Dietz.) The entire sequence is less than a minute

225. R Ebert, "*The Exorcist.*" *Chicago Sun-Times*, Sep. 22, 2000.

long, realized better than any of the dream sequences in *Exorcist II*, and clearly demarcated from the rest of the film—for *The Exorcist* presents its story as an extension of reality. Karras' dream excepted, audiences are asked to relate to the events depicted as though they actually happened; they are asked to respond as they would had the events happened in real life. *Exorcist II* diverges wildly from this approach: its story is a surreal psychodrama, reliant on dream-logic—the visualization of the bizarre thoughts and feelings of the characters (Regan and Lamont in particular). The film constantly makes it difficult to discern which events are real and which are imagined. Realism and plausibility are not on *Exorcist II*'s agenda; or at least, they are subservient to emotions and symbolism. Putting aside whether this is an artistically valid approach, it at least points to one of the reasons the film failed its audience. *The Exorcist* seeks to immerse viewers in a vicarious experience, to convince them it's *real*. It is a film that invites engagement—a participatory experience. Chafing against what he perceived to be the excesses of Friedkin's film and the restrictions of the horror genre, John Boorman denied *Exorcist II*'s audience an emotional participation in favor of an approach that immediately invited viewers to approach the film from a disengaged, critical perspective—inadvertently making the film's manifold flaws more obvious. Inevitably, filmgoers instinctively rejected *Exorcist II* in 1977. In the wake of the film's disaster, Boorman—who believed his approach to be more artistic and highbrow than Friedkin's—regarded the filmgoing masses as too dull-minded and violence-seeking to appreciate *Exorcist II*. This position was echoed by Michel Ciment, who effectively delineated the gnostics who "get" *Exorcist II* from the philistines who don't.

Despite its trappings, *Exorcist II* does not submit to the fantasy genre's trope of the natural world being more valid than the industrial one. After all, the Synchronizer—a product of the technological age—is presented as a good and necessary thing. Nevertheless, science comes off poorly in *Exorcist II*. In *The Exorcist*, Regan is subjected to a series of physical and psychiatric treatments to no avail, and as her ordeal intensifies, baffling the medical specialists and consultants, Blatty gradually strips away the rational explanations for her behavior, ultimately asking the audience to accept the supernatural as the *only* explanation. (Believing in the *real-life* authenticity of demonic possession is beside the point; in the diegetic context, possession *is* the reason for Regan's plight.) The gradual transition from science to the supernatural is absent in *Exorcist II*; the scientific world it depicts is only slightly more credible than the world of supernatural fantasy presented alongside it. Whereas *The Exorcist* labored to depict realistic, state-of-the-art medical procedures (including arteriography and pneumoen-cephalography), *Exorcist II* conjures up an allegedly scientific procedure that is farfetched in the 21st century, let alone 1977. The film's dubious science is exemplified by the Synchronizer, a hypnotherapy device that puts its subjects in a trance and allows them to explore suppressed memories together. Immersing oneself in a patient's memories, virtual-reality-style, is farfetched *before* Pazuzu commandeers the session, yet Boorman would have audiences believe *Exorcist II* is on the periphery of legitimate science:

> When I finished reading Bill Goodhart's screenplay my hands were sweating and I was terrified but immensely stimulated by the ideas that it contained, particularly this idea of exploring the possibility of a kind of "world mind." In the last few years there's been an explosion of research into these areas of ESP and thought transference and related phenomena. In our script we have what is really a logical extension of this research, very close to what is being done, it's called "synchronized hypnosis." We have the psychiatrist and the priest, each in their different ways concerned about this girl who is possessed by two forces, one of good and one of evil, which are warring within her.[226]

Despite Boorman's insistence that the Synchronizer has its roots in genuine hypnotherapy research, the machine's applications as depicted on onscreen have little realistic grounding. *Exorcist II* contends that the production of memories is akin to recording on videotape, and that by connecting two brains with a few wires, one person's memories can be projected onto another's subconscious. Since memories are formed by neural connections within the brain, these connections *cannot* be transferred by wire. Reading minds may be at the forefront of scientific endeavor *today*, but even now, these memories would take on entirely different shapes and make use of enormously complex machines. The idea of reading minds by connecting two heads with a couple of wires is pure comedy, as is *Exorcist II*'s insistence that Tuskin's boondoggle be recognized as legitimate science. (Linda Blair recalled the on-set presence of a consultant hypnotist was a joke.) In any case, *Exorcist II*'s "science" is the pretext for sequences in which characters *talk... slowly... like... this*, while staring blankly at flashing lightbulbs. It's not thrilling stuff. The Synchronizer is essentially a magic machine that does

---

226. J Boorman, quoted in *Exorcist II: The Heretic* production featurette.

crazy things because the script needs it to, as risible as the satellite in *Superman III* (1983) that is capable of *creating* as well as monitoring the weather.

Risible, too, is *Exorcist II*'s contention that the demon remains dormant within Regan after the conclusion of *The Exorcist*, because it invalidates (or at least undermines) Damien Karras' fatal sacrifice. (So Pazuzu jumped out of Regan and into Karras, and after Karras' death, Pazuzu went *back* into Regan but didn't do much of anything until the Synchronizer unlocked Regan's mind four years later?) Regan's story should have ended with the first film, but Linda Blair was too closely identified with *The Exorcist* for Warners to avoid using her in the sequel. Unfortunately, by insinuating that Regan is at least partially inhabited by the demon, *Exorcist II* reduces Karras' martyrdom to a mere delaying tactic. It's especially galling when Tuskin says, "I think the exorcism made the problem worse!" to Lamont. Obviously Tuskin isn't in full possession of the facts, because how is partial amnesia *worse* than a complete personality change, assaulting and killing people, desecrating churches, speaking in tongues, profane language, self-mutilation with a cross, projectile vomiting, head-spinning, and levitation? This is another example of Boorman undermining *The Exorcist*, implying the actual exorcism in the film was not what it was cracked out to be. Yet the plot of *The Heretic* is so flimsy, it provides little evidence that there is anything actually wrong with Regan prior to her first session with the Synchronizer. Yes, she is in therapy, but as Regan herself tells Dr Tuskin, this is at the behest of her overanxious mother. Tuskin then launches into an incredible assault on the poor girl, trying to convince her there *is* something wrong with her, and basically doing the opposite of what her job should be: she sows seeds of doubt in Regan and undermines her confidence and sense of normality because she wants to try out the Synchronizer on her, before a jabbering priest comes out of nowhere and demands to know everything about an event that is best left undisturbed. (Regan probably would have been just fine had she *not* been roped into Dr Tuskin's experiments with the Synchronizer. This plot-hole could have been averted had Boorman included a scene demonstrating that Regan was having problems with Pazuzu *before* she went "in sync." As the film stands, it seems to implicate the Synchronizer as what unleashed Pazuzu to begin with.)

Boorman's filmic attitude towards sexuality is perhaps not as liberal as it seems. *Zardoz* depicts a future in which the obsolete status of procreation has rendered males fey and impotent and females the dominant gender—but *this* matriarchal society is stifled and dull, requiring Sean Connery's virile he-man to save it. Is *Exorcist II* more sexually progressive than *The Ex-*

orcist? Citing the latter's "repressive sexual economy," Peter Biskind wrote:

> It's easy to see why people, especially women, detested the picture. It presents a male nightmare of female puberty. Emergent female sexuality is equated with demonic possession, and the men in the picture—almost all celibate priests—unite to abuse and torture Regan, as John Boorman recognized, in their efforts to return her to presexual innocence... *The Exorcist* is filled with disgust toward female bodily functions... *The Exorcist* is drenched in a kind of menstrual panic.[227]

Biskind's handwringing obscures the practical reason the victim of possession in *The Exorcist* is female. Blatty had intended for the character to be a boy before making the change to distance the novel from the Maryland case that inspired it. (He figured making the character a 12-year-old girl rather than a 14-year-old boy would reduce unwanted publicity for the real-life victim.) Regardless, many people share Biskind's contention that *The Exorcist* displays a reactionary attitude towards sexuality. Yet Boorman, in spite of himself, made *The Heretic* puritan in a different way. It's not as obvious because the film is far less visceral, but *Exorcist II* presents a blinkered view of sexuality. Boorman has Regan wear a midriff-baring top, various tight blouses, and a diaphanous nightgown, yet her emerging sexuality is only *visual*. In terms of *dialogue*, Regan is somewhat asexual—she's written like she is still twelve years old. (The infamous "I was possessed by a demon!" line certainly would have gotten fewer laughs had it been delivered by a twelve-year-old.) The only willfully sexual Regan is her nightwear-clad, Pazuzu-spawned doppelganger who attempts to seduce Father Lamont. Thanks to Richard Burton's casting, the age gap between Lamont and Regan widened enough to make their sexual tension practically non-existent. Michel Ciment claimed American audiences were infuriated with "the sacrilegious union of the priest and the young girl" at the end of *Exorcist II* but there is nothing especially suggestive about the chaste manner in which Lamont and Regan depart at picture's end. (Ciment, in fact, claims that Lamont represents "the absent father whom Regan has been seeking," but this is a stretch—if anything, the older European man whisking the American teenage girl to a hotel has vague connotations of Humbert Humbert and Lolita.) With its Ma-

---

227. P Biskind, *Easy Riders, Raging Bulls: How the Sex 'n' Drugs 'n' Rock 'n' Roll Generation Saved Hollywood* (London: Bloomsbury, 1999), p. 223.

donna/Whore juxtaposition of the asexual "good" Regan and sexual "evil" Regan, *Exorcist II* equates female sexuality with duplicity and perversion, a notion that recurs in Boorman's next film, *Excalibur* (1981).

Another massive fault of the *Exorcist II* script is the way it presents the source of evil in its tale; namely, the aforementioned (and, in the film, oft-mentioned) demon Pazuzu. "We have a fascinating character in the film, the demon Pazuzu," Boorman explained in 1977. "We try to give the audience the experience of riding on the wings of a demon, and he can go anywhere, go through walls, inside people's heads, travelling at immense speeds. The priest is seduced and carried away in this exhilarating flight towards the gates of hell."[228] In his review of *Exorcist II* for the A.V. Club website, Nathan Rabin suggests the film's central miscalculation "is expecting audiences to fear a villain named "Pazuzu." Now Pazuzu is an actual figure from Assyrian and Babylonian mythology... but that doesn't make his name any less ridiculous. No matter how scary the film makes him out to be, "Pazuzu" still sounds like a zany sound effect a slide whistle might make or a baggy-pants vaudevillian's catchphrase."[229] Blatty recalled, "I wanted a powerful demon who had a name. I wanted to get away from the notion that this girl was possessed by Satan himself."[230] Many viewers *did* assume Regan was possessed by Satan in *The Exorcist*—understandable enough, given that the entity within Regan barks "I'm the Devil!" upon its first encounter with Father Karras, and Karras later tells Chris, "Your daughter doesn't say she's a demon, she says she's the Devil himself." However, in both Blatty's novel and the first-draft screenplay, the entity later clarifies its identity as a demon—"*a* devil," a distinction missing in the final version of the film. It is explicitly stated in the novel's prologue that the "ancient enemy" whom Merrin must face is "the demon Pazuzu." In the film's prologue, we see the statue of Pazuzu, and a vision of the statue reappears in Regan's bedroom at one point during the exorcism. Blatty himself attempted to clear up the confusion of the demon's identity, writing the following in his 1974 book *William Peter Blatty on The Exorcist: From Novel to Film*:

228. J Boorman, quoted in *Exorcist II: The Heretic* production featurette.

229. N Rabin, "My Year of Flops: *Exorcist II*." The A.V. Club, May 15, 2007, http://www.avclub.com/articles/my-year-of-flops-case-file-32-exorcist-ii-the-here,15004/

230. William Peter Blatty, quoted in "William Peter Blatty on *The Exorcist*." *Cinema Retro: The Essential Guide to Movies of the '60s and '70s*, vol.7, issue 19, 2011.

... is Satan a single personal intelligence? Or Legion, a horde of evil entities? Or even, as been conjectured, the stuff of the universe: matter itself, of physical evolution, that ends in Teilhard de Chardin's "omega point." I surely do not know, nor can I even make a prudent judgement. Whatever my beliefs concerning Satan's existence, however, we have no reliable data that would link him to possession. I know that will surprise many readers and reviewers. But historically, the "demons" involved in possession and pseudopossession only rarely identify themselves as Satan. And surely the chief of the fallen angels has far worse things that he could be doing. Even in terms of my novel, I have never known the demon's identity. I strongly doubt he is Satan; and he is certainly none of the spirits of the dead whose identity he sometimes assumes. If I had to guess, I would say he is Pazuzu, the Assyrian demon of the southwest wind. But I'm really not sure. I know only that he's real and powerful and evil and apparently one of many—and aligned with whatever is opposed to love.[231]

Blatty believes the spirit that possessed Regan is the demon Pazuzu, but "Pazuzu" could just be a human designation for something older and much more malevolent, something beyond normal comprehension and which cannot be named. The name "Pazuzu" is never actually uttered in the film version of *The Exorcist*—Merrin refers to the entity as "the demon"—which is a smart move. Had Merrin, upon his arrival in the Mac-Neil household, announced portentously he was to do battle with "Pazuzu," the nerve-wracking tension would have stopped dead in its tracks and audiences would have guffawed. In *Exorcist II*, not only is the demonic referred to explicitly as "Pazuzu," the name is recited *incessantly throughout the picture*. Sharon *demands* that Tuskin utter the name "Pazuzu," and one of the film's biggest laughs comes earlier in the piece, during a flashback when the young Merrin turns over the possessed Kokumo, and the boy helpfully announces, *"I am Pazuzu!"* and hisses to the camera. Louise Fletcher, for one, was aware of the comedic value of the demon's name: "I knew that the name Pazuzu would never go over. I remember saying, "As long as I don't have to say it, I won't make a big deal out of it." I thought it was a funny word and it was. Nobody would listen to me. Pazuzu is not a

---

231. Blatty, p. 37.

word you can say seriously."[232] The makers of the animated comedy series *Futurama* (1999-2013) thought "Pazuzu" sounded funny enough to bestow upon Professor Hubert Farnsworth's pet gargoyle.

It's not just the name and unambiguous identity that undermine the gravitas of the demon of *Exorcist II*. The film never gives the demon much of a chance to actually do anything scary or unsettling—committing the cardinal sin of *lowering* the stakes from the first movie, despite its plot being more overtly eschatological than that of its predecessor. *Exorcist II* tilts toward the apocalyptic and ruminates on the existence of evil, but Boorman's insistence on making a riposte to the "ugliness" of *The Exorcist* resulted in a diluted depiction of the diabolical. In *The Exorcist*, the demon prompted Regan to desecrate a church, foretell people's deaths, utter profane language in an ungodly voice, become physically repulsive, and injure and *kill* people. In *Exorcist II*, the demon prompts Regan to draw a weird picture of Father Lamont, subverts a few hypnotherapy sessions, and sets fire to a box of dolls. The generally unthreatening nature of Pazuzu undermines the film's lofty ambition to illustrate the notion that good brings evil upon itself. The story doesn't provide any real justification for Lamont's determination to drive the demonic spirit out of Regan, and therein lays one massive reason why *Exorcist II* didn't just fail with audiences, it *outraged* them—the movie is *not scary*. Considering *The Exorcist* was generally considered to be the scariest film ever made at that time, it was galling for audiences that there was nothing even remotely frightening in the sequel. (The Motion Picture Association of America bestowed an R-rating upon *Exorcist II*—the same rating *The Exorcist* received four years prior—but with only slight trims, one suspects *Exorcist II* could have been PG-rated. Warners *had* pushed for a PG rating on the grounds *Exorcist II* did not contain *The Exorcist*'s strong language and potentially blasphemous content. In hindsight, the MPAA's R-rating of *Exorcist II* in 1977 is as incredible as the same body *not* giving *The Exorcist* an X rating in 1973.)

The Exorcist generated controversy for being so frightening that audience members would faint, throw up, or hastily exit theatres. Even if these reports were exaggerated and sensationalistic, were audiences necessarily *wrong* to expect the second film to be scary? Did Boorman think audiences would quiver in their seats at the sight of a tap-dancing Regan being hit by invisible stones and falling over, or cower at close-up shots of the airborne locust? The hallucinatory sequence in which Pazuzu tries to

---

232. L Fletcher, quoted in L Goldberg, "Louise Fletcher, Schoolteacher from Mars." *Starlog* magazine #109, May 1986.

stop Merrin/Tuskin's hearts culminates in the exposition of a *visible* heart being handled, like slippery chicken innards, but this feels like a clumsy, gratuitous imposition on the story rather than something germane to the plot—and it's not especially terrifying, either. All too often, horror films are weakened by their visualization of otherworldly monsters. In the *Exorcist* films, the demon is properly frightening when it possesses people, and less impressive when it manifests itself as a mass of insects. (In Friedkin's film, the twelve-year-old Regan conceptualizing the insidious entity as her "imaginary" friend "Captain Howdy" is arguably more unnerving than anything Pazuzu does to the older Regan in *Exorcist II*.)

The Heretic's lack of visceral thrills accounts, at least partially, for the film's lack of staying power with audiences; as writer Calum Waddell noted, "It is hard to imagine anyone saying to a friend "You have to see *Exorcist II*—there is a tremendous scene with locusts that cannot be missed!""[233] (On the first *Exorcist II* video cassette release, Warner Home Video claimed the film's "vision of the demon Pazuzu, an evil spirit of the air first encountered by Father Merrin in Africa, is more chilling than anything seen in the first film," and that *Exorcist II* is "brilliantly directed by John Boorman from a complex and challenging original script by William Goodhart." Subsequent *Exorcist II* blurbs are less ostentatious—the blurb on the 2001 VHS, for example, describes *Exorcist II* as "different [to *The Exorcist*] but equally haunting...")

In *The Exorcist*, the demon hurled obscene comments like "Stick your cock up her ass, you motherfucking, worthless cocksucker" and "Your mother sucks cocks in hell, Karras! You faithless slime!" These are *not* gratuitous profanities serving only to shock or titillate viewers—they form a psychological attack on the exorcists (Karras in particular), demonstrating just how vile this demonic entity is. As William Peter Blatty has explained:

> ... [the] film does not purport to be a cop-out. Our demon was not someone with whom you could make a pact; our demon was real, and since we were representing a reflection of ultimate evil we could not, as Stanley Kauffmann has noted, simply have Regan say "Darn," or have a Greek chorus enter and announce that Regan had done "some very naughty things" off camera.[234]

---

233. C Waddell, "Exorcising the Liberal" in Olson, p. 138.

234. Blatty, pp. 281-282.

What is the vilest thing the demon says in *Exorcist II*? "Once the wings have brushed you, you're mine forever!"? Pazuzu's effectiveness is further muted by the awful voice the demon employs. Unable to get Mercedes McCambridge to recreate her chilling, androgynous rasp from *The Exorcist*, Boorman resorted to use of a poor imitation for *The Heretic*. Pazuzu's voice in *Exorcist II*—provided by an uncredited Karen Knapp—is not dissimilar to the demon voice later employed by Linda Blair herself in the *Exorcist* spoof *Repossessed* (1990).

The most effective scare in *Exorcist II* is arguably Lamont's hallucinatory encounter with Kokumo in Jepti, when the priest must test his faith by crossing a moat of nails barefoot. Boorman renders the suspense well, and the moment the nails graphically pierce Lamont's feet and Lamont pitches face-first towards the deadly moat is jolting. One can imagine a receptive audience gasping with relief when Jepti itself proves to be a hallucination from which Lamont awakens in the real Kokumo's laboratory. *Exorcist II* would have been improved by more moments like this. The deaths of the South American woman and Sharon are not rendered particularly well onscreen, but as real-life incidents of death by self-immolation (for political or protest reasons) had become increasingly publicized in the 1960s and 1970s, these scenes might have resonated disturbingly with some viewers. Regan's "sleepwalking" sequence begins well but it builds to little payoff. Obviously, the story was not going to have Regan, under the influence of Pazuzu, take a walk off a skyscraper halfway through the movie. The film has Regan *actually* walking to the edge of the building and *screaming* when she appears to be suspended in mid-air; the next scene has Sharon finding Regan happily feeding birds, apparently unaffected by her brush with Pazuzu and her near-death. Had Boorman depicted Regan actually *plummeting off the building* and then *waking up in bed* from a dream, audiences might have felt just as cheated, but they at least would have gotten a bigger scare for a fleeting moment. Pazuzu's defeat as originally planned, in which Regan's doppelganger is subject to visceral decomposition, would not have saved the film entirely but it would have elicited a better response from viewers than the ending Boorman and Pallenberg subsequently devised. (A horrific vision of the possessed Lamont, with a void for a mouth filled with crawling, gnawing locusts, was another unfortunate omission.) Beyond commercial considerations, heightening the horror would have aided the film narratively: surely Regan and Lamont's final victory over Pazuzu would have meant more had the demon's malign influence and threatening power been illustrated more graphically and effectively beforehand. (It's telling that when Boorman had to revise the film during its first release, without the capacity to reshoot, he was severely limited when it came to how much "horror" he could put into the film, even resorting to splicing in shots from *The Exorcist*.) Ultimately, Boorman was undermined by his own stated ambition to make a film about "healing" and "goodness"—when it came to generating shock and horror, his heart simply wasn't in it.

Poster for the British double-bill re-release of *The Exorcist* and *Exorcist II: The Heretic* (1980).

10

"New Age"

The Discontinuity of

Exorcist II

"... One should point out that neither William Friedkin, who directed the smash movie version of The Exorcist, *nor novelist-screenwriter William Peter Blatty were associated with this misbegotten sequel.* Exorcist II *seems to have evolved out of delusions of cinematic grandeur shared by Boorman and writer William Goodhart. It's obvious that they wanted to contrive a metaphysical thriller that would be astonishing and spiritually inspiring, but their thought processes are so muddled that the movie degenerates almost instantly into a confounded shambles."*

– Gary Arnold[235]

".... the scripts for John Boorman movies are usually lousy."

– Quentin Tarantino[236]

THE EXORCIST WAS RELEASED in 1973, a year often cited as the end of "the Long Sixties." America was still fighting the Vietnam War and although the Watergate scandal was raging, impeachment proceedings

---

235. Arnold.

236. Q Tarantino, "Tarantino on *Deliverance.*" *New Beverly Cinema*, Apr. 23, 2020, https://thenewbev.com/tarantinos-reviews/tarantino-on-deliverance/

against Richard Nixon had not begun. *The Exorcist* tapped into a feeling of disillusionment, of a world falling apart after the supercharged optimism of the 1960s turned sour. *Exorcist II* was released in what we could refer to as the 1970s proper: the US had withdrawn from Vietnam; Nixon and his successor Gerald Ford were both gone; and the country was still some years away from the resurgence of broad conservatism under Ronald Reagan. In a cultural/sociopolitical environment changed from that of its predecessor, should *Exorcist II* be admonished for having staked its own territory?

Continuing instalments are under no obligation to adhere totally to the tone of the works from which they derive, and in lieu of slavishly aping their predecessors, many sequels bring something new to the table (1986's *Aliens*, for example, diverges effectively from 1979's *Alien* without disgracing it). The problem with *Exorcist II* is that its sensibilities are so incompatible with *The Exorcist*, Boorman should have applied them to an entirely different film rather than grafting them into a pre-existing continuity. Boorman was motivated to direct *Exorcist II* because it gave him the opportunity to draw upon a readymade audience, but although he was aware of audience expectations ("They were ready for more"), he had no wish to indulge them. William Friedkin claimed that Boorman "didn't understand what *The Exorcist* was all about. He wanted to do his own thing. That's fine, but then don't call it *Exorcist II!*"[237] As they did with their unproduced *Lord of the Rings* screenplay, Boorman and Rospo Pallenberg strayed far from the author's original intentions, riding as roughshod over Blatty as they did over Tolkien.

Exorcist II's central notion is to tie *The Exorcist* to a convoluted New Age theory, using locusts as a metaphor. The film reveals that Father Merrin exorcised the demon Pazuzu from a boy in Africa who has a magic power over locusts and later becomes a scientist studying the insects. Like the boy, Regan McNeil is a spiritual healer ("the good locust"), possessed by Pazuzu at a time when everyone in the world is a figuratively "brushing their wings" against the evil inherent in humanity as the world reaches global consciousness. It's far from edifying, and *Exorcist II* contains many plot points that are difficult to reconcile with the events of *The Exorcist*. Here are the most glaring examples:

---

237. W Friedkin, quoted in R.A. Thorburn, "R.A. interviews William Friedkin, Academy Award-winning director of The Exorcist," Nov. 22, 2011, http://ratheruggedman. net/2011/11/r-a-interviews-william-friedkin-academy-award-winning-director-of-the-exorcist/

In *Exorcist II*, the Catholic Church indicts Father Merrin posthumously on charges of heresy for performing Regan's exorcism, yet in the first movie, the Church officially approved the exorcism and selected Merrin specifically to perform it. Here is the relevant expository dialogue, as it is presented in the original cut of *Exorcist II*:

> *Jaros:* Merrin's reputation is in jeopardy. His writings have been impounded!
> *Lamont:* I'm not surprised. No one in the Church wants to hear about the Devil. Satan has become an embarrassment to our "progressive" views.
> *Jaros:* Merrin was rather more extreme, I'm afraid... He argued that the power of evil threatens to overthrow the power of God himself!
> *Lamont:*... so they found a heresy to nail him to?
> *Jaros:* Well, many of the theological college believe that... he died at the hands of the Devil, during that... American exorcism. Some, and they're close to the Pontiff, go so far as to suggest that he was a Satanist... At the end, I mean.
> *Lamont:* Perhaps Father Merrin led us astray. Perhaps he took a path that no one could follow.

It's incomprehensible as to why the Vatican higher-ups consider Merrin to be a Satanist, or why they waited *four years* after Merrin's death to implement their investigation. (The film does make a half-hearted implication as to the duplicitous nature of the Church, for hanging Merrin's reputation out to dry, even though he was only following orders.) The reference to Merrin's writings being impounded evokes Teilhard de Chardin running afoul of Catholic orthodoxy, but this doesn't fit with the events of the first movie: if Merrin was such a controversial figure, why did the Church involve him in the MacNeil case to begin with—especially since Father Karras volunteered to perform the exorcism himself, before being assigned to assist Merrin? Boorman presumably thought to correct this inconsistency, as all references to the indictment of Merrin for heresy are removed from the Revised Version of *Exorcist II*. This has the added effect of weakening the title of *The Heretic*. (The title bears more relevance in the original cut in the film—the suspicion that Merrin is a heretic is a pretext to involve Lamont in the story, and since "heretics" are defined as people who hold beliefs contrary to the tenets of the religion they belong to,

Lamont *could* be considered one, as he comes to embrace Merrin's "controversial" philosophy.) In Boorman's *Zardoz*, the ruling class uses (false) religion to subjugate the primitive populace—but this isn't the theme in *Exorcist II*, which, if anything, accuses the Catholic Church of not being religious enough: "No one in the church wants to hear about the Devil. Satan has become an embarrassment to our *progressive* views," Lamont tells Jaros wearily. Boorman would have audiences believe that the upper echelons of the Vatican have swept Satan under the carpet, and no longer believe in the Devil—an implication that contradicts Church doctrine. In an address delivered on November 15, 1972, Pope Paul VI warned against the danger of ignoring Satan:

> Evil is not merely an absence of something but an active force, a living, spiritual being that is perverted and that perverts others. It is a terrible reality, mysterious and frightening... So we know that this dark disturbing being exists and that he is still at work with his treacherous cunning; he is the hidden enemy who sows errors and misfortunes in human history... This matter of the Devil and of the influence he can exert on individuals as well as on communities, entire societies or events, is a very important chapter of Catholic doctrine which should be studied again, although it is given little attention today.[238]

Considering Lamont is presented as a radical defying the Church's official line, it's galling that *Exorcist II* has him utter a line of dialogue taken almost verbatim from the Pope's address: "Evil is a spiritual being, alive and living, perverted and perverting, weaving its way insidiously into the very fabric of life!" *Exorcist II* is the rare film that accuses the Catholic Church of being too *secular*. In *The Exorcist*, the Church—in the person of Karras—was reluctant to believe in a supernatural explanation because a medical explanation seemed more valid. In *Exorcist II*, the Church (in the person of Cardinal Jaros) refuses to believe in a supernatural explanation because the Church has fallen out of touch with its "spirituality."

In *The Exorcist*, it is clearly demonstrated that the rite of exorcism is a matter of doctrine. There is a formal procedure to be followed, and

---

238. "Confronting the Devil's Power." (Address of Pope Paul VI to a General Audience, Nov. 15, 1972). Cited at Papal Encyclicals Online, http://www.papalencyclicals.net/Paul06/p6devil.htm

Church-authorized exorcisms are rare: Father Karras tells Chris MacNeil, "It just doesn't happen anymore... Since the day I joined the Jesuits, I've never met one priest who has performed an exorcism." Blatty claimed that, prior to writing *The Exorcist*, he was aware of only three Church-approved exorcisms performed in America in the 20th century. Friedkin later explained, "There were three cases that the Catholic Church acknowledged in the 20th century in America... [Exorcism] is a very, very rare procedure and not easily sanctioned by the Catholic Church. That's one of the things we try to point out in the film, that it was not commonplace."[239] This serves to emphasize the unique nature of Regan's plight. *Exorcist II* has a faint disregard for the notion of exorcism—the movie begins with Lamont botching an exorcism (not that he puts much effort in—he stands around and sweats as the possessed woman incinerates herself); Cardinal Jaros later says to Lamont, "I'm not asking you to perform another exorcism" and "You've performed exorcisms." The implication that Lamont is an old hand at the ritual doesn't mesh with *The Exorcist's* claim that it is rarely authorized, and there is *no* exorcism to speak of in *Exorcist II's* climax: the demon conveniently manifests a separate physical form, rather than possessing Regan or anyone else. No wonder Lamont foregoes the ritual of exorcism in favor of simply ripping the demon's heart out. (The film was *supposed* to climax with an exorcism, in which Pazuzu would morph through various identities, including a locust face, a Kabuki face, and flesh peeling off a skull, all of which would have been more impressive than what was filmed.) Boorman's dismissive view of the Church illustrates the hilarious scene in which Cardinal Jaros suspends Lamont from the investigation into Merrin's death, *Exorcist II's* equivalent of the belligerent police chief telling the insubordinate, loose-cannon cop he's "off the case!" Although we are supposed to regard Jaros as obtuse, he is quite sound in light of what Lamont says. (If Lamont simply asked Jaros for permission to go to Africa to meet someone who knew Merrin, the Cardinal would have given his authorization, but Lamont shoots himself in the foot by babbling about *"Evil!"* and seeing things in visions.)

Although Boorman was raised a Protestant, his education was Catholic, and his memoirs demonstrate an antipathy towards Catholic ritualism. Unsurprisingly, then, *Exorcist II* treats the rite of exorcism with disdain and Catholicism in general with disregard. Boorman told Michel

---

239. W Friedkin, quoted in K Jagernauth, "Exclusive: William Friedkin Talks Making *Killer Joe*, The Problem With Exorcism Movies, *Sorcerer* & Much More." *The Playlist*, Jul. 26, 2012.

Ciment that Catholicism is represented as "a dead religion" in *The Heretic*. (One of Boorman's school mentors, Father John Maguire, ran afoul of Church superiors; this obviously influenced the Lamont/Jaros conflict in *Exorcist II*. Boorman also admitted that the "poignancy of unresolvable sexuality" originally envisioned for Father Lamont reminded him of Father Maguire.) Despite Boorman's background, *Exorcist II* resembles the work of someone with little familiarity with Catholicism or at least no interest in depicting it as anything other than a narrative obstruction. This represents a huge tonal shift from *The Exorcist*, which was written by a Jesuit-educated Catholic, directed by an agnostic Jew immersed in Catholic research, and employed three Jesuit priests as technical consultants, two of whom appear in the film. Colleen McDannell wrote in *Catholics in the Movies*, "It is [the] creative tension between Friedkin and Blatty—between good horror and good story—that gives *The Exorcist* its energy and endurance. *The Exorcist* then is not merely a horror film; it is a *Catholic* horror film. And, more specifically than that, it is a *Jesuit* horror film."[240] Friedkin told Mick Garris in 2011, "The only way I could have made *The Exorcist* the way I did was if I believed it. If you look at the film, it's a film made by people who believe this. We're not kidding!"[241] For all its sensationalism and controversy, *The Exorcist* is deferential to Catholicism. (It is telling that *The Exorcist* did not receive the censorship that Ken Russell's *The Devils* [1971] was subjected to. Russell's film incriminates the Catholic hierarchy and is extremely cynical on the topics of demonic possession and exorcism, and Warners—after funding and releasing the film—practically disavowed it, a stance the studio has maintained to the present day.) *Ideologically*, there is little Catholicism in *Exorcist II*—Father Lamont invokes Father Merrin's name in prayer more than he does God or Jesus—and the film presents a vague metaphysical philosophy as a superior alternative to Christianity. Boorman's philosophical bent differs sharply from Blatty's earnest Catholicism and is more akin to the "New Age" mindset of the 1970s, if not the existentialist movements proclaiming "God is dead" in the 1960s. Growing dissatisfaction with Christianity (the accepted religion of the establishment) led hippie and counter-culture movements to seek alternative ways of thinking and new modes of spirituality. The re-emergence in the late 1960s of

---

240. C McDannell (ed), *Catholics in the Movies* (London: Oxford University Press, 2008), pp. 198-199.

241. W Friedkin, quoted in M Garris, "Post-Mortem with Mick Garris: William Friedkin." Mar. 2011.

the occult, astrology, esoteric gnosticism, and pagan folklore influenced film, television, and music in the following decade. Post-Woodstock and pre-Reaganism, the 1970s was arguably the heyday of high strangeness, a decade in which Ufology became a cultural pastime and mysticism and shamanism emerged as alternatives to modernism and capitalism. To a certain degree, Boorman was part of this informal movement, not only via *Exorcist II*, but by virtue of his long-running ambition to film *Excalibur* and his personal disillusionment with Christianity. Ewen Millar identified *Exorcist II* as tapping into the *zeitgeist* of 1970s spiritualism:

> The 1970s saw the explosion of the so-called New Age, a sort of eclectic pick 'n' mix approach to the "spirituality" that saw Asian religious traditions strip-mined for authentically-flavored sound bites that were repackaged into books on peak experiences, near-death experiences, self-help, meditation, yoga, the healing power of crystals, angels, and possession... and sold by the truckload via the "Mind Body Spirit" section in local bookstores.[242]

If *The Exorcist* is read as Catholic proselytism—and there is a strong argument it can be—*Exorcist II* represents the countercultural revolt against the spiritually "dead" Western world, emphasizing quality of consciousness and advocating enlightenment through mysticism (supplanted with mind-expanding agents, with the Synchronizer replacing the hallucinogens of hippiedom). In his memoirs, Boorman—not without good reason—bemoans the repressive influence of Catholic theocracy upon his adopted homeland of Ireland. *Excalibur* is elegiac in its depiction of pagan magic giving way to Christianity; had Boorman made *Excalibur* after *Exorcist II*, he would have presented the cycle of Christianity ascending in *Excalibur* before receding in *Exorcist II*. *The Exorcist* drew the ire of Christian commentators, but its depiction of religion is largely devout. *Exorcist II*'s dismissal of Christianity was not a talking point upon the film's release (indicating either the film's cultural irrelevancy or its ideology was dwarfed by its banality and aesthetic shortcomings). Unfortunately—and despite Boorman's intentions—*Exorcist II*'s portrayal of African religion (the "stronger" faith in the context of the story) veers uncomfortably close to racial fetishization. (To the surprise of Warner Brothers, *The Exorcist* generated substantial enthusiasm within African American audiences,

---

242. E Millar, "On Otherness and Illusion in *Exorcist II: The Heretic*," in Olson, p. 377.

even prompting a stand-up routine Richard Pryor included in his 1974 live comedy album *That N*****'s Crazy*. It is possible Warners encouraged the African angle of *Exorcist II's* narrative to capitalize on *The Exorcist's* substantial box office support from the Black community, but this is pure speculation.) In any case, the film presents a subtle visual reference to Lamont representing the hybridization of Western and Eastern faiths: after his return from Africa, Lamont wears an African-design-print shirt (and no Roman collar) under his Church-issue black suit.

Throughout *Exorcist II*, Father Merrin is frequently mentioned by the characters as having saved Regan, yet no mention is made of Father Karras, or *his* part in saving Regan. The closest we get is Tuskin mentioning "three deaths" in relation to Regan's incident in Georgetown (Burke Dennings, Merrin, and Karras). This discrepancy is another example of Boorman showing contempt, or at least indifference, towards *The Exorcist*. It's amazing that Jaros and Lamont concern themselves with the death of an elderly priest who had a pre-existing heart condition, yet ignore the fact that, during the same exorcism that claimed Merrin's life, a much younger priest flung himself out of a second-story window, rolled down a massive flight of concrete steps, and died in a pool of blood. Merrin *was* the worldly theologian, and it makes sense that he would be under scrutiny—but surely Karras' death would need to be investigated as well? Yet *Exorcist II* pretends Damien Karras never existed. (To Blatty's consternation, many viewers of *The Exorcist* did not understand that Karras lured the demon into his body and regained control of himself to avoid killing Regan before *deliberately* throwing himself out of the window. In his critique of *The Exorcist*—included in his 1976 book-length essay *The Devil Finds Work*—James Baldwin supposes it was the Devil who forced Karras out of the window. One feels if there was a mysterious death from the first film to be investigated and clarified, it was the death of *Karras*, not Merrin.) Merrin's death is retroactively contradicted: *Exorcist II* contends that Pazuzu deliberately killed Father Merrin by stopping his heart. In *The Exorcist*, Merrin had a heart condition and died from a cardiac arrest brought on by the strain of the ritual. (Merrin couldn't make it through an archaeological dig without taking nitroglycerin tablets, giving the impression that even *without* confronting the demon, he was not long for this world.) Lamont seems to think that Merrin's death was mysterious and unexplainable, but since *we* know what happened, and it *should* be obvious to Lamont, the "investigation" is devoid of mystery, serving only as a pretext to get Lamont involved with Regan. The suggestion in *Exorcist II* is that the demon "won" by killing Merrin—but Merrin wasn't the demon's target; nor was Regan (despite what *Exorcist II* purports). Blatty's contention is that the demon's target all along was Karras: this is implied when the demon tells Karras, ominously, that an exorcism would bring the two of *them* closer together. *Exorcist II* illustrates the fact that Merrin died *before* Regan was exorcised, yet it doesn't mention at all how the exorcism was completed.

A key element in *Exorcist II* is Father Merrin's formative encounter with the demon Pazuzu, via the exorcism of a young boy in Africa. This exorcism is referenced in *The Exorcist* and is illustrated with flashbacks in *Exorcist II*, although the latter makes little effort to be consistent with what we learned in the former. In *The Exorcist*, the Georgetown University President tells the Archbishop that Father Merrin's previous exorcism took place "Ten, twelve years ago, I think, in Africa. The exorcism supposedly lasted months. I heard it damn near killed him." The flashback scenes in *Exorcist II* purport to depict this exorcism—but they take place *forty* years before the events of the first film. It is possible the President's dialogue in *The Exorcist* is conjecture rather than a statement of fact, but would he mistake forty years for a period of time a *quarter* of that size? Perhaps Merrin performed more than one exorcism in Africa; it's possible this exorcism takes place forty years before *The Exorcist* simply to allow Kokumo to be closer to middle-age when Lamont meets him. It becomes more problematic when one considers *Dominion: Prequel to the Exorcist* and its remake, *Exorcist: The Beginning*. Since *The Beginning* replaced *Dominion*, both prequels contradict each other, but they also contradict *Exorcist II*—the locations and circumstances of the prequels' exorcisms don't resemble *Exorcist II* at all. In *Dominion* and *The Beginning*, the exorcism takes place in Kenya in 1947; in *Exorcist II*, the exorcism takes place in Ethiopia in the early 1930s (forty years prior to the events of *The Exorcist*). The exorcised boy is "Kokumo" in *Exorcist II*, "Cheche" in *Dominion*, and "Joseph" in *The Beginning*—and Joseph is ultimately a red herring: a female adult is the real victim. (Kokumo means "immortal" or "the one who will not die." Given that it is a name from the [West African] Yorùbá dialect, it is an odd choice of name for an [East African] Ethiopian character.) So even if one accepts *Dominion* over *The Beginning* (or vice versa), Merrin still apparently performed at least three different exorcisms in Africa prior to the events of *The Exorcist*: one *before* World War II, one *after* World War II, and one roughly a decade before exorcising Regan MacNeil in the early 1970s. No wonder Pazuzu had it in for Merrin… and no wonder Merrin eventually died from exhaustion.

The demon's powers change between *The Exorcist* and *Exorcist II*. In *The Exorcist*, the demon was capable of possessing one person at a time (Regan and, briefly, Karras) and causing poltergeist-like phenomena (levitation, telekinesis). In *Exorcist II*, the demon is capable of controlling the thoughts and actions of people without possessing them outright (Lamont and, possibly, Sharon), assuming a separate physical form (locusts), and spawning an evil double of Regan. Pazuzu is even capable of jostling the plane Sharon and Tuskin ride in and flinging a taxicab around. It's possible the Synchronizer somehow amplified Pazuzu's powers, but it's more likely that Boorman did not intend or care to keep the demon's powers consistent between the films. (This leads to the argument that the best way to appreciate *Exorcist II* is to pretend it is totally unrelated to *The Exorcist*—but this is patently absurd for a film titled *Exorcist II* and which makes use of characters and situations from the previous film.)

The Exorcist is deliberately vague as to why Regan had been possessed. Blatty's novel is more forthcoming: when Merrin and Karras rest in the hallway mid-exorcism, Karras asks Merrin why Regan has been possessed, and Merrin posits a theory. This expository scene was reproduced faithfully in Blatty's first-draft screenplay of *The Exorcist*:

> *Karras:* If it's possession, why her? Why this girl?
> *Merrin:* Who can know? Who can really hope to know? Yet I think—the demon's target is not the possessed; it is us... the observers... every person in this house. And I think—I think the point is to make us despair; to reject our own humanity, Damien; to see ourselves as vile and putrescent; without dignity; ugly— unworthy. And there lies the heart of it, perhaps: in worthiness. For I think belief in God is not a matter of reason at all; I think it is finally a matter of love; of accepting the possibility that God could love us... Yet even from this... from evil... will come good. In some way. In some way that we may never understand or ever see. And perhaps even Satan... Satan, in spite of himself... somehow serves to work out the will of God.[243]

This exchange is missing from the original theatrical cut of *The Exorcist*, and Blatty argued against its absence:

---

243. From the first-draft screenplay of *The Exorcist* by William Peter Blatty, reproduced in Blatty, p. 240.

> Here we had an explicit articulation of the theme that gave
> the film clarity and a definite moral weight: clarity because it
> focused the story on Karras and his problem of faith; and moral
> weight because it put the obscene and repellent elements of
> the film into the context of evil's primary attack on mankind:
> namely, the inducement of despair... The revised (and final)
> screenplay retained the bare bones of the hallway scene. Then
> we cut it down further, although in rehearsal Max von Sydow
> argued for expanding on it somewhat. This was done and
> the scene was shot. But later it was cut from the film because
> Billy said it was a "showstopper," not in the usual sense but
> in that it stopped the action dead in its tracks by pausing for
> a "theological commercial." Regardless, I still disagree very
> strongly with the scene's absence from the film.[244]

William Friedkin, on the other hand, believed the scene articulated too
much to the audience. He later changed his mind. When *The Exorcist* was
re-released to theatres in 2000, the film featured ten minutes of restored
footage, and one of the scenes Friedkin re-inserted into the film was the
"theological commercial" from Father Merrin. Reviewing the revised cut
of *The Exorcist*, Roger Ebert felt the hallway conversation is theologically
interesting, but noted it interrupts the film's momentum. In any case, here
is the brief hallway conversation between Karras and Merrin in the ex-
tended version of *The Exorcist*:

> **Karras:** Why her? Why this girl?... It doesn't make sense.
> **Merrin:** I think the point is to make us despair. To see
> ourselves as... animal and ugly. To make us reject the
> possibility that God could love us.

This is more concise and less ponderous than the same scene in the original screenplay, but it gets the point across. Merrin, not entirely certain
why Regan has been possessed, hazards a guess that has merit in the context of the film without being conclusive enough to dissuade viewers from
formulating their own ideas. Unfortunately, by excluding this scene from
The Exorcist, Friedkin inadvertently gave *Exorcist II* free rein to make
Merrin proclaim a very different explanation for demonic possession.
Speaking from beyond the grave in *The Heretic*, Merrin tells Lamont,

---

244. Blatty, pp. 278-279.

"Not only Kokumo, but others like him began to appear in the world. I found these people where I could and tried to protect them against evil. So Satan has sent Pazuzu to destroy this goodness. Phillip, you must take my place. [Regan]'s precious, and I entrust her to you!" This explanation would have been problematic had *The Exorcist* retained the stairway conversation between Merrin and Karras. It could also be argued that the evil force in *The Exorcist* is especially insidious by its ambiguity, whereas *Exorcist II* errs by imposing tangibility upon the demon and articulating

Lamont (Richard Burton)'s assault by rock-flinging Ethiopians results in Regan (Linda Blair) suffering a seizure during her tap dance recital in New York.

Pazuzu as Satan's flunky in a supervillain-like plot for world domination. Furthermore, by centralizing Regan, *Exorcist II* ignores the fact the demon's target was Karras—a character *Exorcist II* ignores. In any case, it's more frightening for a *normal* girl to be demonically possessed than for a girl to be targeted by a demon because she's the pre-destined telepathic harbinger of a New Age of human consciousness. In this respect, *Exorcist II*'s attempt to address global implications negates the universality of *The Exorcist*.

A selection of locales filmed inside studio soundstages. Top row (L-R): The Institute; the exterior of the MacNeil house; and the African landscape. Middle row (L-R): The African village; the rock church; and the mud city of Jepti. Bottom row (L-R): The Hitchcock Steps; Prospect Street, Georgetown; and the ruins of the MacNeil house.

Dr. Gene Tuskin (Louise Fletcher) presents the Synchronizer to
Regan MacNeil (Linda Blair).

11

"Visual magic"

The Production Design and Visual Effects of *Exorcist II*

"John's phenomenal—tough, but phenomenal."

– William A. Fraker[245]

ONE OF THE REASONS William Peter Blatty lobbied Warner Brothers to hire William Friedkin to direct *The Exorcist* was because Blatty felt the film desperately needed the look of documentary realism Friedkin brought to *The French Connection*. Friedkin and his *French Connection* cinematographer, Owen Roizman, duly shot *The Exorcist* in a documentarian style, filming in real locations, and grounding the events of the story in a recognizably *real* world—from the excavation sequence in sun-drenched Northern Iraq, to the bulk of the story in and around autumnal Georgetown. *The Exorcist*, like *Rosemary's Baby*, was a horror in a modern, urban environment (no gothic castles or exotic landscapes) contemporary viewers could relate to. It was, as Friedkin told *Cinemafantastique* in 1974, "an attempt to make a realistic story of inexplicable things."[246] The documentary style prevalent in *The Exorcist* is

245. WA Fraker, quoted in "The Photography of *Exorcist II: The Heretic.*"

246. W Friedkin, quoted in W Crouch, "Friedkin on *The Exorcist.*" *Cinemafantastique* vol

almost totally absent in *Exorcist II*; at very few points in the movie do we feel like we are seeing *real* exterior locations—John Boorman told Michel Ciment that production designer Richard Macdonald regarded any exterior filming "as a kind of defeat."[247] Like *The Exorcist, Exorcist II* was filmed on 1:85:1 Panavision, but the production design and use of color and lighting resulted in a very different visual experience. While *The Exorcist* used location photography and naturalistic lighting to create a *realistic* world—as mundane as the bleak London suburbia in Boorman's *Leo the Last*—*Exorcist II* opted for stylization over naturalism. This was a throwback to Hollywood's stagey past, despite Boorman's demonstrated skill in location photography: *Hell in the Pacific, Deliverance,* and *The Emerald Forest* exhibit superb exterior cinematography. (*The Emerald Forest* [1985], another Boorman/Pallenberg project, shares some of *The Heretic*'s flaws, including heavy-handed mysticism and a curious emotional detachment from the characters. However, these problems barely register thanks to the authenticity of the film's evocative visuals, shot in the Amazon rainforest.)

"When you work on location, you tend to seek out the strange configurations in the landscape, anything out of the ordinary, and you shoot it with the assurance that it is real. You concentrate on using the qualities that appeal to you," Boorman explained to Barbara Pallenberg in 1976. "The tendency on a set, however, is to make everything look ordinary, because you start to worry that it won't look "real." My word to Richard [Macdonald] on this set was to make it look as daring as possible, and the reality would take care of itself."[248] *Exorcist II*'s Director of Photography, William Fraker, shared Boorman's enthusiasm with the challenge of filming the majority of the film's exterior shots on soundstages:

> It was rather exciting, trying to shoot a basically exterior picture on the stage. It was a tremendous undertaking. People ask, "How do you shoot the Ethiopian desert on a stage?" I say, "The only way I know how to do it is the way I do it outside—by stopping down to f/8 or f/11." Of course, in order to be able to stop down that far, you must have enough light to allow you to do it. That means that instead of 20 arcs,

3, no. 3 (Fall 1974). Reprinted in Olson, p. 66.

247. Ciment, p. 169.

248. J Boorman, quoted in Pallenberg, p. 84.

you end up with 123 arcs—which is what we used on the stage. Okay—now, how do you put up 123 arcs and have 100 people on the set and cast one shadow? It breaks down to taking eight hours to light one shot.[249]

Fraker claimed the film sought to achieve a "theatrical effect, but at the same time, very realistic… Stylizing a look that is basically believable, so that you accept it as real, while knowing it's phenomenal."[250] Can *Exorcist II* be forgiven for its abundance of plywood, hardboard, plaster, and Styrofoam? Admittedly, Garrett Brown's tracking shots were innovative for their time; in the Jepti set, the Steadicam-wielding Brown was required to energetically "race through the narrow streets, up steps, leap from wall to wall, scattering people, chickens, goats, and dogs."[251] But even these moments are undermined by the poorly-conceived set design—the African sequences make liberal use of a "village" all too obviously filmed indoors (with orange lighting), like something out of a swords-and-sorcery movie or an old adventure serial. (The African sequences take place in Ethiopia—the setting suggests the northern province of Tigray, where rock-hewn monolithic Ethiopian Orthodox churches are located—and the priests can be heard speaking Amharic.) "That [Ethiopian] set was probably one of the toughest and I doubt I would ever try to do anything like that again. It just takes too much out of a person," Fraker admitted years later. "The other set involved all the special effects that were required for the picture; the deterioration of the Georgetown house, the reflections in the train windows which are just so time consuming and very difficult to achieve."[252] The closing scenes in Georgetown, filmed on a soundstage, largely fail to evince an exterior location: the film ends with Regan and Lamont supposedly walking off into the distance, with Blair and Burton striding towards a phony backdrop that renders the Georgetown neighborhood as a sort of foggy wasteland. Fraker claimed, "We changed the colors on the backings so that they would be a little theatrical… When an effect began to look very realistic, we would move it beyond almost anything you have ever seen before."[253] John Boorman admitted the intended

---

249. WA Fraker, quoted in "The Photography of *Exorcist II: The Heretic*."

250. WA Fraker, quoted in "The Photography of *Exorcist II: The Heretic*."

251. Pallenberg, pp. 175-176.

252. WA Fraker, quoted in Schaefer & Salvato, p. 148.

253. WA Fraker, quoted in "The Photography of *Exorcist II: The Heretic*."

scale of the set was muted on film: "We built a huge Georgetown street set on the stage for the climax. It was much admired. It is often the way with street sets: people are impressed with their size, but once it is on film, it is simply a rather small street."[254]

The worst manifestation of Boorman's set design edict is Dr Tuskin's psychotherapy institute: a large room consisting of smaller, free-standing hexagonal rooms and offices, made almost entirely from glass. The rooms, the lights, and even the foam toys rolled around by the kids are all hexagon-shaped—hexagons being something of a visual trope in 1970s sci-fi. Contextually, the décor in this labyrinthine locale is impractical at best and dangerous at worst. The glass offices bathed in fluorescent light ensure people can see into therapy sessions (with no curtains or blinds to protect visual privacy), and we see groups of *children* scampering, running around chaotically and playing around in the walkways. Putting aside the fact these children supposedly have various physical and mental problems, surely *any* child should not be allowed to run around, day-care-style, in rooms made from floor-length panes of glass? William Goodhart, in fact, envisioned a more practical look for the Institute, as Boorman explained:

> We devoted a lot of thought and work to the film's visuals; and it was a point on which William Goodhart and I disagreed. He thought that, because of the visionary element in the African episodes, the New York sequences ought to be prosaic, banal, 'realistic', from a visual point of view. In his script, for example, the clinic was a simple psychiatrist's surgery. It was my opinion that, on the contrary, as so much of the film was set there, it would have been impossible to cut from the Ethiopian scenes to a single, drably-designed room without creating a sense of anticlimax, without lowering the tension. What was important, rather, was to 'elevate' reality, to give it another dimension in order to create a sort of correspondence. That's why we thought of this clinic, with its infinite reflections and its strange children in the background—a complex space which would also serve to symbolize, through its technology, the scientific aspect of the conflict. As for the patients imprisoned in their separate cells, what made the situation so poignant was that, despite their

---

254. Boorman, p. 224.

efforts, neither science nor religion could reach them. And when Regan succeeds in communicating with a little girl and cures her, in the simplest possible manner, the fact that it happens in such a context makes it all the more forceful.[255]

The "daring" design on display in the Institute scenes does *Exorcist II* no favors. In order to contrast with the hallucinatory and surreal world in the dream and flashback sequences, the Institute scenes should look as "real" as possible—akin to the stark manner in which Friedkin filmed the clinic and arteriography scenes in *The Exorcist*. Making the Institute a house of mirrors gives the story no realistic foothold and distances the viewer from the story. Describing the Institute in *The Cinema of John Boorman*, Brian Hoyle writes, "The construction of this set and the materials used to build it... defamiliarize the audience by not providing a clear sense of scale or space."[256] In a strange way, the ill-advised set design and resultant lack of verisimilitude is visual shorthand for the flaws inherent in the script: this is not religion vs. science, as the film contends—it's New Age spirituality vs. Pseudoscience. If anything, Tuskin's Institute is more cult than clinic: an obsessive devotion to one symbol (the hexagon); no privacy; and patients being persuaded to do things against their will.

The impractical set-design extends to the bizarre stainless-steel-and-glass design of Regan's apartment: the rooftop terrace boasts a slippery-looking floor surrounded by flimsy glass panels with human-sized, building-code-defying gaps in the surrounding rails. The Synchronizer, much-lauded in the context of the story, is nothing more than a pair of flashing lights and vinyl head-straps attached to a stick on a box. "*Exorcist II* features a lot of scientific mumbo-jumbo about two people learning to train their brain waves to communicate at a subconscious level," Gene Siskel wrote. "That sounds great, but on screen it looks ridiculous as Burton and Blair don cheap leather headbands rigged with wires and simultaneously stare into a pulsating lightbulb."[257] Boorman argued that the machine would be more impressive if it looked "rougher" and "more experimental," but one suspects the device is improbably small to facilitate the plot-point of Regan stealing and carrying it around. (*The Exorcist* was menacingly documentarian in its depiction of medical technology,

---

255. J Boorman, quoted in Ciment, pp. 169-172.

256. Hoyle, p. 111.

257. Siskel.

which makes the tacky sci-fi of the Synchronizer in *Exorcist II* look even sillier by comparison.) *Exorcist II* also attempts to simulate a billowing plague of locusts by blowing around painted Styrofoam, the mountains of Ethiopia via obvious miniatures, and a young woman burning to death with a dummy and a jarring jump-cut. (Sharon's fiery demise is also rendered ineptly: the flames appear *around* her, but not *on* her.) It's amazing to consider that *Star Wars*—the highest-grossing film of 1977, released a month before *Exorcist II*—was hailed for its ground-breaking special effects, yet its budget was $3 million *lower* than that of *Exorcist II*, a film that boasts far less-impressive visuals.

Contrasting with Friedkin's documentarian approach, Boorman's aesthetic is rooted not in logic or realism, but in fables and the subconscious. The intention to stylize *Exorcist II* with a dreamlike tone is fine in theory but the application is faulty. Boorman's approach should have been akin to Nicolas Roeg's brilliant psychological drama/occult thriller *Don't Look Now* (1973), which used innovative photographic and editing techniques as well as authentic location filming to maintain its unnerving, ominous tone. *Exorcist II* also compares unfavorably to Robert Altman's hallucinatory masterpiece *3 Women* (released several months prior) and to Dario Argento's balletic Italian horror film *Suspiria*, which received its American release two months after *Exorcist II*'s premiere. (The highly-stylized *Suspiria* deliberately draws attention to its artifice and performative nature, and the fact it subjugates narrative to aesthetics is not a flaw—the style *is* the substance. It would be difficult to mount the same case for *Exorcist II*, in which narrative weakness is an unintended consequence rather than deliberate design. Incidentally, Dario Argento's underrated 1985 horror film *Phenomena* bears interesting similarities to *Exorcist II*: like Regan, the protagonist of *Phenomena* is the teenage daughter of an American actor, has paranormal abilities, and suffers from a perilous sleepwalking disorder; the film also features an entomologist as a supporting character, and large, billowing insect-swarms figure into the plot.)

An interesting comparison can be made between *Exorcist II* and Boorman's own *Deliverance*. Not only does *Deliverance* avoid the schematic heavy-handedness of Boorman's next two films, *Zardoz* and *Exorcist II*, it proved to be more influential on the horror genre. The dream sequence at the end of *Deliverance* was transmogrified into the final jump-scare of Brian De Palma's *Carrie* (1976) which, in turn, was appropriated by Sean S. Cunningham's *Friday the 13th* (1980)—an effective synthesis of Boorman, De Palma, and Cunningham. Another comparison can be made between *Exorcist II* and the film Boorman made after it, *Excalibur*. The foreboding dialogue and hallucinatory world so gauche in *Exorcist II* are appropriate in *Excalibur*. Much of *Excalibur*'s dialogue is ponderous, and the characterizations are threadbare—but the film is populated by mythic archetypes, not characters, and the uneven narrative befits the episodic nature of its source, Thomas Malory's *Le Morte d'Arthur*. *Excalibur* also *looks* marvelous, with sumptuous locations, costumes, production design, and Alex Thomson's Oscar-nominated cinematography. In *Exorcist II* and *Excalibur*, Boorman's "vision" trumps dialogue and characterization: problematic for *Exorcist II*, but not for *Excalibur*.

Exorcist II's most obvious point of comparison is, of course, *The Exorcist*. Although some of its special effects have inevitably aged, Friedkin's film looks remarkably contemporary today: the documentarian style achieves a texture, verticality, and spatial awareness that eludes Boorman's warm-toned psychedelic haze and clunky studio sets. The most unnerving moments of Friedkin's film are those which depict the *frisson* between the ordinary, *explicable* world and the realm of the supernatural (as its theatrical trailer intoned gravely in words that could have been written by Rod Serling: "*Somewhere between science and superstition, there is another world. A world of darkness…*"). *The Exorcist*'s most famous shot is Father Merrin's approach of the MacNeil house, which features prominently in the film's trailers, posters, and soundtrack, VHS, and DVD releases. Merrin's arrival comes at a pivotal point of the narrative—setting up the film's riveting exorcism sequence—and up until this point, Friedkin and Roizman have shot *The Exorcist* in a fairly realistic style. (Even when supernatural things are happening on screen, the scenes are staged matter-of-factly. Friedkin doesn't drown the scenes with music or augment them with overly stylized editing.) After doing his best to convince audiences that this fantastical story takes place in the "real world," by the time Merrin arrives, Friedkin foregoes "realism" and shoots the scene in a stylized manner, with the expressionistic lighting and fog. (The shot—which took two nights to stage—was inspired by René Magritte's painting, *L'Empire des Lumières*.) Friedkin doesn't hold the shot for too long, so it doesn't become a distraction. A major reason one can't buy into anything in *Exorcist II* is because too much of the film reeks of artifice. Boorman slathers his film with self-consciously "arty" shots; for example, when Regan enters the Institute and comes face to face with a blank-staring Father Lamont, the priest is reflected by one of the glass panels, which slides back to reveal Dr Tuskin in the same pose. An even less subtle moment occurs during Regan's sleepwalking sequence. One of Regan's drawings—a stylized portrait of a woman with narrowed eyes and pursed lips—is displayed on an easel next to Regan's bed. Linda Blair rises from her bed, leans forward, and turns to face the camera, so her head occupies the same space the drawn face was at. Then, for no apparent reason, Regan narrows her eyes and purses her lips, doing an *impression* of her picture for the audience. Is this an example of the "visual magic" Pauline Kael referred to?

To be fair, there *are* some genuinely impressive visual moments in *Exorcist II*, most of which were probably underappreciated by the general audience and the majority of critics in 1977. The destruction of the MacNeil house, achieved on set with no optical effects, is rendered very effectively. There is old-school Hollywood charm in the Pazuzu fly-past scenes, in which genuine locust footage is composited over second-unit photography in Africa. The Holy Communion sequence in the (Coptic Christian) rock church is well-realized. The scene in which Tuskin's life is endangered when the Synchronizer conjures up Merrin and the demon is fairly striking, with parallel footage combined seamlessly to create the spectral effect of the demon grasping at Tuskin's heart. Garrett Brown's Steadicam photography amid the full-scale sets and above the miniature sets is applied effectively for the scenes which assume the point of view of the airborne Pazuzu, although the technology to film smooth overhead gliding shots high above the full-scale set was still some years away. (After inventing the Steadicam, Brown spent years and much of his own money developing the SkyCam—a computer-controlled lightweight camera operated by a system of high posts, wires, and gyros—which Alan Parker used in the film *Birdy* [1984] to simulate the title character's fantasy of flying over South Philadelphia. The SkyCam has since been used most commonly for telecasts of sporting events.) There is also a nifty visual moment to end the final Synchronizer session: an unbroken shot of Father Merrin getting up from the floor of Regan's bedroom to stagger through the interior of the Ethiopian rock church.

There are recurring visual motifs employed subtly and effectively throughout the course of *Exorcist II*—most notably, strobe-light effects used to evoke the Synchronizer. (A light flashes behind Lamont's head when he is conversing with Tuskin on the street after the hospital fire; there are flashing lights in the backdrop of Regan's tap dance recital and reflected on the window of the Washington Express bus; the sun as photographed by William Fraker connotes a flashing light; and the final shot of the film is Tuskin's tear-stricken face flashed by Synchronizer-like lights, suggesting Tuskin has been psychically linked as Regan and Lamont have been.) Even if the exterior scenes are hampered narratively by hermetically sealed interior photography, the artifice is at least appreciable as filmmaking of a set-oriented age that is largely bygone.

Against the backdrop of her artwork, Regan (Linda Blair) is roused in her sleep by the demon Pazuzu.

Regan MacNeil (Linda Blair) and Father Lamont (Richard Burton)
in the Institute in New York City...

... and in the MacNeil house in Georgetown.

12

"There's nothing wrong with me!"
The Acting In
Exorcist II

"In Exorcist II: The Heretic, *Richard Burton explores new areas of his craft, and calls upon his great experience to bring forth the terror and compassion called for in the story."*

– Excerpt from *Exorcist II: The Heretic's* press kit, 1977

"I loathe loathe loathe acting. In studios. In England. I shudder at the thought of going to work with the same horror as a bank-clerk must loathe that stinking tube-journey every morning and the rush-hour madness at night. I loathe it, hate it, despise, despise, for Christ's sake, it."

– Diary entry by Richard Burton, August 4, 1969[258]

Herman (**Michael J. Pollard**): *A drink for Mr. Richard Burton. Drink up!*
Eva (**Anne Ramsey**): *Drink, just for me. For you, Dick.*
Herman: *That Dick knows how to live!*
Frank Cross (**Bill Murray**): *Why do you keep calling me "Dick"?*

---

258. R Burton, quoted in *The Richard Burton Diaries* (London: Yale University Press, 2012), p. 312.

> **Herman:** *I'm sorry, Mr. Burton. Maybe we don't know you*
> *well enough to call you "Dick", but after* Exorcist II *and*
> Night of the Iguana, *we thought we had something special...*
>
> – From *Scrooged* (1988) by
> Mitch Glazer & Michael O'Donoghue

THE CAST ASSEMBLED for *The Heretic* was a distinguished one for its time and is no less impressive today, including as it does two Oscar winners (Louise Fletcher and James Earl Jones) and four Oscar nominees (Linda Blair, Richard Burton, Max von Sydow, and Ned Beatty)—even if none of those accolades resulted from *Exorcist II*. Whereas William Friedkin managed to convince the cast of *The Exorcist* to feign—and even *feel*—fear, John Boorman failed to inspire or provoke the same level of commitment from his players. William Peter Blatty found the performances in *Exorcist II* "appalling," but the script is a mitigating factor—and, as Brian Hoyle notes in *The Cinema of John Boorman*, "the performances in *The Heretic* clearly suffer from a paucity of directorial attention."[259] This is flatly evident from what is onscreen, much of which seems to comprise first-takes. Boorman freely admitted that he paid less attention to his actors as the shoot became more problematic:

> The film represented an enormous amount of work, a struggle that never seemed to end... You don't want to be swallowed up in the terrifying logistics which such a project represents. Then there's the pressure on you of the fact that a film of this dimension costs two hundred thousand dollars an hour. It's like commanding an army; and though the shoot lasted twice as long as usual, I actually had less time to spend on the camera and the actors.[260]

An *Exorcist II* starring either Jon Voigt or Christopher Walken as Lamont and George Segal or Chris Sarandon as Tuskin would almost certainly have been better, or at least more interesting, than the version made with Richard Burton and Louise Fletcher. Yet (mis)casting is only half the story; the other half is the lack of effort to make the best of the situation.

---

259. Hoyle, p. 105.

260. J Boorman, quoted in Ciment, p. 177.

Louise Fletcher, as Dr Gene Tuskin, delivers the definition of a phoned-in performance. Tuskin was conceived as a hip New Yorker (George Segal would have been ideal) and this would have added humor and spice to the character's verbal clashes with Father Lamont. However, Burton and Fletcher's casting and the ensuing rewrites pitted one desultory character against another, with Fletcher listlessly delivering verbiage like "The psychological effects of synching with another mind last a long time, it's very powerful…" with faint disregard. To be fair to Fletcher, she does not have much to work with. *Exorcist II* tries to replicate its predecessor's juxtaposition of a female atheist with a lapsed priest, but the dynamic isn't there: Tuskin's emotional investment in Regan falls short of Chris MacNeil's, and she is effectively a bystander for the film's last third. No wonder Fletcher's lack of effort is so palpable. Perhaps she was so fed-up with the constant rewrites that she gave up; maybe she underplayed her role because she knew she was amid a disaster. A devastating account in Barbara Pallenberg's book reveals Fletcher's dissatisfaction with the script's direction:

> Word has come through that Louise is dissatisfied with the new rewrite, because the one scene in which she can be seen as a person, not merely a doctor—she is dressed up to go out on a date—has been cut. Aside from that, she thinks her last speech in the film is awful. She has told Guy McElwaine and Dick Lederer that she won't say it. She has also told [makeup supervisor] Gary Liddiard and [supervising hairstylist] Lynda Gurasich. Lederer relays this to Boorman and Pallenberg. [Script supervisor] Bonnie Prendergast overhears, and when she gets Pallenberg alone she tells him she *hates* the ending of the movie now. She says there are so many catastrophes, it is almost a joke… Although he is used to her bluntness, Pallenberg is nonetheless shocked into silence for a moment. "It won't be a joke," he says finally.[261]

Fletcher later remarked, "The project was so technical, with footage I shot intended to be part of something else, that I couldn't be sure how it would turn out. I did rewrite a lot of the dialogue, which I felt was terribly stilted."[262] Fletcher won an Oscar for *One Flew Over the Cuckoo's Nest*, and her one-note performance as Nurse Ratched was appropriate for

261. Pallenberg, p. 126.

262. L Fletcher, quoted in Talbot, p. 22.

the soulless character. (Fletcher effectively replaced Ellen Burstyn as the adult female lead in *Exorcist II*. Burstyn regretted turning down the role of Nurse Ratched for *Cuckoo's Nest*, although she later played the Ratched-like Nurse Cooder in *When You Remember Me* [1990] and the villainous grandmother in the 2014 remake of *Flowers in the Attic*—Louise Fletcher played the role in the 1987 version.) Perhaps Ratched's shadow loomed too largely in audience's imaginations, making Tuskin difficult to sympathize with. In hindsight, *Cuckoo's Nest* pointed the way for Louise Fletcher's frequently disappointing screen career, in which the actor would rarely bring depth to her characters. (*Exorcist II* is far from the worst film Fletcher appeared in, considering she has *Two-Moon Junction* [1988] and *Return to Two-Moon Junction* [1995] on her résumé.) Fletcher does have some good moments in *Exorcist II*, including her opening scene in which Tuskin is briefly seen interacting with a deaf child. (Fletcher was pleased with how this scene turned out, and it meant a lot to her. Fletcher was raised by deaf parents who worked with the deaf and hard of hearing, and she memorably used sign language to thank her parents when accepting her Oscar for *Cuckoo's Nest*.) Fletcher later appeared in Douglas Trumbull's science-fiction film *Brainstorm* (1983), once again playing a character engaged in experimental technology involving thought-transference and the linking of minds (alongside a character played by Christopher Walken, the Father Lamont who never was). In *Brainstorm*, however, Fletcher's scientist is somewhat flippant and obstinate—permitting Fletcher to demonstrate just how much more lively her performance as Dr Tuskin *could* have been.

Kitty Winn's performance as Sharon is less risible, although Winn had less to do onscreen: Sharon was foisted onto the story at the insistence of Warners and despite Boorman's efforts to justify her importance to the story (and his claim the film is enlivened by tension between Sharon and Tuskin), Sharon's role could have been taken by a generic housekeeper. If anything, her presence exemplifies a tendency of sequels to bring back characters as a sop to audiences rather than for any practical dramatic purpose, a metatextual capitulation over narrative logic. It's also unfortunate that Sharon, delicate and relatable in the first movie, becomes dysfunctional and *deranged* in the second: character development is one thing, but in the second film Sharon barely feels like the same character from the first. (Boorman believed Sharon barely registered with audiences in the first film and was therefore hesitant to hire Kitty Winn for the sequel—but it could be argued that in *The Exorcist*, as an onlooker in the MacNeil house, and not being an actor, priest, doctor, or child, Sharon is an identification character for much of the general audience. She serves no such function in *Exorcist II*, being a figure of "spiritual torment" and vaguely sketched treachery.) Brian Hoyle contends Sharon was the greatest victim of *Exorcist II*'s script rewrites:

> …one does not really understand why [Sharon] kills herself, and there is no previous implication that she has "chosen evil." Rather, this decision seems to be in part because the writers did not know what else to do with the character, and because they wanted to add a further element of drama to the film's already ill-conceived climax."[263]

Rospo Pallenberg wrote Sharon's death by flames into the script to counterpoint the fiery death of the girl healer: "In the beginning, Lamont is impotent; he can neither save nor redeem to girl. By the end, he has the power, born in the face of the ultimate evil, of restored faith, and he absolves Sharon before she dies."[264] Pallenberg does not make a convincing case: Lamont isn't powerful enough to *prevent* Sharon from torching herself—and in the Revised Version of *Exorcist II*, he's not around to *absolve* her, either. Sharon's abrupt self-immolation seems to serve no purpose other than to block Tuskin from entering the MacNeil house—a fairly paltry reason for a sequence that is far less effective than Lee Grant's near-identical heel-turn/death-by-incineration in *Damien: Omen II* (1978).

Max von Sydow escapes largely unscathed from *Exorcist II*; von Sydow retains his dignity by virtue of the fact the Father Merrin scenes are relatively tangential to the plot. Paul Henreid has insufficient screen time to make a good *or* bad impression (although his onscreen billing as "THE CARDINAL" brings to mind Monty Python's "THE BISHOP" sketch). Ned Beatty's minute-long appearance as Edwards is practically a cameo, as the character's contributions to the narrative were whittled down. Boorman told Ciment,

> There was a conversation between Lamont and Edwards, the pilot of the aircraft, which I finally cut… When Lamont asked him how he happened to take up his profession, Edwards replied: 'Ex-priest, ex-pilot. I'm still trying to believe. I'm still trying to fly.' And he added: 'It was I who introduced

---

263. Hoyle, p. 105.

264. R Pallenberg, quoted in Pallenberg, p. 155.

those plaster Madonnas into darkest Africa. And one day, in exchange, I'm going to steal an African soul and put it into this empty shell.' He ended the sentence by beating his chest and, with the other hand, throwing the statue out the aeroplane window. The idea was that Edwards was a disillusioned priest who was desperately searching in Africa for the relationship with spirituality which he'd lost. [265]

Despite spending half his screen time outfitted in an insect costume and the other half delivering atrocious dialogue about "the Good Locust," James Earl Jones has the gravitas to get away with his appearance as Kokumo. It's with the two leads that *Exorcist II*'s acting front becomes more objectionable.

"I never wanted Richard Burton, really," John Boorman admitted. "The studio kind of imposed him." [266] Many *Exorcist II* detractors criticize Burton's performance as Father Philip Lamont, throwing around adjectives such as "stilted," "wooden," "hammy," "Shatnerian," and "sweaty." It's hard to disagree: Burton's performance—which brings to mind other unhinged, sweat-sodden clerics like Rod Steiger's nauseated priest in *The Amityville Horror* (1979) and Anthony Perkins' nitrate-huffing preacher in *Crimes of Passion* (1984)—ranges from seeming like he desperately needs a stiff drink to the impression he's already had a few. "Burton lurches through this film like a man in the grip of a profound, if not terminal, hangover," Desmond Ryan noted in his *Exorcist II* review for *The Philadelphia Enquirer*. [267] Having directed Lee Marvin in two consecutive films, John Boorman was not inexperienced when it came to dealing with hard-drinking actors. In reference to Burton's alcoholism, Boorman griped, "He's like all these drunks. Impossible when he's drunk and only half there when he's sober. Wooden as a board with his body, relies on doing all his acting with his voice." [268] With more sensitivity, Boorman in his autobiography elaborated on working with Burton on *Exorcist II*:

---

265. Ciment, p. 177.

266. J Boorman, quoted in Abrams.

267. D Ryan, "'Exorcist II' lacks originality, polish." *The Philadelphia Enquirer*, Jun. 21, 1977.

268. J Boorman, quoted in A Malone, *Censoring Hollywood: Sex and Violence in Film and on the Cutting Room Floor* (Jefferson: McFarland & Company, Inc., 2011), p. 54.

Richard kept his drinking to the weekends. However, he made no contribution to the enterprise. I told him what was required and he did it. If I asked him to adjust his reading, he simply changed it without comment. He expressed no preference, he had no view of the character, and it was, I suspect, of no interest to him. He acted from the neck up, face and voice. His body was rigid, completely inexpressive. When alcoholics are on the wagon there is a hollowness about them. Some of their humanity drains away when they pour the booze down the sink. I persuaded myself that this emptiness could work for the film.[269]

Boorman's claim that Burton was sober on the set differs from the recollection of *Exorcist II* camera operator Nick McLean, who claimed Burton was "scarier" than the film itself:

He was something else. Richard didn't like to do Take Two. As a camera operator, you had to have your act together or he would get extremely pissed off. He was a really big drinker, sometimes he would be drunk by noon, so that was another thing you had to deal with. One time the camera wouldn't pan down all the way, it was one of those old-time deals where you had to get the camera on kind of a plate to get the device go down on an angle. I remember trying to tilt the camera down to where it needed to go but it just wouldn't tilt at the right angle, and Burton yelled, "Get it together, boys! Get it together!" And we just thought, "Jesus Christ, we better get this thing to work." He was one intense guy. I endured the wrath of Richard on several occasions.[270]

By other accounts, however, Burton was punctual and professional on the *Exorcist II* set and was reportedly protective of Linda Blair when the young star incurred discontent for her habitual lateness. Burton knew who the real star of the film was, and no doubt he was aware of the pressure Blair was under. Blair, for her part, recalled working with Burton as one of the highlights of her career. If Burton's behavior on set was largely beyond reproach—yelled-at cameramen notwithstanding—his onscreen

269. Boorman, p. 221.

270. N McLean, quoted in Byrne & McLean, p. 50.

presence in the finished film is questionable, though not without its admirers. Michel Ciment, for one, was persuaded that Burton's dubious performance was simpatico with the film's intentions: "Burton's somnambulistic performance," Ciment wrote, "dovetails with Regan's hypnosis and her oneiric adventures."[271] It is difficult to agree. Burton—like Marlon Brando and Dirk Bogarde—was an actor who came to believe acting was beyond contempt. (What Burton really wanted to do was *write*.) Simon Callow, reviewing *The Richard Burton Diaries*, wrote:

> …even when [Burton]'s trying—especially when he's trying—he's playing neither a character nor an action; he's simply intoning words, narcissistically resonating them through his superb vocal instrument. This is not acting: it is speaking. And this is why Burton found acting so unsatisfying; he was using so little of himself. He is bored by it.[272]

Callow opined that Burton's acting is "disappointing" and while that judgement is difficult to apply to *Look Back in Anger*, *The Spy Who Came in from the Cold*, or *Who's Afraid of Virginia Woolf?* (to name some obvious examples), phrases like "simply intoning words," "narcissistically resonating," and "bored" accurately describe Burton's performance in *Exorcist II*. The truth is, although Burton squandered his talents in films that were clearly beneath him, he *was* a brilliant actor, and one could argue that a credible and nuanced performance from Burton in *Exorcist II* would have chafed against the lunacy surrounding the actor. Given that the grim-faced and lugubrious Lamont is clobbered with most of the film's worst dialogue—to say nothing of the fact he is required to say and do most of the movie's idiotic things in order to advance the plot—it's difficult to see *how* Burton could have made the character convincing. In the contextual daftness of *Exorcist II*, Burton's mostly-somnambulant, occasionally-raging-ham, thoroughly flushed performance is almost a plus. Much of the pleasure to be gleaned from *Exorcist II* derives from Richard Burton wrapping his famous voice around the verbal garbage John Boorman and Rospo Pallenberg saddled him with—his cultured, portentous drone is like something out of a Hammer or Amicus horror film, albeit without

---

271. Ciment, p. 162.

272. S Callow, "The Richard Burton Diaries edited by Chris Williams—review." *The Guardian*, Nov. 29, 2012, https://www.theguardian.com/books/2012/nov/29/richard-burton-diaries-chris-williams-review

the knowing flamboyance of Peter Cushing, Christopher Lee, or Vincent Price, or the bug-eyed intensity of Donald Pleasence. Contrary to popular belief, Richard Burton's performance is *not* the worst on display in *The Heretic.*

One of *Exorcist II*'s most fundamental problems is the performance of Linda Blair as Regan. Blair has a natural, wholesome beauty, but her presence in *Exorcist II* has a cloying artificiality: it's like watching Gidget wandering through a horror film. There is simply no *depth* to Regan. Blair *might* have managed to deliver a less annoying performance had she been properly guided by John Boorman, but this was not to be; in his review of *Exorcist II*, Nathan Rabin of the A.V. Club notes, "Without Friedkin around to terrorize her into excellence, Blair comes off as a total ditz. Her fetching airhead never seems to have experienced anything as traumatic as watching a movie as scary as *The Exorcist*, let alone experiencing its most agonizing moments firsthand."[273] There *was* a precedent for Regan not remembering the events of her original possession—she had no memory of the experience in the closing scenes of *The Exorcist*—but watching *Exorcist II*, one feels the reason Regan still has no memories of her possession has less to do with the purposes of storytelling, and more to do with the fact that Linda Blair's sole recourse was to play the role as an oblivious, perky twit. The fault is not Blair's. From *Hope and Glory* (1987) onwards, Boorman could be considered an "actor's director" in a way he wasn't for the first two decades of his career; *Exorcist II* is one of many films Boorman made which are not based on characterization and performance. (It's telling that one of the reasons Boorman was not interested in directing *The Exorcist* was the fact much of the film depended on the *performance* of a child.) Blair needed a director who could work with her limitations, and the John Boorman of 1976 was *not* that director. At the outset of the *Exorcist II* shoot, Boorman informed his cast he did not wish to consult with them during the filming process, for aesthetic reasons: "Once we start shooting, I will keep a certain distance, because it is very easy for us to be too close... I have to be detached, to know only what I see on the camera. I'm not interested in what you're thinking what your motivations are, unless I can see it through the glass of the viewfinder."[274] Near the end of production, Boorman told Barbara Pallenberg that Blair "knew her character thoroughly, and her responses were just terrific. I often did extra takes with her, giving her advice along the way, because

---

273. Rabin.

274. J Boorman, quoted in Pallenberg, p. 57.

this is what she was used to and thought she needed. But in actuality she was so right most of the time that it wasn't necessary."[275] This is as difficult to believe as Boorman's fatuous claim that no suitable male actor could be found for the role of Dr Tuskin. Boorman was clearly aware of Blair's deficiencies, as he later told Michel Ciment that casting Kitty Winn enabled him "to solve to problem posed by Linda Blair, who's physically attractive and has a real screen presence, but lacks spirituality. And, as that was the film's subject, it was Kitty Winn, her friend, who would communicate the sensation of fear, a strange form of spirituality."[276] (Considering the emphasis *Exorcist II* places on humankind's spiritual evolution, humanity's avatar being played by someone who fails to convey spirituality could be considered a galling flaw.)

In *Exorcist II* there is, perhaps, no figure to feel sorrier for than Linda Blair. While filming *The Exorcist* in 1972, William Friedkin told *The New York Times* that Blair was the most remarkable actress he'd ever worked with. Blair did the hard yard in *The Exorcist* and deserved her Academy Award nomination—her Regan is still one of the finest and most uninhibited performances by a child actor in film history. However, without taking anything away from Blair, it *was* a performance that relied a great deal upon combined mechanics: Dick Smith's makeup and prosthetics, Marcel Vercoutere's special effects, and Mercedes McCambridge's dubbed voice. Without such cinematic trickery in *Exorcist II*, Blair was left to her own devices—and she delivered a gee-whiz performance that exposed her, as Nathan Rabin noted, as "the kind of terrible actress who delivers a line like "I was possessed by a demon" with the off-handed casualness of someone ordering lunch from a Chinese take-out place."[277] It is true that the *Exorcist II* script did Blair no favors: be it the fault of William Goodhart, John Boorman, or Rospo Pallenberg (or all three), *Exorcist II* has little to no inclination to make Regan sound like the mid-1970s female teenager she is supposed to be. (On top of that is the problem that saintliness is often difficult to convey without slipping into insipidness.) However, it's not just the bad lines that show Blair up; in the first scene in the Institute, Blair botches the simple line "There's *nothing wrong* with me!" Her unconvincing delivery is on ample display throughout the rest of the film. (The rooftop scene between Regan and Tuskin is particularly bad.) The carnality and villainy

---

275. J Boorman, quoted in Pallenberg, p. 207.

276. J Boorman, quoted in Ciment, p. 165.

277. Rabin.

Blair attempts to convey as "Pazuzu's Regan" are almost totally lacking, although Blair is hampered by bad dialogue ("Once the wings have brushed you, you're mine *forever!*") and clumsy dubbing.

Despite the blurb of *Exorcist II*'s original home video release claiming that "Linda Blair recreates her original role as Regan, acting with new maturity and depth," Blair's performance in that film effectively presaged the acting style she would bring to most of her subsequent screen outings: well into adulthood, Blair generally lacked credibility as a *mature* actor. One could argue that the notoriety of *Exorcist II* did irreparable damage to Blair's big screen career, drop-kicking her from mainstream Hollywood into a filmography consisting mostly of schlocky exploitation films and bad comedies. The titles alone are a giveaway: anyone interested in the dubious pleasures of the Linda Blair cult canon are advised to seek out *Roller Boogie* (1979), *Hell Night* (1981), *Chained Heat* (1983), *Savage Streets* (1984), *Night Patrol* (1984), *Red Heat* (1985), *Savage Island* (1985), *Nightforce* (1987), *Witchcraft* (1988), and *Fatal Bond* (1991). (Blair's best post-*Exorcist* performance was spoofing her Regan MacNeil role in Bob Logan's 1990 *Airplane!*-style *Exorcist* parody, *Repossessed*.) If nothing else, Blair never fell into obscurity; on the contrary, she retained a fanbase thanks to the violent action and prison pictures she made in the 1980s, and cult films enthusiast Danny Peary noted, "Though she has always been a competent actress, Blair seems completely miscast in these films, but that, I suppose, is what makes them funny rather than repulsive. Anyway, Blair tries and has spirit."[278] One can only wonder as to how Blair's career would have evolved had she refused to appear in *Exorcist II*. (Would there even have *been* an *Exorcist II*?) Had Blair been given the opportunity to star in a better caliber of films, perhaps she would have broadened her range and developed into a more accomplished performer. In any case, the contrast onscreen between Blair (unskilled, but earnest) and Burton (skilled, but non-committed) contributes to *Exorcist II*'s wobbly tone. Blair spends most of her screen time in *Exorcist II* playing Regan either cherubic and chipper or in a trance-induced monotone—in short, nothing to connote the state of mortal terror the character *should* be feeling. (After the sleepwalking sequence, why does Regan act so perky and cheerful, given she's just had a traumatic near-death experience?) Regan doesn't get perturbed much at all throughout *Exorcist II*, which reduces the film's scare-factor. If *Regan* is not particularly disturbed by the demon, why should *viewers* be?

---

278. D Peary, *Cult Movie Stars*. Simon & Schuster (1991), p. 60.

In his 2003 autobiography, John Boorman makes only one reference to the top-billed star of *Exorcist II*: "Linda Blair, who played Regan, was incapable of arriving on time and lingered even longer in make-up. One day she said to me, proudly and without irony, 'John. Did they tell you I was only in ten minutes late today?'"[279] Boorman's lack of empathy, during filming and a quarter-century later, is unfortunate. In a television documentary produced in 2001, Blair revealed that the dissolution of a personal relationship, combined with the pressures of the *Exorcist II* shoot, drove her to develop a drinking problem:

> I was so troubled and so hurt, and I didn't know where to put that pain, and I'm supposed to be doing a professional job, holding up this huge motion picture. For me to drink what I could find... It was enough for me to know that I could get to bed, and that I would pass out, get up, go to work... [280]

Out of her depth and insecure about her abilities, Blair practically confessed to Barbara Pallenberg in 1976 Boorman's inability to help her. What should have been validation of Boorman became praise for his predecessor:

> I think John Boorman and Billy Friedkin both are geniuses. John, I think, will be more visual and not into the performance, and I do like help with the performance. Billy was my first teacher, and I would really like to work with him again... Billy gives a lot of support to actors. *The Exorcist* wouldn't have been anything without him... *The Exorcist* was hard to do. I was sure embarrassed, but Billy was there to help.[281]

Friedkin himself did not fault Blair for *Exorcist II*: "It had a very distinguished cast of people... but the story was a load of bollocks, you know, and it was *beyond* stupid, but you can't hold the actors responsible for *that*."[282]

279. Boorman, p. 221.

280. L Blair, quoted in *Intimate Portrait: Linda Blair.* Lifetime Productions Inc, 2001.

281. L Blair, quoted in Pallenberg, pp. 75-76.

282. W Friedkin, quoted in *Intimate Portrait: Linda Blair.* Lifetime Productions Inc, 2001.

13

"How about adulation?"
The Aftermath of
Exorcist II

"A disaster like The Heretic *just makes it very difficult to make your next film... After* The Heretic *I didn't work for a while. It took me a while to recover and wait for people to forget it... My judgement was severely dented, it felt that my relationship with the audience was completely skewed."*

– John Boorman[283]

"[Exorcist II] is really a dumb movie. The 15 minutes I saw are the product of a demented mind."

– William Friedkin[284]

EXORCIST II: THE HERETIC HAS BEEN haunted by its derided reputation since its original theatrical run. In *The Warner Brothers Story* (1979), Clive Hirschhorn described *Exorcist II* as "a disappointing sequel" that "was not nearly as effective or profitable as its predecessor, took itself far too seriously, and emerged as little more than arrant nonsense parading as authentic mysticism."[285] *Exorcist II* was ridiculed at

---

283. J Boorman, quoted in Thrift.

284. W Friedkin, quoted in T & D Lucas, *Video Watchdog* Issues 1-8 (1990), p. 90.

285. C Hirschhorn, *The Warner Bros. Story* (London: Octopus Books Limited, 1980), p. 429.

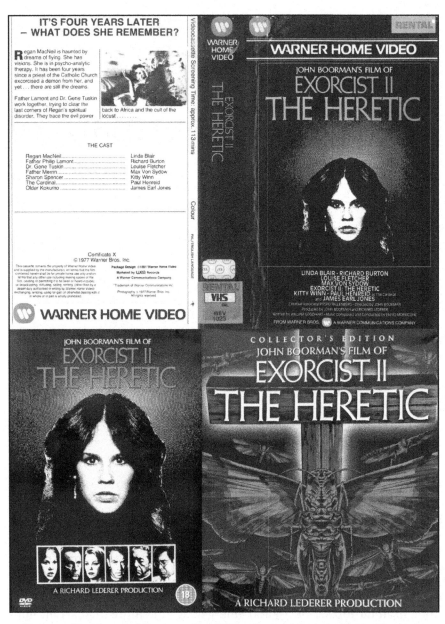

Top row: The sleeve of the Australian VHS release of *Exorcist II: The Heretic* by Warner Home Video (1981). Bottom row, L-R: The sleeve of the British DVD release of *Exorcist II* by Warner Bros. Entertainment Inc. (2003) and the sleeve of the American Blu-ray Collector's Edition of *Exorcist II* by Shout! Factory (2018), cover design by The CRP Group.

length in Michael and Harry Medved's book, *The Golden Turkey Awards* (1980). In their 1978 book *The Fifty Worst Films of All Time (And How They Got That Way)*, the Medveds and co-writer Randy Dreyfus invited readers to nominate their favorite "worst films." They later claimed to have received 3,000 replies. In *The Golden Turkey Awards*, *Exorcist II* was named "the worst sequel ever" and the second-worst movie ever made, beaten in the latter category by Edward D. Wood, Jr.'s shoestring sci-fi *Plan 9 from Outer Space* (1959). The Medveds claimed *Exorcist II* received 384 votes—nine less than *Plan 9*—but they overplayed their hand, attempting humor over accuracy in their *Exorcist II* assessment. Take this excerpt:

> Psychiatrist Louise Fletcher asks [Richard] Burton, who plays a haunted priest, "What am I up against, Father?" In response, he is supposed to say a single word: "Evil." But what actually emerges from his mouth is a long, canine howl that makes the word nearly unintelligible. "Eee-ville!!!" he shrieks, with enough extra breath to blow out all the candles on his fifty-fifth birthday cake.[286]

Now, in the scene in question, Richard Burton *actually* replies with a clipped and perfectly normal and intelligible utterance of the word "evil." John Kenneth Muir made a thinly veiled swipe at the Medveds and their ilk in his more measured assessment of *Exorcist II*:

> *Exorcist II: The Heretic* is not a good film, but nor is it the "worst movie ever," as many critics have claimed for years. Instead, it is merely mediocre, and the authors of certain "niche" books have exaggerated the film's worst qualities, particularly Richard Burton's performance, for purposes of humour... By trying to be different, by attempting to establish an identity different from its successful predecessor, the film went against expectations... and maybe, just maybe, deserves a little credit for not being a carbon copy of the original material... In summation, *Exorcist II: The Heretic* is sabotaged by a ridiculous contraption, weakened by unintended humour, and unfaithful to what came before. On

---

286. M & H Medved, *The Golden Turkey Awards* (London: Angus & Robertson Publishers, 1982), p. 191.

top of these issues, the ending is one of the funniest in horror movie history.[287]

Film-guide books generally dismiss Boorman's film. Danny Peary refers to *Exorcist II* as "absurd" and a "camp classic" in his *Guide for the Film Fanatic* (1986).[288] Leslie Halliwell described *Exorcist II* as "a highly unsatisfactory psychic melodrama" that "falls flat on its face along some wayward path of metaphysical and religious fancy" and "was released in two versions and is unintelligible in either."[289] Leonard Maltin dismissed *Exorcist II* as "preposterous... Special effects are the only virtue in this turkey."[290] In *Revenge of the Creature Features Movie Guide*, John Stanley summarizes *Exorcist II* as "an absolute fiasco... Audiences laughed this hunkajunk off the screen, and it deserved debasing, being the funniest unintentional parody in movie history."[291] In *Cinema of the Psychic Realm: A Critical Journey*, Paul Meehan writes, "A howler of a bad movie, *Exorcist II* appears on many a "worst of" list, and its cinematic depredations have been extensively analyzed in print elsewhere... Burton's way over-the-top performance as the demon-obsessed cleric is one of the comedic highpoints of his illustrious career. The acclaimed British thesp adopts a laughingly intent manner as he mumbles inane dialogue about "Kokumo" and "Pazuzu" while chewing on the scenery like a nest of termites."[292] In *Cinema of the Occult: New Age, Satanism, Wicca, and Spiritualism in Film*, Carrol Lee Fry notes that *Exorcist II* was "panned by critics for its muddled plot and bad acting. Script writer William Goodhart and director John Boorman tried to make the film a mediation on human nature and the reality of evil, but the result is confused and too philosophical for the metroplex horror audience."[293]

287. JK Muir, *Horror Films of the 1970s: Volume 2* (Jefferson: McFarland & Company, Inc., 2002), pp. 476-477.

288. D Peary, *Guide for the Film Fanatic* (New York: Simon & Schuster, 1986), pp. 143, 498.

289. L Halliwell, *Halliwell's Film Guide: Fifth Edition* (London: HarperCollins, 1995), p. 370.

290. L Maltin, *Leonard Maltin's 2009 Movie Guide* (New York: Plume, 2008), p. 427.

291. J Stanley, *Revenge of the Creature Features Movie Guide: An A to Z Encyclopedia to the Cinema of the Fantastic* (Pacifica: Creatures at Large Press, 1988), p. 100.

292. P Meehan, *Cinema of the Psychic Realm: A Critical Journey* (Jefferson: McFarland & Company, Inc., 2009), p. 83.

293. CL Fry, *Cinema of the Occult: New Age, Satanism, Wicca, and Spiritualism in Film* (Cranbury: Associated University Press, 2010), p. 137.

American Exorcist: Critical Essays on William Peter Blatty (2008) contains several derisive asides to *Exorcist II*: Scott D. Briggs claims the film has "a well-deserved reputation for being nothing short of execrable"[294] and Michael Garrett describes it as a "senseless, batty concoction."[295] John Wilson, founder of the Golden Raspberry Awards, writes *Exorcist II* "is among the most insanely idiotic sequels ever made" in *The Official Razzie Movie Guide* (2005).[296]

There have, however, been some high-profile recommendations of *Exorcist II*. "It's mildly shocking that virtually no one has stepped out to acknowledge the film's truly lofty intentions, its occasional success in conveying complex ideas, and its amazing technical achievement," Todd McCarthy wrote in the September-October 1977 issue of *Film Comment*. "*Exorcist II: The Heretic* is arguably the first $10 million-plus avant-garde film ever made on Hollywood sound stages."[297] One year later, *Film Comment* ran an article titled "Martin Scorsese's Guilty Pleasures." Regarded today as one of the greatest and most influential film directors in history, Scorsese in 1978 was one of the Young Turks of New Hollywood, with a half-dozen feature films—including *Mean Streets* (1973), *Alice Doesn't Live Here Anymore* (1974), *Taxi Driver* (1976), and *New York, New York* (1977)—under his belt. In his *Film Comment* piece Scorsese claimed *Exorcist II* is better than its reputation:

> … we're dealing with metaphysics. The picture asks: Does great goodness bring upon itself great evil? This goes back to the Book of Job; it's God testing the good. In this sense, Regan (Linda Blair) is a modern-day saint; like Ingrid Bergman in *Europa '51*, and in a way, like Charlie in *Mean Streets*. I like the first *Exorcist*, because of the Catholic guilt I have, and because it scared the hell out of me; but *The Heretic* surpasses it. Maybe Boorman failed to execute the material, but the movie still deserved better than it got.[298]

---

294. SD Briggs, ""So Much Mystery...": The Fiction of William Peter Blatty," in B Szumskyj (ed.), *American Exorcist: Critical Essays on William Peter Blatty* (Jefferson: McFarland & Company, Inc., 2008), p. 16.

295. M Garrett, "*Demons Five, Exorcists Nothing—A Fable*: The Theo-illogical, Semi-Autobiographical Epic Film That Never Was," in Szumskyj, p. 142.

296. Wilson, p. 305.

297. T McCarthy, "The Exorcism of *The Heretic*." *Film Comment*, Sep.-Oct. 1977.

298. M Scorsese, "Martin Scorsese's Guilty Pleasures," *Film Comment*, Sept.-Oct. 1978.

Scorsese's sincerity should not be doubted even if it was *Exorcist II's* ideas (and not necessarily their execution) that appealed to him. (He might have viewed *Exorcist II* with sympathy as his musical *New York, New York*, which opened two days after *Exorcist II* to generally negative reviews, also made extensive use of soundstages substituting for exterior locations.) Of his list, Scorsese clarified, "On the whole, these films are not good. They're guilty. But there are things in them that make you like them, that make them worthwhile."[299]

In *Nightmare Movies: Horror on Screen Since the 1960s*, Kim Newman wrote, "[*Exorcist II*] doesn't work in all sorts of ways; as a horror film, as a study of people under stress, as a discourse upon good and evil or as a piece of Catholic propaganda. However, like Ennio Morricone's mixture of tribal and liturgical music, it does manage to be very interesting."[300] Indeed, Morricone's *Exorcist II* score has worn better than the film itself and could well be the most laudable aspect of *The Heretic's* legacy. Demonstrating the composer's sonic eclecticism and interest in World Music, the *Exorcist II* soundtrack album exemplifies film journalist Dennis Lim's declaration that "Morricone's attentiveness to pop fashions has given his less enduring work the flavor of kitsch time capsules."[301] Cues which are sliced up and sprinkled around the film flower more fully in the album; divorced from the film's visuals, the soundtrack makes the strings, woodwinds, and tribal rhythms less obvious and overwrought, and "Regan's Theme" less schmaltzy. In 2019, *Rolling Stone* magazine ranked *Exorcist II* #21 in its list of "35 Greatest Horror Soundtracks," writing,

> A box office disaster that's regarded as one of the worst films of all time, [*Exorcist II's*] lone saving grace is that they budgeted for Ennio Morricone. In one of his first forays into big budget Hollywood, the Maestro handed in one of his weirdest, eeriest scores. There's the Afro-Cuban tribal thunder of "Pazuzu," the prog-rock stomp of "Magic and Ecstasy" as well as the ethereal voice and orchestra of

299. M Scorsese.

300. K Newman, *Nightmare Movies: Horror on Screen Since the 1960s: Updated Edition* (London: Bloomsbury Publishing, 2011), p. 63.

301. D Lim, "Bernard Herrmann vs. Ennio Morricone" in S Manning (Ed.), *Rock and Roll Cage Match: Music's Greatest Rivalries Decided* (New York: Three Rivers Press, 2008), p.107.

"Regan's Theme (Floating Sound)"... "Night Flight"—a mash-up of ritualistic Haitian drumming, strings, moaning and a children's choir—might sound cluttered on paper, but Morricone blends it into a horror film confection of the skin-prickling and sublime.[302]

Morricone remained proud of the score and the film itself. "Unfortunately, despite the emotional beauty of that experience and the good craft of the film itself, the movie was not as successful as its predecessor," he recalled. "Curiously enough, in 1987, William Friedkin, the director of the first *The Exorcist,* called me as well, asking me to collaborate on *Rampage.*"[303]

In his book *More Classics of the Horror Film* (1986), William K. Everson claims, "*Exorcist II: The Heretic* was a far better film [than *The Exorcist*], and perhaps because of that a less successful one commercially. It made little sense; in fact, it was often downright bewildering, but it was a beautiful film to watch, with some extremely powerful set pieces."[304] Upon the film's 40th anniversary in 2017, Rob Skvarla of *Cinepunx* wrote,

> When placed in the context of the *Exorcist* series, *Exorcist II: The Heretic* holds a place similar to that of *Halloween III: Season of the Witch.* Both films abandon their predecessors in an attempt to exist as separate entities, and both are regarded as black sheep because of that. Like *Halloween III*, *Exorcist II* isn't nearly as bad as its legacy may lead you to believe, and in fact, holds up against other entries in its series... [you] could make a case that it's the best AND worst film in the series. Its highs match those of the original but its lows are so misguided and so off-the-charts bad, it's hard to argue that anything else in the series comes close. What isn't up for debate is that, of the five *Exorcist* films, it's the most

---

302. CR Weingarten, B Soderberg, S Smith, A Beta, A Battaglia, K Grow, P Orlov & D Epstein, "35 Greatest Horror Soundtracks: Modern Masters, Gatekeepers Choose." *Rolling Stone*, Oct. 17, 2019, https://www.rollingstone.com/music/music-lists/35-greatest-horror-soundtracks-modern-masters-gatekeepers-choose-126190/xtro-harry-bromley-davenport-1983-105371/

303. E Morricone, quoted in De Rosa, p.109.

304. WK Everson, quoted in Talbot, p. 29.

interesting of all because it takes chances none of the other films are willing to risk.[305]

To date, the most thorough attempted validation of *Exorcist II* came from Michel Ciment in his book *Boorman: Un visionnaire en son temps* (1985). Ciment argued that "by virtue of energy and calculation, in spite of all the inherent difficulties, [Boorman] succeeded in imposing his personality on a super-production, in wresting a film d'auteur out of the least 'noble' of Hollywood genres: the horror movie."[306] Ciment blamed *Exorcist II*'s failure on the American critics who "have rarely been equal to the dimension of [Boorman's] talent and originality" and the audiences "who were no doubt hoping for effects even more gruesome than those of *The Exorcist*."[307] No blame is assigned to Boorman. Arguing *The Heretic* is deeply misunderstood and only *intended* to be the sequel to *The Exorcist* (the inference being it is not *actually* a sequel), Ciment's defense of the film boils down to the rather patronizing claim that audiences and critics just didn't *get* it:

> *The Heretic* is the product of poeticism—a fact which no doubt explains why it is still so misunderstood... Just as Boorman refuses to sacrifice the autonomous power and visual splendour of a composition to either movement or duration...but strives instead to develop them in tandem, so his poetic sensibility is never allowed to weaken the narrative continuity... *The Heretic* is not—as some of its fiercest defenders will doubtless claim—a great film in spite of its screenplay. Its pivotal idea—the therapy of the synchronizer and the visions which it engenders—is, on the contrary, rich in thematic possibilities and wholly consistent with the filmmaker's obsessions... We can measure his success by the fact that he does so without a hint of intellectual aridity but with a totally consummate artistry... Like the English metaphysical poets, he renders the idea tangible with the highest possible degree of physical presence... *The Heretic*, a speculation on the individual and its place in history, an interrogation into

---

305. R Skvarla, "*Exorcist II: The Heretic* is the best and worst *Exorcist* movie." Cinepunx. com, Jun. 29, 2017, https://cinepunx.com/exorcist-ii-the-heretic-is-the-best-and-worst-exorcist-movie/

306. Ciment, pp. 157-158.

307. Ciment, p. 158.

the meaning of the future, is confirmation of his phase... Boorman offers us in *The Heretic* a new image of his personal cosmogony in which are blended the songs of innocence and experience, in which are united Heaven and Hell.[308]

Ciment likens Lamont to other Boorman protagonists who undergo spiritual awakenings, and Boorman himself to *Point Blank*'s anti-hero: "A man sets himself a challenge, deploys all the resources of his talent and intelligence to meet it, overcomes one by one every obstacle in his path without ever allowing himself to be distracted from it, then discovers at the end of his adventure that he has been engulfed by the system he hoped to defeat."[309] However, Ciment's analysis of *Exorcist II*—which invokes William Blake, Sigmund Freud, Hermann Broch, D.W. Griffith, Jerry Schatzberg, and André Breton—is a mélange of purple prose. Ciment is entitled to his opinion of *Exorcist II*, but his laudatory overview says a lot without really saying anything; referring to the film's metaphysical aspirations but practically silent on dialogue and acting, Ciment contends dubiously that Boorman's "poetic sensibility is never allowed to weaken the narrative continuity." Brian Hoyle, author of *The Cinema of John Boorman*, finds positive elements in *Exorcist II*, but his summation is sager than Ciment's:

> In its attempt to engage with [its] ideas, one must count *The Heretic* as one of Boorman's most visionary films. However, by rather foolishly trying to do so within the context of a big-budget Hollywood blockbuster, it also became his greatest folly—the work in which his reach most exceeds his grasp... The dialogue is littered with the same kind of mystical babble that marred *Zardoz*... The countless references to the names Pazuzu and Kokumo can be unintentionally amusing... The script is also rather incoherent... Many curial points are curiously underdeveloped... [The] performances clearly suffer from a paucity of directorial attention... The ending is the script's greatest weakness; it is simply at odds with all that preceded it.[310]

308. Ciment, pp. 160-164.

309. Ciment, p.157.

310. Hoyle, pp. 105-106.

Tony Williams, like Ciment, claimed *Exorcist II* is "misunderstood," and blamed its fate on the "traditionally-minded audience" rather than on Boorman:

> Deliberately intended as an alternative philosophic answer to the original film, John Boorman attempted a significant breach with many restrictive codes preventing dialectical movement toward new goals the horror genre should, and must, attempt... However, its innovatory techniques resulted in serious misunderstanding. It did not give audiences what they wanted. Boorman tried to blend opposites, engaging viewers within a sophisticated visual interplay, avoiding traditional gothic codes, and attempting to move towards new generic horizons.[311]

Williams' intellectualization of *Exorcist II* refers to the film's "higher meanings," "dialectical interplay," "higher metaphysical unity," and "utopian goal." Addressing *Exorcist II*'s supposedly esoteric nature, Aubrey Malone remarked,

> *Exorcist II* gives us a New Age devil movie, an elaboration of its predecessor rather than a re-tread, but the golden age of sequels is: if it ain't broke, don't fix it. Intellectuals should stick to intellectual fare rather than flirt around with commercial genres in the vague hope of injecting some metaphysical juice. The result was a flat and flaccid hybrid that did nobody any favors.[312]

There *is* room for intellect in the horror film—David Cronenberg and George A. Romero, for example, crafted horror films that appeal to the intellect as well as the senses, and 1977 *did* see the release of arguably cinema's best fusion of horror, surrealism, and poeticism: *Eraserhead*, the feature film directorial debut of David Lynch. Filmed between 1971 and 1976 on a budget of $20,000 (a fraction of *Exorcist II*'s cost), Lynch's "dream of dark and troubling things" became a midnight movie cult hit and an enduring, unsettling, classic.

---

311. T Williams, *Hearts of Darkness: The Family in the American Horror Film* (London: Associated University Presses, 1996), p. 123.

312. A Malone, *Sacred Profanity: Spirituality at the Movies* (Santa Barbara: Praeger, 2010), p. 275.

In *Chinatown*, Noah Cross (John Huston) remarks that "Politicians, ugly buildings, and whores all get respectable if they last long enough." To that list we might add a number of once-notorious film failures. Roundly despised initially, films like *Peeping Tom* (1960), *Sorcerer* (1977), *Heaven's Gate* (1980), *The Thing* (1982), and *Twin Peaks: Fire Walk with Me* (1992) have undergone critical re-evaluation decades after their theatrical releases. It would be difficult, however, to argue that posterity has granted *Exorcist II* that same kind of respectability. Like film fiascos as disparate as *Caligula* (1979), *The Apple* (1980), *Howard the Duck* (1986), *Super Mario Bros.* (1993), and *Showgirls* (1995), *Exorcist II* has acquired fans and defenders, if not widespread re-evaluation. In 2013, film critic Mark Kermode stated, "Today it has become fashionable for people to attempt to reclaim *The Heretic* as some kind of misunderstood gem, a flawed masterpiece in the manner of *Heaven's Gate*."[313] Yet, despite its partisans' efforts, *Exorcist II*'s reputation remains overwhelmingly negative—in direct contrast to *The Exorcist*, which has grown in esteem and was selected for preservation in the Library of Congress' National Film Registry. If anything, *Exorcist II*'s notoriety has become *more* pronounced in the age of online message boards, blogs, and review aggregator sites. *Exorcist II* currently holds a 3.8/10 rating on the Internet Movie Database; it has been reviewed on many "bad movie" websites; it appears frequently on "Worst Sequels of All Time" lists; and online discussions of the film generally convey affection or hatred for the film's perceived campiness. (The positive reviews display a Ciment-like tendency to praise the film from a distance: discussing it broadly whilst shying away from the plot-holes, loopy dialogue, and dubious acting.)

Praise for *Exorcist II* has been scarce from those involved with the film's production; a pervasive sense of regret colors most of their recollections. When biographer Michael Munn asked Richard Burton why he had agreed to star in *Exorcist II*, the actor replied,

> It looked a whole lot better going in than coming out. It had a good director but he was lost with the material. He said, "I made the wrong film." Well, didn't we all? It seemed like a certainty to be a success because of the original, but nobody was fooled this time. I could have done with a hit film. My agent thought it was a wise move, maybe because the money was good.[314]

---

313. Kermode, p.185.

314. R Burton, quoted in Munn, p. 220.

In the wake of *Exorcist II*'s underwhelming reception, Burton told Janet Maslin of *The New York Times*, "I had a choice of three or four indifferent films at the time—I was actually waiting to do *Equus*... I should, I suppose, if I had been sensible, just have taken three or four months off." Burton had not actually watched *Exorcist II*, nor had he any interest in doing so, remarking to Maslin, "You've obviously seen the film, poor thing."[315] In early 1977—half a year before *Exorcist II*'s release—Linda Blair told Liz Derringer of Andy Warhol's *Interview* magazine, "I think it came out pretty good. But when we first started, it was the sort of thing where so many people were expecting something great."[316] Blair has since been much more vocal about the film's failure:

> With *The Heretic*, they had discussed making a Part Two for a long time. They brought me a script that was very good, they brought in Richard Burton and Louise Fletcher and Director John Boorman. There were several re-writes, John Boorman brought in Rospo Pallenberg to work on the script, which I still don't understand. Pallenberg directed a lot of the film. Other people on the set were getting sick with a weird 'flu, I wasn't a part of that. There were so many factors that just didn't work in association with the film. It just wasn't the project that I signed on to do.[317]

Blair has also claimed, "John Boorman got scared. He brought in it Rospo Pallenberg to finish filming [*Exorcist II*]."[318] In 2013, she elaborated on her misgivings about Pallenberg:

> I remember all of the rehearsal with Richard, myself and Louise and I remember that the next thing we knew there was another person who was part of the process named Rospo Pallenberg.

315. R Burton, quoted in J Maslin, "Burton: 'In Trouble All My Life." *The New York Times*, Oct. 5, 1977.

316. L Blair, quoted in L Derringer, "Linda Blair exorcises twice daily." *Interview*, Feb. 1977.

317. L Blair, quoted in "Interview: Linda Blair of *The Exorcist* Reflects of the Devil Inside." HollywoodChicago.com, Jul. 15, 2010, http://www.hollywoodchicago.com/news/11312/interview-linda-blair-of-the-exorcist-reflects-on-the-devil-inside

318. L Blair, quoted on Suicide Girls.com, Oct. 8, 2010, suicidegirls.com/interviews/2732/Linda-Blair---The-Exorcist/

Everybody was, "What?" He was always whispering in John's ear and you could tell, Richard and I did not like this Rospo, and I can't speak for Louise at all because I don't remember. It's Richard and I that I remember so much. We were not comfortable... I remember that we just were not pleased with the constant rewrites and then my makeup people came to see me and they brought me something that was a storyboard, and it was not acceptable at all what Rospo presented. Let me put it this way: it had a sexual content to it. To see it physically drawn out as a storyboard was unacceptable... So I'll never exactly know what happened, whether John lost his path. I still don't know who this Rospo Pallenberg is. Some people do. In my opinion, he destroyed the film. I think that John had just maybe lost his way. He should've trusted his gut... I think it's a shame whatever happened.[319]

The 1981 *The New York Times* article "The Movies That Drew Hatred" described *Exorcist II* as "the classic example of a movie to which audiences brought the wrong expectations" and "a mystical, pseudo-science-fiction movie" rather than a demonic possession film. Quoted in the piece, *Exorcist II* producer Richard Lederer owned up to "a conceptual mistake":

We were always terribly afraid of what the first week's audience would bring to the theater in the way of expectation... Stanley Kubrick warned me that, in order to work, the second picture would have to out-vomit the first, perhaps by having the characters vomit in rainbow colors... An extremely nervous and tension-filled audience came and wasn't rewarded... So they responded with derision and couldn't wait to tell other people not to come.[320]

In 1986, Louise Fletcher admitted to having mixed feelings about *Exorcist II*:

319. L Blair, quoted in F Topel, "Ahead of My Time: Linda Blair revisits the *Exorcist* movies," Feb. 15, 2013, http://www.craveonline.com/film/interviews/205015-ahead-of-my-time-linda-blair-revisits-the-exorcist-movies

320. R Lederer, quoted in A Harmetz, "The Movies That Drew Hatred." *The New York Times*, May 4, 1981.

> [*Exorcist II*] is something I guess I would *rather* forget about...
> I had been looking for several months for something to do.
> I was beginning to think I was *never* going to make another
> movie... It was a part written for a man and I thought it was
> a good part. I was mesmerized by the fact that they would
> let *me* do a part written for a male star. So, I'm not sorry,
> it was a good experience. I'm not ashamed of what I did in
> *Exorcist II* but I think everybody involved in it would rather
> forget about it. It was a movie that didn't do well... OK, it was
> monumental failure.[321]

Exorcist II camera operator Nick McLean felt he was working on a film
worthy of *The Exorcist*, and then he saw the finished product. "When I
went to the premiere, I really hoped that I was going to get screen credit,"
McLean recalled. "And then about halfway through the film, I thought,
"Jeez, do I really want to have credit on this thing?" It was pretty rough.
There were no scares, so it didn't work well as a horror film."[322] Director of
Photography William Fraker was happy with his work, if not the film itself:

> The gratification of doing a picture like that came at the end
> of the year when it made the top ten in the preliminary Oscar
> nominations for cinematography. Which proved to me that
> my peers felt it was extraordinary enough to be one of the
> top ten pictures photographically, even though it didn't work
> commercially. I felt very good about that.[323]

Editor Tom Priestley believed *Exorcist II* was compromised by lack of time:

> There were many experimental scenes with no proper time to
> try once and fail, and then try something different. John and
> I seemed to spend less time together than on the previous
> films... Sadly, once the film had been released, it was very
> clear it was not working properly with audiences, so John
> had to supervise an amended version. It was a shame that
> we have not been allowed the time to finish the film properly

321. L Fletcher, quoted in Goldberg.

322. N McLean, quoted in Byrne & McLean, p. 50.

323. WA Fraker, quoted in Schaefer & Salvato, p. 149.

in the first place, and to stand back and review it critically. Experiments must be allowed to fail.[324]

John Boorman admitted, "[Failure] has always embarrassed me, and confessing it to others is even more painful than the failure itself."[325] Boorman's position on *Exorcist II*'s failure is interesting; at various times Boorman has vacillated between penitent and churlish, between blaming himself and blaming the public. Shortly after the film's release, Boorman bemoaned that "audiences were laughing at all the wrong things" and "created a kind of hostility" towards the film. Recalling in his memoirs *Exorcist II*'s torturous production, Boorman admits the film was blighted by miscasting and subpar performances and concedes he was rash to accept it in the first place: "I was found out, humiliated... This would surely end my career. As ever, I had tried to do too much, put too much in, been too ambitious. As [Pauline] Kael said, my judgement was faulty—I had taken something on without thinking out the consequences."[326] Boorman's accusation that the audience was complicit in the film's failure, and his "No one is interested in goodness" line, are nonsense. (Audiences didn't pelt objects at the beatific denouement of *Close Encounters of the Third Kind*, a film that captures the rapturous sense of cosmic oneness that *Exorcist II*'s Teilhard de Chardin pastiche can only hint at.) The claim of ambitious overreach might be Boorman's attempt to excuse himself on the grounds of noble failure, but there is nothing innately admirable in ambition—and attempting something avant-garde and failing is *not* equivalent to succeeding at it. After all, Boorman also claimed *Zardoz* was "too ambitious," and while it cannot be denied that *Zardoz* and *Exorcist II* are both ambitious renditions of a personal vision, both films are also Boorman's biggest follies. As Mark Kermode wrote, "Staggering as it may seem, the man who made *Deliverance*—one of the outstanding works of seventies cinema—followed it up with the worst science-fiction movie ever made, and then followed that up with the worst movie ever made. As falls from grace go, that is surely one of the most spectacular."[327] In 2005, Boorman was more contrite about why *Exorcist II* was unsuccessful:

---

324. T Priestley, quoted in Ciment, p. 243.

325. Boorman, p. 25.

326. Boorman, pp. 228–229.

327. M Kermode, *Hatchet Job: Love Movies, Hate Critics* (London: Picador, 2013), p. 183.

... it all comes down to audience expectations. The film that I made, I saw as a kind of riposte to the ugliness and darkness of *The Exorcist*—I wanted a film about journeys that were positive, about good, essentially. And I think that audiences, in hindsight, were right. I denied them what they wanted and they were pissed off about it -- quite rightly, I knew I wasn't giving them what they wanted and it was a really foolish choice. The film itself, I think, is an interesting one—there's some good work in it... But it had one of the most disastrous openings ever—there were riots! And we recut the actual prints in the theatres, about six a day, but it didn't help of course and I couldn't bear to talk about it, or look at it, for years.[328]

In his 2020 book *Conclusions*, Boorman wrote that *Exorcist II* "included some of the best work I have ever done, but I still find it painful to watch. The scorn and ridicule have clung to it," adding,

[Alfred] Hitchcock said a successful film has many fathers, but failure is an orphan. I am glad that two of my orphans, *Zardoz* and *The Heretic*, have gained foster-parents through their cult status... I recently received a letter which surprised me. It was from a man, David Kerridge, who wanted to make a documentary about *The Heretic*. He and his cinephile friends were great admirers of the film. He claimed that its enthusiasts were legion. He called and asked me about the making of the film.[329]

No such admirer is William Friedkin. Rarely one to mince his words, Friedkin has, on multiple occasions, been witheringly blunt on the subject of *Exorcist II*:

I saw half an hour of it. I was at Technicolor and a guy said "We just finished a print of *Exorcist II*, do you wanna have a

---

328. J Boorman, quoted in "Rich Man, Boorman: Film Freak Central Interviews John Boorman John Boorman." Film Freak, Mar. 13, 2005, http://filmfreakcentral.net/notes/jboormaninterview.htm

329. J Boorman, quoted in John Boorman, *Conclusions* (London: Faber & Faber, 2020), p. 66.

look at it?' And I looked at half an hour of it and I thought it was as bad as seeing a traffic accident in the street. It was horrible. It's just a stupid mess made by a dumb guy—John Boorman by name, somebody who should be nameless but in this case should be named. Scurrilous. A horrible picture.[330]

Although by his own admission he has never seen *Exorcist II* in its entirety, Friedkin has felt qualified to describe *The Heretic* as "possibly the worst film I've ever seen."[331] On another occasion, Friedkin stated, "I find [*Exorcist II*] worse than terrible; I find it disgusting."[332] He has also proclaimed, "All of the [*Exorcist*] sequels suck... I wouldn't piss on them if they were on fire. They are all shit. One of the reasons they are is because the people that made them have no belief in the original story. It was about shtick and putting their own imprimatur on it rather than a belief in the story, or an understanding of what that story was about."[333] In 2008, filmmaker Mick Garris discussed Friedkin's 1980 guest spot on *Fantasy Film Festival*, recorded for Los Angeles' pioneering cable station Z Channel:

> I did an interview with William Friedkin, and he was so insulting about the makers of *Exorcist II* and the fact that we dared show *Exorcist II* and have those people on, that the Z Channel thought—the legal staff thought it might be libel and they never ran that show... So there is a great "lost" *Fantasy Film Festival* with William Friedkin. I was on my honeymoon when they said they needed to redo it and I couldn't redo it, so they ended up just not doing that show.[334]

330. W Friedkin, quoted in McCabe, p. 165.

331. W Friedkin, quoted in G Macnab's interview with Friedkin for *The Independent*, 19 Dec. 2003

332. W Friedkin, quoted in M Hogan, "William Friedkin, 'Exorcist' Director, Says Film's Sequels Aren't 'Worth A Bucket Of Warm Spit.'" *The Huffington Post*, Apr. 15, 2013, https://www.huffpost.com/entry/william-friedkin-exorcist_n_3085477

333. W Friedkin, quoted in BA Orange, "Exclusive: William Friedkin Says No to *The Exorcist* in 3D." MovieWeb, Feb. 19, 2010, http://www.movieweb.com/news/exclusive-william-friedkin-says-no-to-the-exorcist-in-3d

334. Mick Garris on Icons of Fright.com, Sep. 2008 (http://www.iconsoffright.com/IV_Mick.htm).

In raconteur mode, Friedkin claimed *Exorcist II* "set a record for the number of people who demanded their money back" before regaling a likely apocryphal story about its debut:

> This is what happened when they had the sneak preview of that film. The people who were at Warners then are no longer there now, they called me and Blatty and said, "You guys are grandfathers! This thing is great. You're going to love this. This really works!" Well, then they had the first preview. The Warners guys pulled up in limousines, and they went in. Customarily, they sat in the back of the theatre while the preview audience saw the first screening of [*The Heretic*], and they let their limousine drivers go. You know, "The movie runs two hours. Go out and get a hamburger, and get back in an hour-and-a-half or so." They sat in the back, and the movie started. After about ten minutes of it, someone in the audience yelled out, "The people who made this piece of shit are in this room!" Somebody else yelled out, "Where?" And he turned around and said, "There they are!" These Warner guys got up and started heading for the back. They ran the hell out of there as quickly as they could. No limousines! They were literally chased down the street![335]

Exorcist II's dubious reputation is celebrated by other filmmakers. Horror director Eli Roth neatly summarized *Exorcist II* as part of YouTube's "Trailers from Hell" series:

> There was *so much* anticipation for this movie, and they had the director of *Deliverance*… and then, it just all goes wrong… It's fantastic. This is just one of the most *wrong* movies on so many levels, because you're watching this, going, "What in God's name is going on??"… It's so ridiculously cheesy on so many levels… This movie was so ridiculed and maligned and laughed at when it opened in theatres that people were actually *throwing things* at the screen… A really terrible movie.[336]

335. W Friedkin, quoted in S Biodrowski, "William Friedkin at the Fangoria Weekend of Horrors, Part Two," Aug. 27, 2000, http://www.mania.com/william-friedkin-fangoria-weekend-of-horrors-part-two_article_23746.html

336. E Roth, transcript from "Trailers from Hell: *Exorcist II: The Heretic*," Aug. 9, 2011,

Studies in the Horror Film: The Exorcist (2011) comprises essays and interviews relating to *The Exorcist* and its sequels, with little championing of *Exorcist II*. Ewen Millar contributes a thoughtful, "admittedly playful" reading of the film—discussing its take on sexuality, psychology, and science—concluding that the narrative offers "a pastiche of themes and marshalling none of the singular vision of its progenitor... Like its main protagonist Father Lamont, in the end, despite its protestations to the contrary, *Exorcist II* comes across as irrelevant, obsessive, and oddly disquieting."[337] James Kloda's spirited overview does not mount a defense of *Exorcist II* ("Judge Dredd could not protect this film from reproach") but an explanation for the fascination it inspires: "Upon first encounter, the feverish insanity and befuddled inanity of the first *Exorcist* sequel provides cringing gasps of disbelief... With its catatonic performances, deranged plotting, and sheer lack of common sense, the film is as misguided as a Michael Bay project... In short, *The Heretic* is a ludicrous piece of crap."[338]

Perhaps the most amusing declamations of *Exorcist II* have come from Mark Kermode, author of the book *BFI Modern Classics: The Exorcist* and host of the BBC documentary *The Fear of God: 25 Years of The Exorcist*. Making reference to *Exorcist II* in his book *Hatchet Job: Love Movies, Hate Critics*, Kermode wrote "if there's one thing worse than a really bad horror movie, it's a really bad horror movie made by someone who thinks they are somehow above horror movies."[339] On his video blog in 2009, Kermode explained his antipathy for John Boorman whilst acknowledging admiration for his earlier films:

> What *is* my problem with John Boorman?... In his early years, Boorman did *Leo the Last*, *Hell in the Pacific*, *Point Blank*, and, of course, *Deliverance*—and *then* something happened, and it may be a critic's fault: People started saying to Boorman, "You're a good filmmaker. You know what? You're not just a good filmmaker. You're an *auteur*. You're the kind of person about whom Michel Ciment will write books saying *how much* of an auteur you are. John, you are a

http://youtu.be/86alyErlXAU

337. E Millar, "On Otherness and Illusion in *Exorcist II: The Heretic*," in Olson, p. 397.

338. J Kloda, "Burn *The Heretic*! The Apocalyptic Folly of *Exorcist II*," in Olson, p. 405.

339. Kermode, p. 184.

true artist." And *then* what happens? *Zardoz. Exorcist II: The Heretic. The Emerald Forest. Where the Heart Is. Excalibur!* All of these films, which, fundamentally, I have had a massive problem dealing with. Now, I started to wonder if, perhaps, all of my problems came down to my resentment of *Exorcist II: The Heretic*, and let me be quite clear: I HATE *Exorcist II: The Heretic*, for two reasons. One: it is *clearly* the *worst* film ever made, by *anyone, ever*. I know in *The Golden Turkey Awards* it comes in at Number 2 after *Plan 9 from Outer Space*, but Ed Wood had *no* money, he had *nothing* to work with. John Boorman had *an entire studio* at his disposal and *look* what he did! The second thing is, *Exorcist II: The Heretic* TRASHED my favourite movie of all time, and it seemed to me to be the work of somebody who had a contempt for *The Exorcist*, and a contempt for the horror genre. In fact, I'm *not* just imagining this: if you read [*The Making of Exorcist II: The Heretic*], we hear Boorman saying things like, "Well, the problem with the original was, that I was trying with my sequel to repair the *damage* that the original had done." He somehow felt that he was *above* horror; he somehow felt that the original was a shock-fest and he could do something to remake the world with *Exorcist II: The Heretic*, and consequently made something that wasn't just terrible on its own terms, but terrible in what it did to a great film... *Zardoz* is a similar problem. *Zardoz* is a science-fiction film about Sean Connery in a red leather jockstrap that manages to be *boring. Why* is it boring? Because it's the work of someone who doesn't think that science-fiction is up to very much, who thinks, "I am an *artist!* I am an *auteur!* I'm going to take a genre that is essentially trash and I'm going to do something uplifting and interesting and full of ideas, unlike all of those other people who make science-fiction films!" So, back-to-back... he makes *two* genre movies which seem to have *contempt* for the genres they came from.[340]

In spite of Boorman's insistence that *The Heretic* is about "goodness," the film *does* reek of contempt—primarily towards *The Exorcist. Exorcist II*

---

340. M Kermode, transcript from "Kermode Uncut: John Boorman," Aug. 4, 2009, http://www.bbc.co.uk/blogs/markkermode/2009/08/boorman_040809.html

is what Harold Bloom would refer to as a "clinamen"—the conscious turning away from the influence of a predecessor. *Exorcist II* does not belong to the "possessed child" subgenre virtually created by *The Exorcist*, nor does it qualify as an entrant in the telekinesis subgenre. (Despite the contrivance of spiritual abilities in *Exorcist II*, the film has little in common with the likes of *Carrie*, *The Fury*, *The Medusa Touch*, or *The Shining*. If anything, an older, alienated, investigative male figure teaming up with a young, psychologically-fragile woman—backed with a Morricone score—makes *Exorcist II* resemble a *giallo* film, albeit a defanged and relatively desexualized one.) There is nothing inherently wrong with Boorman's approach, but it proved catastrophic in the hands of a director with no empathy for *The Exorcist*, whose assignation to *Exorcist II* doomed the film *before* it incurred production difficulties. While it is easy to admire directors who undertake ambitious, challenging projects, it is hard to forgive directors who have no regard for the genres they choose. Danny Peary was surely being kind when he wrote, "When [Boorman] flops we feel badly for *him* because we know how much effort he puts into each project; we don't reject him as we would a Ken Russell."[341] (Russell's *Altered States* [1980], incidentally, is the film *Exorcist II* wants to be: a phantasmagorical collision of science, metaphysics and hallucinatory mysticism.) Reviewing *Zardoz* in 1974, Pauline Kael wrote:

> John Boorman is an intoxicated moviemaker, with a wonderful kind of zeal—a greed to encompass more and more and more in his pictures. His action scenes are rarely comprehensible. He can't get any suspense going. He doesn't seem to understand the first thing about melodrama. He has no particular affection for humor. And his skills are eccentric and his ideas ponderously woozy.[342]

It's mildly damning that these words are from someone who *liked* Boorman's films. (*With friends like these…*) Kael's perception that Boorman has no affection for humor is correct; in fact, there is much *intentional* humor in *The Exorcist*—not surprising, given Blatty's background as a comedy writer—but none in *Exorcist II*. A unique film in many respects, *Zardoz*

---

341. D Peary, *Cult Movies 2: Fifty More of the Classics, the Sleepers, the Weird, and the Wonderful* (New York: Dell Publishing Co., 1983), p. 175.

342. P Kael, "Boorman's Plunge." *The New Yorker*, Apr. 20, 1981. Reprinted in *Taking It All In* (London: Arrow Books, 1987), p. 182.

does share *Exorcist II*'s half-baked intellectualism, earnestness transmuted into humorlessness, and the sense of revelatory ambition missing the mark. In a retrospective review of *Zardoz*, Will Thomas of *Empire* magazine remarked, "You have to hand it to John Boorman. When he's brilliant, he's brilliant... but when he's terrible, he's *really terrible*."[343]

Although he made fine films before and after *Exorcist II*, Boorman was ill-suited to direct an *Exorcist* sequel. "I admired it in many ways but I didn't like it" is one of the nicer things Boorman has said about *The Exorcist*.[344] Boorman's admitted distaste for Blatty's book and Friedkin's film should have disqualified him from *The Heretic*. (Surely *liking* the first film should be a basic prerequisite for making the *sequel*.) Intending to exploit *The Exorcist*'s success and hijack its audience, Boorman created a film that displayed acrimony towards *The Exorcist* and its fans. "In other words, he could take all the hard work which William Friedkin and William Peter Blatty had putting into making a movie he found "repulsive" and then hijack it to his own 'metaphysical' ends without having to bother with all that tedious nonsense of actually getting the audience to care about or invest in your characters or their stories," Mark Kermode wrote in *Hatchet Job*. "In effect, *The Exorcist* had warmed the audience up; now *The Heretic* could jump in and give them all a collective spiritual orgasm."[345]

Boorman's myopic view of *The Exorcist* was the crux of *Exorcist II*'s failure, but the film was not sunk by Boorman alone. Rospo Pallenberg certainly bears responsibility for his detrimental script revisions, and producer Richard Lederer was on the same page as Boorman when he proclaimed that, with the *Exorcist* sequel, "no attempt would be made to reproduce the hideous vulgarity of the original."[346] The hands-off approach of John Calley allowed *Exorcist II* to blatantly disregard its progenitor. Calley was largely absent from *The Heretic* (present only during pre-production and the very end of production), but it was he who offered the project to Boorman. Encouraging director autonomy during his time at Warners, Calley facilitated fine work from many directors (including Robert Altman, Mel Brooks, Stanley Kubrick, Sidney Lumet, Terrence

343. W Thomas, "*Zardoz* review." *Empire*, Mar. 3, 2007, https://www.empireonline.com/movies/reviews/zardoz-review/

344. J Boorman, quoted in M Thrift, "John Boorman on Kubrick, Connery and the lost Lord of the Rings script." *Little White Lies*, Jan. 18, 2018, https://lwlies.com/interviews/john-boorman-lost-lord-of-the-rings-script/

345. Kermode, pp. 184-185.

346. R Lederer, quoted in McCarthy.

Malick, Mike Nichols, Alan J. Pakula, Arthur Penn, Sydney Pollack, and Martin Scorsese). For *Exorcist II*, Calley banked on the John Boorman of *Deliverance* but got the John Boorman of *Zardoz*. The studio's parent company had no qualms with the development of *The Heretic*, if only because it wasn't paying much attention to it. In 1976, Warner Communications Vice-President Jay Emmett told Barbara Pallenberg, "I haven't got the vaguest idea what is going on with *The Heretic*. We give the people in our divisions complete autonomy: Frank Wells, Ted Ashley, and before him John Calley—made the decisions... We think [*The Heretic*] will be enormously successful; otherwise we wouldn't have invested in it what we have."[347] When the film snowballed out of control, why was Boorman not reined in? Guy McElwaine had his concerns, but Warners in general didn't seem to be aware of the disaster until *after* the film's completion, and even then the studio made the fatal mistake of not test-screening the film. Was the studio's faith in Boorman well-placed? Contemporaneous films like *Jaws* and *Star Wars* survived—and were strengthened—by adverse production developments. Brian De Palma recalled the 1970s as "the era where everyone saw the directors as the geniuses, so we got a lot of opportunities to make any crazy movie that happened to occur to us."[348] Boorman said, "In the seventies, the studios believed in directors. They left it to us."[349] Fine in principle, but *Exorcist II* exemplifies when this approach goes wrong. During the film's troubled production, Warners seemingly gave little to no serious consideration to the idea of admonishing or replacing Boorman. Perhaps *The Exorcist* served as a precedent: Warners panicked over the film's schedule and budget overruns but didn't want to take William Friedkin off the film, whatever discontent he had caused in the meantime. Ultimately, Friedkin delivered. The studio, evidently, believed Boorman would too.

By the dawn of the 1980s, film studios had become wary of profligate directors. The business side of the industry—the executives and dealmakers—reasserted control, blunting the creative freedom of the New Hollywood's *cinéliterate* generation of directors. Although *Jaws* (1975) and *Star Wars* (1977) are routinely blamed for ending America's 1970s film renaissance, New Hollywood's hubristic overreach was a contributing factor. Studios took beatings for financing flops like Peter Bog-

347. J Emmett, quoted in Pallenberg, p. 141.

348. B De Palma, quoted in J Carucci, "De Palma reminisces on the Hollywood 'genius' era." *Associated Press*, Sep. 16, 2012.

349. Boorman, p. 294.

danovich's *At Long Last Love* (1975), William Friedkin's *Sorcerer* (1977), and Martin Scorsese's *New York, New York* (1977). The failure of Michael Cimino's *Heaven's Gate* (1980) ruined United Artists almost entirely. A string of flops and a whisper campaign alleging drug-fueled eccentricity sent Hal Ashby's career into terminal decline. Francis Ford Coppola declared bankruptcy after *One from the Heart* (1982) failed to recoup its production costs. John Boorman—a non-American—was at best a peripheral figure in New Hollywood, but *Exorcist II* merits consideration in the context of the movement's end: *Exorcist II* was *not* a studio-bankrupting financial disaster, but it *was* a cautionary tale of a "personal" filmmaker being given a sizeable budget and total creative freedom, the latter less common in the 1980s "high-concept" era of film projects intensely scrutinized by studio executives. By giving Boorman free rein, Warners befouled its own nest. There are many fateful situations and circumstances one can point to throughout *Exorcist II*'s production: Rospo Pallenberg rewriting William Goodhart's script; the casting of Richard Burton and Louise Fletcher; John Boorman's freak illness and Pallenberg's subsequent assumption of directorial duties; Warners refusing to test-screen the film before an audience... Any one of these things was damaging on its own; the aggregate was calamitous. However, the initial hiring of John Boorman to direct *The Heretic* was, in retrospect, the most damaging factor. Boorman unapologetically hated *The Exorcist* and if he had his way, there would have been no *Exorcist* film franchise in the first place. Entrusting *Exorcist II* to this man was one of the most baffling and catastrophic decisions a major film studio has ever made.

The *Exorcist* film franchise survived *The Heretic*, thanks to the enduring popularity of the original film—although a dozen years would elapse before the release of a further instalment. A pseudo-sequel emerged in the meantime: *The Ninth Configuration* (1980), written and directed by William Peter Blatty, and based on his 1978 novel of the same name (itself a reworking of his 1966 novel *Twinkle, Twinkle, "Killer" Kane!*). An almost unclassifiable mélange of absurdist comedy, gothic horror, metaphysics, and theological melodrama, *The Ninth Configuration* won Blatty a Golden Globe Award for Best Screenplay and has oblique connections to *The Exorcist*. (Tonally, the absurdism of *The Ninth Configuration* is at odds with the somberness of *The Exorcist*, but both films are linked by common themes—human suffering, the existence of God, self-sacrifice—and a Christian medal as a symbol of faith. *The Ninth Configuration* also uses dialogue Blatty discarded from the first-draft screenplay of *The Exorcist* and Blatty has stated that Billy Cutshaw in *The Ninth Configuration* is the astronaut warned "You're going to die up there!" by Regan in *The Exorcist*. Indeed, *The Exorcist*, *The Ninth Configuration*, and *The Exorcist III* have been referred to as Blatty's "Faith Trilogy.") Blatty subsequently warmed to the idea of a more explicit continuation of *The Exorcist*. *Legion* would return the *Exorcist* series to its theological/horror roots by exploring the connection between Regan's exorcism and the execution of a serial killer that occurred on the same night. Blatty envisioned *Legion* as a William Friedkin film, but the backlash against *Cruising* (1980) made Friedkin wary of making another violent movie centered on a serial killer. After Friedkin opted to direct the (dire) Chevy Chase arms-dealing comedy *Deal of the Century* (1983), Blatty wrote *Legion* as a novel. Published to strong sales in 1983, *Legion* was the basis for the 1990 film *The Exorcist III*, scripted and directed by Blatty. The film featured the return of Detective William Kinderman and Father Joe Dyer from *The Exorcist* (now played by George C. Scott and Ed Flanders respectively), and Jason Miller reprised his role of Damien Karras. (Miller, along with fellow *Exorcist III* cast members Scott Wilson, Ed Flanders, and George DiCenzo, had appeared in *The Ninth Configuration*.) According to Brad Dourif, who played James Venamun ("the Gemini Killer"), those involved in the production of *The Exorcist III* pretended *Exorcist II* never happened:

> [*Exorcist II*] was the biggest piece of shit—probably—ever made... and they had a great cast and everybody was *terrible*, and the movie was ridiculous and boring, and I just cannot understand why they did that. I mean, why would they think to have James Earl Jones riding a big bug would be *scary?*[350]

Blatty's film, which had retained the title *Legion* during production, was filmed on location in Georgetown in mid-1989, with interior studio scenes filmed in Wilmington, North Carolina. *Legion* was altered significantly during post-production at the behest of Morgan Creek Productions (then a subsidiary of Twentieth Century-Fox), the studio that bought Blatty's script and funded the film's production. Ordered to re-shoot scenes and rectify the film's abrupt ending, Blatty shot new sequences featuring actors Jason Miller and Nicol Williamson, neither of whom appeared in the previous cut of the film. (Williamson, incidentally, had played Merlin in

---

350. B Dourif, quoted in *Death Be Not Proud: The Making of "The Exorcist III*," Shout! Factory LLC, 2016.

John Boorman's *Excalibur*.) Blatty also trimmed some dialogue and added a gory, special effects-saturated exorcism sequence into the climax. (The original cut featured no exorcism and ended with Kinderman simply shooting the Gemini Killer.) The film's title remained a bone of contention between Blatty and the studio. Envisioned as *Legion*, and known at various times throughout production as *The Exorcist 1990*, *The Exorcist: Fifteen Years After* and *The Exorcist III: Legion*, the film was finally released as *The Exorcist III*, against Blatty's wishes:

> I begged them when they were considering titles not to name it *Exorcist* anything, because *Exorcist II* was a disaster beyond imagination. You can't call it *Exorcist III* because people will shun the box office. But they went and named it *Exorcist III*, then they called me after the third week when we were beginning to fade at the box office and they said 'We'll tell you the reason, it's gonna hurt, you're not gonna like this—the reason is *Exorcist II*.' I couldn't believe it! They had total amnesia.[351]

The studio's mandate regarding the title was unfortunate if not unsurprising, given the film was released when numerically titled horror sequels were especially rampant: to put it into context, *The Exorcist III* came out the year after *Friday the 13th Part VIII*, *A Nightmare on Elm Street 5*, and *Halloween 5*, and in the same year as *The Texas Chainsaw Massacre III*, *Child's Play 2*, and *Psycho IV*. Despite Blatty's film contradicting *Exorcist II*—the MacNeil house demolished at the end of *Exorcist II* still stands in *The Exorcist III*—its title implied continuation from *Exorcist II*, even if its tagline, "From the creator of the original *Exorcist*," was the studio's tacit disavowal of responsibility for *Exorcist II*. (Blatty's film is not a repudiation of Boorman's as much as it simply does not acknowledge the previous film's existence.) A murder mystery with theological overtones and emphases on characterization, dialogue, suspense, jump-scares, and violence, *The Exorcist III* could not contrast more starkly with *Exorcist II*; its authentic location cinematography and offbeat humor also differ from *Exorcist II*'s staginess and humorless, self-important tone. Released in August 1990—four months after Friedkin's return to horror, *The Guardian*, and one month before the *Exorcist* parody *Repossessed*—*The Exorcist III* opened in first place during its opening weekend. However, as Blatty had

---

351. WP Blatty, quoted in McCabe, p. 175.

anticipated, the film's theatrical run proved to be a box office disappointment, due at least in part to residual antipathy towards *Exorcist II*. The *Exorcist III* received some complimentary reviews upon its release and has since gained a cult following, being cited frequently as an underrated horror film. (Less laudably, it was reportedly the favorite film of American serial killer Jeffrey Dahmer.) "It's still a superior film," Blatty has remarked. "And in my opinion, and excuse me if I utter heresy here, but for me it's a more frightening film than *The Exorcist*."[352] In 2010, *Legion* was adapted by writer Charley Sherman and staged by director Anne Adams for Chicago's WildClaw Theatre.

Fans of *The Exorcist* were treated to the film's DVD release in 1997 and the BBC's 75-minute documentary, *The Fear of God: 25 Years of The Exorcist*, in 1998. In 2000, *The Exorcist* was re-released to cinemas worldwide, boasting remastered sound and picture, new digital effects, and ten minutes of footage Blatty had lobbied Friedkin to reinstate. The revisions were not without controversy—Roger Ebert, for example, docked the film from **** to ***½—but the release was a commercial success. In 2001, Morgan Creek (by this time, under the ownership of Warner Brothers, and keen to exploit the *Exorcist* franchise further) began preparation of an *Exorcist* prequel, a project initiated in 1997. Taking a cue from *Exorcist II* but otherwise ignoring Boorman's film, *Exorcist: The Beginning*, written by William Wisher and Caleb Carr, would focus on the formative encounter between Father Merrin and the demon in Africa, decades before their rematch in *The Exorcist*. *Exorcist: The Beginning* suffered a production even more troubled than that of the *Exorcist* sequels. Veteran director John Frankenheimer—who made the 1975 sequel to Friedkin's *The French Connection* and was, for a time, attached to the project that became Friedkin's 1978 comedy *The Brink's Job*—was hired to direct before bowing out due to ill health. (He died months later, in July 2002.) The film was assigned to Paul Schrader, who rewrote the screenplay sans credit. A successful screenwriter (with credits including Martin Scorsese's *Taxi Driver* and *Raging Bull*) and an experienced director in his own right, Schrader was no stranger to horror, having directed the 1982 *Cat People* remake (which was edited by Friedkin collaborator Bud Smith, editor of *The Exorcist*'s Iraq sequence and the film's infamous, banned original trailer). However, Morgan Creek—in the person of CEO James G. Robinson—found Schrader's film too cerebral and insufficiently gory for a horror film. Robinson had felt similarly about *The Exorcist III* (of

---

352. WP Blatty, quoted in McCabe, p. 175.

which he was the executive producer), but his solution this time was even more drastic. Schrader's film was shelved, and *The Beginning* was re-filmed almost entirely from scratch by Renny Harlin (director of *A Nightmare on Elm Street 4* and *Die Hard 2*) from a retooled script by Alexi Hawley. Harlin's *Exorcist: The Beginning* was released to middling box of-fice and negative reviews in August 2004. Schrader's film was granted a limited theatrical release in May 2005 under the title *Dominion: Prequel to The Exorcist*. Although it elicited a better response from critics and an endorsement from William Peter Blatty, *Dominion's* general reception was mixed. *The Beginning* and *Dominion* both star Swedish actor Stellan Skarsgård as Father Merrin.

Exorcist II left an indelible mark on the *Exorcist* franchise: directors of subsequent *Exorcist* films were not allowed the autonomy John Boor-man received in 1976. (Not even *Repossessed* was spared from ruinous post-production tinkering. Writer/director Bob Logan's original cut was more referential to *The Exorcist* but tested poorly with audiences unfa-miliar with the specifics of Friedkin's film. *Repossessed* was subsequently re-tooled as a broader comedy, with more contemporaneous cultural ref-erences and generic gags. The film duly limped in and out of theatres and has dated badly.) The *Exorcist* franchise has endured in various media. Friedkin's film received its first Blu-ray release in 2010 and a revised, 40th anniversary edition of Blatty's novel was published in 2011. The follow-ing year, *The Exorcist* was brought to Los Angeles' Geffen Playhouse by playwright John Pielmeir and director John Doyle; the play was re-staged in the UK and Ireland between 2016 and 2019. Reports in 2012 indicated Morgan Creek was preparing an *Exorcist* television series (without the involvement or consent of William Peter Blatty or William Friedkin, both of whom objected publicly to the project). Morgan Creek and Twentieth Century-Fox Television duly commissioned *The Exorcist*, a modern-day interpretation created by Jeremy Slater (who wisely decided against sim-ply re-adapting Blatty's original novel). The series debuted on the FOX network in September 2016; its fifth episode revealed the series as a se-quel to Blatty's story via the plot-twist that lead character "Angela Rance" (Geena Davis) is the middle-aged Regan MacNeil. The second season of *The Exorcist* premiered in September 2017, but the poorly rated series was cancelled the following May. In October 2016, the home media group Shout! Factory, via its sublabel Scream Factory, released *The Exorcist III* on Blu-ray, a "Collector's Edition" package including both the theatri-cal cut and an approximation of the film Blatty assembled before the reshoots. (Advertised as "The Director's Cut" and billed onscreen as "William Peter Blatty's *Legion*," this patchwork version includes low-quality footage excerpted from VHS dailies, as the necessary film footage shot by Blatty had been lost by the studio and not recovered.)

On January 12, 2017—five days after his 89th birthday—William Peter Blatty died. News of Blatty's death was made public the following day by William Friedkin, who described Blatty as his "dear friend and brother." The following year, Scream Factory released a 2-disc "Collector's Edition" Blu-ray of *Exorcist II: The Heretic*, containing two versions of the film and a selection of extra features. The most intriguing supplements are the Linda Blair interview and John Boorman's audio commentary. The diplomatic Blair maintains disappointment in *Exorcist II* but is happy there are people who like the film. Boorman's intermittent commentary is almost entirely superfluous to those who have read his memoirs; his sparse comments include his description of *The Exorcist* as "abhorrent" and his claim that *Exorcist II* "has something important to say."

In July 2021 it was reported that Universal Pictures would pay $400 million for the rights to a new film trilogy of *The Exorcist* with Ellen Burstyn set to reprise her role of Chris MacNeil—which Burstyn refused to do for *Exorcist II* back in 1976. David Gordon Green, who revitalized John Carpenter's *Halloween* series in 2018, will direct the first film in the trilogy, which is expected to continue narratively from the 1973 film rather than reboot the story or follow previous *Exorcist* sequels or the television series. The caretaker apparent of the *Exorcist* franchise, Green has stated, "I like all the *Exorcist* movies… And not only do I like them, I think they can all fall into the acceptable mythology for what I'm doing. It's not like I'm saying, 'Pretend that *The Exorcist 2* never happened.' That's fine to exist. They're all fine to exist, and I enjoy all of them."[353]

353. DG Green, quoted in J Farley & E Garbutt, "*Exorcist* reboot director David Gordon Green says the movie will be a sequel to the original." *Total Film*, 22 Jul. 2021, https://www.gamesradar.com/au/exorcist-reboot-director-david-gordon-green-says-the-movie-will-be-a-sequel-to-the-original/

Regan MacNeil (Linda Blair) sensing Father Lamont's journey.

Father Lamont (Richard Burton) administers the Last Rites to Sharon
(Kitty Winn) while Dr. Gene Tuskin (Louise Fletcher) looks on.
This scene is not present in the revised cut of *Exorcist II*.

Postscript

After *Exorcist II*

Kitty Winn appeared in several more films and some episodic television before retiring from acting in 1984. Winn said, "It wasn't difficult to retire. I have friends who have a family life and do their art and make it work. I realized I couldn't give myself to both."[354] Winn returned to the stage in 2011, appearing in *The Last Romance* at the San Jose Repertory Theatre. As late as 2021, Winn admitted to having never watched *The Exorcist*: "But I heard it's really good. Maybe one day I'll watch it."[355]

Frank Wells continued to serve as vice chairman of Warner Brothers until 1982. In 1984 he became President of the Walt Disney Company, a position he held until his death in a helicopter crash in 1994. He was 61. Disney's *The Lion King* (1994) is dedicated to Wells.

Max von Sydow amassed a prolific filmography. After *Exorcist II* he worked with John Huston, Woody Allen, Steven Spielberg, and Martin Scorsese, and received Oscar nominations for *Pelle the Conqueror* (1987) and *Extremely Loud and Incredibly Close* (2012). Contrasting with *The Greatest Story Ever Told*'s Christ and *The Exorcist*'s saintly Father Merrin, von Sydow adeptly played villains in *Three Days of the Condor* (1975), *Flash Gordon* (1980), *Never Say Never Again* (1983), and *Needful Things* (1993). He also appeared in *Star Wars: The Force Awak-

354. K Winn, quoted in R Stein, "Winn Traded Film for Family." *San Francisco Chronicle*, Aug. 1, 1999.

355. K Winn, quoted in K K Pir, "Kitty Winn and *The Panic in Needle Park* (1971)." The Baram House, 2021, www.baramhouse.com/kitty-winn-and-the-panic-in-needle-park

ens (2015) and TV's *Game of Thrones*. When von Sydow died in 2020 at the age of 90, Peter Bradshaw of *The Guardian* wrote, "An aristocrat of cinema has gone."[356]

Tom Priestley continued editing films until 1987. His post-*Exorcist II* credits include *Tess* (1979), *Times Square* (1980), and *Nineteen Eighty-Four* (1984). Since 1990, Priestley has handled the estate of his late father, English novelist/playwright J.B. Priestley.

Rospo Pallenberg reteamed with John Boorman for *Excalibur* (1981) and *The Emerald Forest* (1985). In the late 1980s, he wrote a screenplay adaptation of Stephen King's novel *The Stand*, but the 1994 miniseries used a teleplay by King himself. Pallenberg made his directorial debut with the 1989 slasher film *Cutting Class* (featuring Brad Pitt) before returning to screenwriting with *The Barber of Siberia* (1998) and *Vercingétorix* (2001).

Barbara Pallenberg had two minor onscreen roles in 1986, in the film *Legal Eagles* and an episode of television's *The Colbys*. She co-wrote with her husband Rospo the screenplay for *Ricochet*, which was set to be directed by South African director William Faure before the film was abandoned due to financial difficulties. In 2001, Pallenberg's book *Guerrilla Gardening: How to Create Gorgeous Gardens for Free* was published by Renaissance Books.

Ennio Morricone reunited with Sergio Leone to score *Once Upon a Time in America* (1984) and received Best Original Score Academy Award nominations for *Days of Heaven* (1979), *The Mission* (1986), *The Untouchables* (1987), *Bugsy* (1991), and *Malèna* (2000). Morricone's other film scores include *The Thing* (1982), *Cinema Paradiso* (1988), *In the Line of Fire* (1993), and *Ripley's Game* (2002). Morricone toured the world extensively, conducting performances of cues from his scores. He received an honorary Oscar in 2007 and in 2016, at the age of 87, he won his first competitive Academy Award, for Quentin Tarantino's *The Hateful Eight* (2015). Morricone died in 2020 at the age of 91. With over 400 film credits to his name, he is acclaimed as one of cinema's greatest composers.

Nick McLean worked as a camera operator on films such as *Looking for Mr. Goodbar* (1977), *Heaven Can Wait* (1978), *The Deer Hunter* (1978), and *The Right Stuff* (1983) and was the Director of Photography of *Staying Alive* (1983), *Cannonball Run II* (1984), *The Goonies* (1984), *Short Circuit* (1986), *Spaceballs* (1987), and *Mac and Me* (1988), among

---

356. P Bradshaw, "Max von Sydow: an aristocrat of cinema who made me weep." *The Guardian*, Mar. 9, 2021, https://www.theguardian.com/film/2020/mar/09/max-von-sydow-an-aristocrat-of-cinema-who-made-me-weep

others. McLean has worked extensively in television and was Director of Photography for close to 100 episodes of the sitcom *Friends*. His book *Behind the Camera: The Life and Works of a Hollywood Cinematographer* was published in 2020.

Guy McElwaine returned to ICM Partners, the talent agency business he helped found, after 18 months at Warner Brothers. He later served as President of Columbia Pictures between 1982 and 1986, when the studio released hits such as *Gandhi* (1982), *Tootsie* (1982), *The Big Chill* (1983), *Ghostbusters* (1984), *The Karate Kid* (1984), *A Passage to India* (1984), *St. Elmo's Fire* (1985), *Silverado* (1985), *Fright Night* (1985), and *Stand by Me* (1986). McElwaine returned to ICM in 1988 before serving as President of Morgan Creek Productions from 2002 until his death in 2008, at the age of 71. During his time at Morgan Creek, McElwaine executive produced *Exorcist: The Beginning* (2004) and *Dominion: Prequel to The Exorcist* (2005).

Richard Macdonald brought his production design expertise to films such as *The Rose* (1979), *Altered States* (1980), *Supergirl* (1984), *Coming to America* (1988), *The Addams Family* (1991), and *The Firm* (1993). He died in 1993, at the age of 73.

Richard Lederer left Warner Brothers—where he had worked since 1950—after the release of *Exorcist II*. He co-wrote and produced the *American Graffiti* knock-off *The Hollywood Knights* (1980) before serving at Orion Pictures as Vice President of worldwide marketing and at Francis Ford Coppola's Zoetrope Studios as a marketing consultant. Lederer died in 2007, at the age of 90.

James Earl Jones voiced Darth Vader in further *Star Wars* installments. His distinctive voice is also famous for CNN's tagline and as Mufasa in both versions of *The Lion King* (1994 and 2019). Jones' other credits include *Conan the Barbarian* (1982), *Coming to America* (1988), *Field of Dreams* (1989), *The Hunt for Red October* (1990), and *Cry, the Beloved Country* (1995). On television, Jones starred in *Paris* (1979-1980), *Gabriel's Fire* (1990-1991) and *Pros and Cons* (1991-1992) and guested in *The Simpsons*, *Homicide: Life on the Street*, and *House, M.D.* Jones' awards include a Tony for *Fences* (1987), Emmys for *Heat Wave* (1990), *Gabriel's Fire* (1990), and *Summer's End* (1999), a Screen Actors Guild Lifetime Achievement Award in 2009, and an Honorary Academy Award in 2011.

Paul Henreid made no further film appearances after *Exorcist II*. He died in 1992, aged 84.

William Goodhart co-wrote the aerobatics drama *Cloud Dancer* (1980), his third and final film credit. Goodhart died in 1999, at the age of 74.

William A. Fraker's post-*Exorcist II* cinematography credits include *Close Encounters of the Third Kind* (1977), *1941* (1979), *The Best Little Whorehouse in Texas* (1982), *WarGames* (1983), *Memoirs of an Invisible Man* (1992), and *Tombstone* (1993). He directed *The Legend of the Lone Ranger* (1981) and episodes of television's *Wiseguy*. Fraker earned five Academy Award nominations in his career and served as President of the American Society of Cinematographers in 1979 and 1980. He died in 2010, at the age of 86.

Louise Fletcher continued to work steadily in films after *Exorcist II*, albeit in little that replicated the acclaim for *One Flew Over the Cuckoo's Nest*. Fletcher's credits include *Brainstorm* (1983), *Strange Invaders* (1983), *Firestarter* (1984), *Invaders from Mars* (1986), *Flowers in the Attic* (1987), *Virtuosity* (1995), and *Cruel Intentions* (1999). She has had greater success on the small screen, earning Emmy nominations for *Picket Fences* and *Joan of Arcadia* and appearing in *Star Trek: Deep Space Nine*, *E.R.*, *Heroes*, and *Shameless*.

Jay Emmett was indicted in September 1980 on charges of racketeering and taking bribes from the mob-connected owners of the Westchester Premier Theater. Emmett received a suspended sentence after pleading guilty to two felony charges. Although he received leniency in exchange for testifying against Warner Communications' assistant treasurer Solomon Weiss, Emmett was summarily dismissed from the Warners board. He served on the boards of several Major League Baseball teams before his death in 2015 at the age of 86.

John Calley quit Warner Brothers in 1981, breaking a five-year $21 million contract. Suffering from occupational burnout, Calley spent the rest of the decade as a virtual recluse from the film industry. He resurfaced to produce *Postcards from the Edge* (1990) and *The Remains of the Day* (1993) before serving as an executive for United Artists in 1993 and as President of Sony Pictures from 1996-2003. Calley returned to producing and received the Irving G. Thalberg Memorial Award in 2009. He died in 2011, aged 81. Journalist David Poland wrote, "To leave this world beloved is a wonderful thing. To leave this business beloved is a fucking miracle. John Calley was that kind of miracle man."[357] William Friedkin

---

357. D Poland, "Obituary: John Calley." MCN Blogs, Sep. 13, 2011, http://moviecitynews. com/2011/09/john-calley/

said, "John Calley was the very best film executive I've ever worked with. His comments and his support of *The Exorcist* made the film what it became. I'm forever grateful to him, I miss him and the industry has not seen anyone comparable since his retirement."[358]

Garrett Brown brought his Steadicam expertise to films such as *The Shining* (1980), *Altered States* (1980), *Reds* (1981), *One from the Heart* (1981), *The King of Comedy* (1983), *Return of the Jedi* (1983), *Twilight Zone: The Movie* (1983), *Indiana Jones and the Temple of Doom* (1984), *Philadelphia* (1993), and *Casino* (1995). Brown invented other stabilized camera systems such as the SkyCam, the DiveCam, and the MobyCam, and since 2005 he has devoted his career to lecturing and inventing. Holding patents for over fifty camera devices, Brown won Academy Awards in 1978, 1999, and 2006, the President's Award from the American Society of Cinematographers in 2001, and the 2014 Nikola Tesla Satellite Award "For visionary achievement in filmmaking technology." Brown was inducted into the National Inventors Hall of Fame in 2013.

Richard Burton received a Best Actor Academy Award nomination for *Equus* (1977) and went on to play a telekinetic misanthrope in *The Medusa Touch* (1978), a mercenary in *The Wild Geese* (1978), another Catholic priest in *Absolution* (1978), the narrator of the prog-rock album *Jeff Wayne's Musical Version of The War of the Worlds* (1978), and Richard Wagner in *Wagner* (1983). Burton reunited with his ex-wife, Elizabeth Taylor, for a Broadway revival of Noël Coward's *Private Lives* in 1983. His final film role was his acclaimed turn as the interrogator O'Brien in Michael Radford's *Nineteen Eighty-Four* (1984); the film was released two months after Burton's death from a cerebral hemorrhage at the age of 58. Burton made over sixty films in a career spanning forty years. Despite seven nominations, he never won an Academy Award, although he did win a BAFTA Award, two Golden Globes, two Tonys, and a Grammy. Burton's diaries were published in 2012; the actor kept no account of filming *Exorcist II*.

Linda Blair encountered trouble with the US Drug Enforcement Administration in late 1977. She was arrested and charged with possessing and conspiring to sell cocaine and amphetamines and received three years' probation after pleading guilty to a lesser charge. (Blair's brush with the

---

358. William Friedkin, quoted in "John Calley Remembered: Hollywood Pays Tribute to the Late Studio Executive" by Stephen Galloway & Gregg Kilday, *The Hollywood Reporter*, Sep. 13, 2011, http://www.hollywoodreporter.com/news/john-calley-remembered-hollywood-pays-234855

law was later referenced in the 1982 song "Linda Blair" by punk rock band Redd Kross). Blair starred in Wes Craven's *Stranger in Our House* (a.k.a. *Summer of Fear*, 1978), the cowgirl drama *Wild Horse Hank* (1979), the disco-fad flick *Roller Boogie* (1979), and the action movie *Ruckus* (1980). She also inspired ex-boyfriend Rick James' 1983 single "Cold Blooded." Blair suffered a paucity of laudable work in the 1980s; her career in that decade comprised lackluster comedies, crude action and women-in-prison films, and nude magazine photoshoots. The Golden Raspberry Awards nominated Blair "Worst Actress" for *Hell Night* (1981) and *Chained Heat* (1983) and awarded her "Worst Career Achievement" in 1985 and "Worst Actress" in 1986 for *Night Patrol, Savage Island* and *Savage Streets*. Blair bounced back with a fine comedic performance opposite Leslie Nielsen in the intermittently amusing *Exorcist* spoof *Repossessed* (1990) and played Rizzo in a 1997 Broadway revival of *Grease*. Blair remains an icon of horror cinema and has continued to work in film and television alongside a career in animal rights activism.

Ned Beatty's post-*Exorcist II* films include *Superman* (1978), *1941* (1979), *Superman II* (1981), *Back to School* (1986), *The Big Easy* (1987), *Repossessed* (1990), *He Got Game* (1994), and *The Killer Inside Me* (2010). Beatty voiced Lots-o'-Huggin' Bear in *Toy Story 3* (2010) and Tortoise John in *Rango* (2011). His television roles include Dan Conner in *Roseanne* and Detective Stanley "The Big Man" Bolander in the first three seasons of *Homicide: Life on the Street*. After Emmy nominations for *Friendly Fire* (1979) and *Last Train Home* (1990) and a Golden Globe nomination for *Hear My Song* (1991), Beatty won a Drama Desk Award for playing Big Daddy in the 2003 revival of *Cat on a Hot Tin Roof*. Beatty died in 2021 at the age of 83; in an epitaph for the actor published by *The Guardian*, John Boorman recalled, "He was a wonderful actor... I loved him dearly."[359]

Ted Ashley remained chairman of Warner Brothers until 1981. He vacated the post to serve as vice chairman of the studio's then-parent company, Warner Communications, a position he held until his retirement in 1988. In his later years, Ashley devoted himself to amassing an extensive art collection, which included works by Fernand Léger, Juan Gris, Joan Miró, Mark Rothko, Constantin Brâncuşi, Henri Matisse, and Edgar Degas. After a long battle with leukemia, Ashley died in 2002 at the age of 80.

---

359. J Boorman quoted in "John Boorman: how a belligerent Ned Beatty won me over." *The Guardian*, Jun. 15, 2021, https://www.theguardian.com/film/2021/jun/15/john-boorman-how-a-belligerent-ned-beatty-won-me-over

John Boorman's career recovered after the failure of *Exorcist II*; Boorman's frequently excellent directorial output over subsequent decades alternated between studio and independent films. In 1979, Boorman informed John Calley of his intention to film Lawrence Kasdan's screenplay *The Bodyguard*, but the project fell apart following the withdrawal of stars Ryan O'Neal and Diana Ross. (*The Bodyguard* was eventually filmed in 1992 by Mick Jackson.) Boorman's first post-*Exorcist II* film was his longtime personal project: the Arthurian fantasy epic *Excalibur* (1981). Written by Boorman and Rospo Pallenberg, filmed in Ireland, and starring Nigel Terry, Nicol Williamson, Helen Mirren, Nicholas Clay, and Cherie Lunghi, *Excalibur* was Boorman's best-reviewed film in years. It was also a box office hit, Boorman's last entry in the fantasy genre, and a boon for the fledgling Irish film industry. Boorman then directed the ecological/anthropological drama *The Emerald Forest* (1985) starring Powers Boothe, Meg Foster, and Boorman's son Charley. Rospo Pallenberg, who wrote the screenplay, objected to Charley Boorman's casting and advised Embassy Pictures to withdraw funding. (Despite the younger Boorman receiving acclaim for his performance, his casting ended the personal and professional relationship between his father and Pallenberg.) Boorman subsequently wrote, produced, directed, and narrated the *roman à clef* World War II dramedy *Hope and Glory* (1987), based on Boorman's childhood experience of London during the Blitz, and starring Sarah Miles, David Hayman, Ian Bannen, and Sebastian Rice-Edwards. *Hope and Glory* won a Golden Globe Award for Best Motion Picture (Musical or Comedy) and was nominated for five Academy Awards, including Best Picture, Best Director, and Best Screenplay. In 1989, Boorman and film producer Kieran Corrigan founded the Dublin-based independent production company Merlin Films. Boorman then directed the romantic comedy *Where the Heart Is* (1990), which he co-wrote with his daughter, Telsche Boorman. Despite a high-profile cast (including Dabney Coleman, Joanna Cassidy, Suzy Amis, Uma Thurman, Crispin Glover, and Christopher Plummer), the film was a critical and commercial failure. Boorman's next project, the post-apocalyptic *Broken Dream*—co-written by Neil Jordan—was to star River Phoenix and Winona Ryder but was shelved after Phoenix's death in 1994. After directing the Burmese-set drama *Beyond Rangoon* (1995) starring Patricia Arquette, Boorman wrote, produced, and directed *The General* (1998), starring Brendan Gleeson as Dublin crime boss Martin Cahill and Jon Voight as the police inspector on his trail. The film was highly acclaimed and won Boorman won a Best Director Award at Cannes—the same award he had won for *Leo the Last* three decades earlier. Boorman subsequently directed the spy film *The Tailor of Panama* (2001), based on the novel by John Le Carré and starring Pierce Brosnan, Geoffrey Rush, Jamie Lee Curtis, and Brendon Gleeson. Boorman's next film, the post-Apartheid South African melodrama *In My Country* (2004), was adapted from Antjie Krog's nonfiction book *Country of My Skull* and starred Samuel L. Jackson, Juliette Binoche, and Brendan Gleeson. Boorman attended a special screening of the film held for Nelson Mandela, who subsequently proclaimed *In My Country* to be "a beautiful and important film." In 2006, Boorman directed the Dostoyevskian Irish black-comic thriller *The Tiger's Tail*, starring Brendon Gleeson (in dual roles), Kim Cattrall, and Gleeson's son Brian; his next film was the *Hope and Glory* sequel *Queen and Country* (2014), depicting the further adventures of Boorman's cinematic alter ego Bill Rohan and based upon Boorman's experience of military service in the early 1950s. Starring Callum Turner, Caleb Landry Jones, Tamsin Egerton, and Vanessa Kirby (with Sinéad Cusack, David Hayman, David Thewlis, and Richard E. Grant in supporting roles), *Queen and Country* premiered at the 2014 Cannes Film Festival and went into general release in 2015, receiving mostly positive reviews. For television, Boorman directed the films *I Dreamt I Woke Up* (1991), *Two Nudes Bathing* (1995), and *Lee Marvin: A Personal Portrait by John Boorman* (1998). Boorman's official accolades include a British Academy of Film and Television Arts fellowship in 2004, an Irish Film and Television Lifetime Achievement Award in 2010, and a British Film Institute fellowship in 2013. Boorman has written the memoirs *Money into Light: The Emerald Forest Diary* (1985), *Adventures of a Suburban Boy* (2003), *Conclusions* (2020), and *John Boorman's Nature Diary: One Eye, One Finger* (2020) and the novel *Crime of Passion* (2016). In 2019, it was announced Boorman will direct *Underground*, a heist thriller set in Boston, as part of a two-film deal between Merlin Films and the American company Film Bridge International.

At the end of *Exorcist II: The Heretic*, Dr Tuskin tells Regan, "I understand now. But the world won't. Not yet." The world *didn't* understand what was going on in *Exorcist II* in 1977, and decades later, perhaps it still doesn't. Yet in spite of *Exorcist II*'s many problems—in fact, *because of* them—the film has endured. Longer, perhaps, than John Boorman might have expected—or wanted. The *Exorcist* franchise survived the brushing of Pazuzu's wings, and *Exorcist II: The Heretic* remains a dubious classic.

Utterly horrible... and fascinating.

Japanese flyer promoting the 1977 release of *Exorcist II.*

A selection of *Exorcist II*-related magazines, 1977-1978.

Warner Books' *The Making of Exorcist II: The Heretic* by Barbara Pallenberg (1977).

Sources

BOOKS

James Baldwin, *James Baldwin: Collected Essays* (ed. Toni Morrison). New York: Library of America, 1998.

Peter Biskind, *Easy Riders, Raging Bulls: How the Sex 'n' Drugs 'n' Rock 'n' Roll Generation Saved Hollywood*. London: Bloomsbury, 1998.

William Peter Blatty, *Classic Screenplays: The Exorcist & Legion*. London: Faber & Faber, 1998.

William Peter Blatty, *The Exorcist*. New York: Harper & Row, 1971.

William Peter Blatty, *William Peter Blatty on The Exorcist: From Novel to Film*. New York: Bantam Books, 1974.

John Boorman, *Adventures of a Suburban Boy*. London: Faber & Faber, 2003.

John Boorman, *Conclusions*. London: Faber & Faber, 2020.

Laurent Bouzereau, *The Cutting Room Floor*. New York: Carol Publishing Group, 1994.

Mark Browning, *Stephen King on the Big Screen*. Chicago: Intellect Books, 2009.

Richard Burton, *The Richard Burton Diaries* (ed. Chris Williams). London: Yale University Press, 2012.

Wayne Byrne & Nick McLean, *Behind the Camera: The Life and Works of a Hollywood Cinematographer.* Jefferson: McFarland & Company, Inc, 2020.

Michel Ciment (trans: Gilbert Adair), *John Boorman.* London: Faber & Faber, 1986.

Michel Ciment (trans: Gilbert Adair), *Kubrick.* New York: Holt, Rinehart and Winston, 1984.

Thomas D. Clagett, *William Friedkin: Films of Aberrations, Obsession and Reality: Expanded and Updated 2nd Edition.* Beverly Hills: Silman-James Press, 2003.

Giulia D'Agnola Vallan. *John Landis.* Milwaukie: Milwaukie Press, 2008.

Alessandra De Rosa (ed., trans: Maurizio Corbella), *Ennio Morricone In His Own Words.* New York: Oxford University Press, 2019.

Alan Frank, *The Horror Film Handbook.* Totowa: Barnes & Noble Books, 1982.

William Friedkin, *The Friedkin Connection: A Memoir.* New York: HarperCollins, 2013.

Carrol Lee Fry, *Cinema of the Occult: New Age, Satanism, Wicca, and Spiritualism in Film.* Cranbury: Associated University Press, 2010.

Brian Hoyle, *The Cinema of John Boorman.* Lanham: Scarecrow Press, Inc., 2012.

Leslie Halliwell, *Halliwell's Film Guide: Eleventh Edition.* London: HarperCollins, 1995.

Clive Hirschhorn, *The Warner Brothers Story.* London: Octopus Books Limited, 1980.

Pauline Kael, *5001 Nights at the Movies.* London: Arrow Books, 1987.

Pauline Kael, *Reeling: Film Writings 1972-1975.* New York: Warner Books, 1976.

Pauline Kael, *Taking It All In: Film Writings 1980-1983.* London: Arrow Books, 1987.

Pauline Kael, *When the Lights Go Down: Complete Reviews 1975-1980.* London: Marion Boyars Publishers Ltd, 2009.

Mark Kermode, *BFI Modern Classics: The Exorcist (Revised 2nd Edition)*. London: Palgrave Macmillan, 2010.

Mark Kermode, *The Exorcist: The Making of a Classic Motion Picture*. Twickenham: Warner Home Video, 1998.

Mark Kermode, *Hatchet Job: Love Movies, Hate Critics*. London: Picador, 2013.

David Konow, *Reel Terror: The Scary, Blood, Gory, Hundred Year History of Classic Horror Films*. New York: St. Martin's Press (2012).

John Landis, *Monsters in the Movies: 100 Years of Cinematic Nightmares*. New York: DK Publishing, 2011.

Aubrey Malone, *Sacred Profanity: Spirituality at the Movies*. Santa Barbara: Praeger, 2010.

Aubrey Malone, *Censoring Hollywood: Sex and Violence in Film and on the Cutting Room Floor*. Jefferson: McFarland & Company, Inc, 2011.

Leonard Maltin, *Leonard Maltin's 2009 Movie Guide*. New York: Plume, 2008.

Sean Manning (ed.), *Rock and Roll Cage Match: Music's Greatest Rivalries Decided*. New York: Three Rivers Press, 2008.

Tony Magistrale & Michael A. Morrison (eds.), *A Dark Night's Dreaming: Contemporary American Horror Fiction*. Columbia: University of South Carolina Press, 1996.

Bob McCabe, *The Exorcist: Out of the Shadows*. London: Omnibus Press, 1999.

Colleen McDannell (ed.). *Catholics in the Movies*. New York: Oxford University Press, 2008.

Michael Medved & Harry Medved, *The Golden Turkey Awards*. London: Angus & Robertson Publishers, 1982.

Paul Meehan, *Cinema of the Psychic Realm: A Critical Journey*. Jefferson: McFarland & Company, Inc, 2009.

John Kenneth Muir, *Horror Films of the 1970s: Volume 2*. Jefferson: McFarland & Company, Inc, 2002.

Michael Munn, *Richard Burton: Prince of Players*. London: JR Books, 2008.

Kim Newman, *Nightmare Movies: Horror on Screen Since the 1960s: Updated Edition*. London: Bloomsbury Publishing, 2011.

Danel Olson (ed.), *Studies in the Horror Film: The Exorcist*. Lakewood: Centipede Press, 2011.

Barbara Pallenberg, *The Making of Exorcist II: The Heretic*. New York: Warner Books, 1977.

Danny Peary, *Cult Films 2: Fifty More of the Classics, the Sleepers, the Weird, and the Wonderful*. New York: Dell Publishing Co., 1983.

Danny Peary, *Cult Movie Stars*. New York: Simon & Schuster, 1991.

Danny Peary, *Guide for the Film Fanatic*. New York: Simon & Schuster, 1986.

Dennis Schaefer & Larry Salvato, *Masters of Light: Conversations with Contemporary Cinematographers*. Berkeley and Los Angeles: University of California Press, 2013.

Steven H. Scheuer, *Movies on TV*. New York: Bantam Books, 1977.

Nat Segaloff, *Hurricane Billy: The Stormy Life and Films of William Friedkin*. New York: William Morrow and Company, Inc, 1990.

John Stanley, *Revenge of the Creature Features Movie Guide: An A to Z Encyclopedia to the Cinema of the Fantastic*. Pacifica: Creatures at Large Press, 1988.

Benjamin Szumskyj (ed.), *American Exorcist: Critical Essays on William Peter Blatty*. Jefferson: McFarland & Company, Inc, 2008.

Pierre Teilhard de Chardin (trans: Bernard Wall), London: *The Phenomenon of Man*. Harper & Row, 1965.

Christopher Tookey, *Named and Shamed: The World's Worst and Wittiest Movie Reviews from Affleck to Zeta-Jones*. Leicester: Troubador Publishing Limited, 2010.

Tony Williams, *Hearts of Darkness: The Family in the American Horror Film*. London: Associated University Presses, 1996.

John Wilson, *The Official Razzies Movie Guide: Enjoying the Best of Hollywood's Worst*. New York: Warner Books, 2005.

Douglas E. Winter, *Faces of Fear: Encounters with Creators of Modern Horror*. New York: Berkley Books, 1985.

Peter Wollen, *Signs and Meaning in the Cinema: New and Enlarged*. Bloomington: Indiana University Press, 1972.

ARTICLES AND WEBSITES

"Confronting the Devil's Power" (Address of Pope Paul VI to General Audience), Nov. 15, 1972, http://www.papalencyclicals.net/Paul06/p6devil.htm

"Richard Burton to Begin 'Heretic' Filming May 17." *The New York Times*, Apr. 21, 1976.

Oalar Hendrek, "What Will 'Jaws' and 'Exorcist' do for an Encore?", *The New York Times*, Jun. 27, 1976.

Bob Lardine, "Peaches and cream Linda's second trip with the Devil for $2 million." *People Weekly*, Jul. 8, 1976.

John Austin, "*The Heretic: Exorcist II*." *Photoplay Film Monthly*, Aug. 1976.

Liz Derringer, "Linda Blair exorcises twice daily." *Interview*, Feb. 1977.

"The Photography of *Exorcist II: The Heretic*." *American Cinematographer* vol. 58 no.8, Aug. 1977.

Gary Arnold, "Giving the Devil His Due." *The Washington Post*, Jun. 18, 1977.

Kevin Thomas, "'Exorcist II' Puts On Straight Face." *Los Angeles Times*, Jun. 18, 1977.

Candice Russell, "'Exorcist II' Confusing Claptrap." *The Miami Herald*, Jun. 18, 1977.

George McKinnon, "Exorcist II is cursed.'" *The Boston Globe*, Jun. 18, 1977.

Katleen Carroll, "'Heretic' Is Bedeviled." *Daily News*, Jun. 18, 1977.

Vincent Canby, "Film: 'Exorcist II: The Heretic' Is Heavy Stuff." *The New York Times*, Jun. 18, 1977.

Gary Arnold, "Exorcising the Laughs from a 'Heretic' Fiasco." *The Washington Post*, Jun. 29, 1977.

Rex Reed, "The second time around: one hit, one error." *Daily News*, Jul. 1, 1977.

Urjo Kareda, "The Devil must have made them do it. There's no other explanation." *Maclean's*, Jul. 11, 1977.

Dave Zurawik, "'Exorcist II': Heresy of Horror." *Detroit Free Press*, Jun. 19, 1977.

R.H. Gardner, "New 'Exorcist' evokes not terror but laughter." *Baltimore Sun*, Jun. 19, 1977.

Gene Siskel, "'Exorcist II' haunted by howlingly awful special effects and script." *Chicago Tribune*, Jun. 20, 1977.

Joel Baltake, "Exorcist II—The Heretic." *Philadelphia Daily News*, Jun. 20, 1977.

Allen Oren, "'Exorcist II' Devilishly Bad Film." *The Charlotte Observer*, Jun. 20, 1977.

Bob Ross, "'Exorcist II': Hollywood's encore for the devil." *St. Petersburg Times*, Jun. 20, 1977.

Patrick Taggart, "'Heretic' a sorry sequel to 'Exorcist.'" *Austin American-Statesman*, Jun. 20, 1977.

Perry Stewart, "'Exorcist II' can go away." *Fort Worth Star-Telegram*, Jun. 21, 1977.

Desmond Ryan, "'Exorcist II' lacks originality, polish." *The Philadelphia Enquirer*, Jun. 21, 1977.

George Anderson, "'The Heretic' Is No 'Exorcist.'" *Pittsburgh Post-Gazette*, Jun. 22, 1977.

Dean Johnson, "The Devil made them do it?" *Sentinel Star*, Jun. 22, 1977.

Malcolm L. Johnson, "'Exorcist II' Defies Belief." *The Hartford Courant*, Jun. 22, 1977.

Mike Petryni, "'Exorcist II' — Did Devil win this time?" *The Arizona Republic*, Jun. 23, 1977.

Joseph McBride, "Boorman Shoulders Responsibility for Heretic, Which He's Recutting." *Daily Variety*, Jun. 24, 1977.

C Nieland, "'Exorcist' is just silly," *Press & Sun-Bulletin*, Jul. 3, 1977.

Christopher Porterfield, "Cinema: Pazuzu Rides Again." *Time*, Jul. 4, 1977.

John Simon, "Flaws." *New York*, Jul. 4, 1977.

Rudy Purificato, "Sounds & Scenes." *Fort Hood Sentinel*, Jul. 7, 1977.

Stan Mieses, "The Devil Made Her Do It (Again): A Grown-Up Linda Blair Talks about 'Exorcist II', Rock & Roll, and Her Life As A Teen Celeb." *Circus*, Jul. 7, 1977.

Tim Yagle, "Cinematic Heresy." *The Michigan Daily*, Jul. 8, 1977.

E Marshall, "Exorcist Sequel Disappointing." *The Daily Times-News*, Jul. 18, 1977.

Molly Haskell, "Boorman Finds the Devil in Africa," *The Village Voice*, Aug. 1, 1977.

Tim Radford, "Bad patches beneath the brilliantine." *The Guardian*, Sep. 15, 1977.

Helen Frizell, "Mumbo-Jumbo mixture brought a few shivers." *The Sydney Morning Herald*, Sep. 16, 1977.

Romola Constantino, "Sight-N-Sound: Films with Romola Constantino." *The Sun-Herald*, Sep. 18, 1977.

Alexander Walker, "Whatever possessed them?" *Evening Standard*, Sep. 22, 1977.

Robert C. Cumbow, *Movietone News* #55, Sep. 1977.

Todd McCarthy, "The Exorcism of *The Heretic*," *Film Comment*, Sep.-Oct. 1977.

Janet Maslin, "Burton: 'In Trouble All My Life." *The New York Times*, Oct. 5, 1977.

The British Monthly Film Bulletin, Oct. 1977.

The New York Times Biographical Record Volume 8, 1977.

Rob Edelman, *Films in Review* Volume 28, 1977.

F.C. Westley, *The Spectator* vol. 239, 1977.

New Times, Volume 9, Number 9, 1977.

New West, Volume 2, 1977.

New Society Vols. 41-42, 1977.

Martin Scorsese, "Martin Scorsese's Guilty Pleasures," *Film Comment*, Sep.-Oct. 1978.

Aljean Harmetz, "The Movies That Drew Hatred." *The New York Times*, May 4, 1981.

Lee Goldberg, "Louise Fletcher, Schoolteacher from Mars." *Starlog* #109, May 1986.

Caryn James, "Book of the Times: Burton's Life and His Love Affair With the Press." *The New York Times*, Feb. 22, 1989.

Mark Kermode, "My Blair Lady," *The Dark Side: The Magazine of the Macabre and Fantastic*, Nov. 1991.

Ruth Stein, "Winn Traded Film for Family." *San Francisco Chronicle*, Aug. 1, 1999.

Roger Ebert, "*The Exorcist*." *Chicago Sun-Times*, Sep. 22, 2000.

"Rich Man, Boorman: Film Freak Central Interviews John Boorman." *Film Freak*, Mar. 13, 2005, http://filmfreakcentral.net/notes/jboormaninterview.htm

Will Thomas, "*Zardoz* review." *Empire*, Mar. 3, 2007, https://www.empireonline.com/movies/reviews/zardoz-review/

Nathan Rabin, "My Year of Flops: *Exorcist II*." *The A.V. Club*, May 15, 2007, http://www.avclub.com/articles/my-year-of-flops-case-file-32-exorcist-ii-the-here,15004/

"Fast Chat: James Earl Jones." *Newsday*, Mar. 16, 2008, http://www.newsday.com/entertainment/stage/ny-c5611250mar16,0,5264743.story

Mick Garris interviewed on *Icons of Fright.com*, Sep. 2008, http://www.iconsoffright.com/IV_Mick.htm

Mark Kermode, transcript from web blog "Kermode Uncut," Aug. 4, 2009, http://www.bbc.co.uk/blogs/markkermode/2009/08/boorman_040809.html

B. Alan Orange, "Exclusive: William Friedkin Says No to *The Exorcist* in 3D." MovieWeb, Feb. 19, 2010, http://www.movieweb.com/news/exclusive-william-friedkin-says-no-to-the-exorcist-in-3d

"Interview: Linda Blair of *The Exorcist* Reflects of the Devil Inside." HollywoodChicago.com, Jul. 15, 2010, http://www.hollywoodchicago.com/news/11312/interview-linda-blair-of-the-exorcist-reflects-on-the-devil-inside

Linda Blair interviewed on *Suicide Girls.com*, Oct. 8, 2010, suicidegirls.com/interviews/2732/Linda-Blair---The-Exorcist/

"William Peter Blatty on *The Exorcist.*" *Cinema Retro: The Essential Guide to Movies of the '60s and '70s*, vol. 7, issue 19, 2011.

William Friedkin, "Post-Mortem with Mick Garris: William Friedkin." Mar. 2011.

"After 40 Years, Grisly 'Exorcist' Book Gets a Rewrite." NPR Books, Oct. 29, 2011, http://www.npr.org/2011/10/29/141683620/after-40-years-grisly-exorcist-book-gets-a-rewrite

Eli Roth, transcript from "Trailers from Hell: *Exorcist II: The Heretic*," Aug. 9, 2011, http://youtu.be/86alyErlXAU

David Poland, "Obituary: John Calley." *MCN Blogs*, Sep. 13, 2011, http://moviecitynews.com/2011/09/john-calley/

R.A. Thorburn, "R.A. interviews William Friedkin, Academy Award-winning director of *The Exorcist*," Nov. 22, 2011, http://ratheruggedman.net/2011/11/r-a-interviews-william-friedkin-academy-award-winning-director-of-the-exorcist/

Simon Reynolds, "Max von Sydow interview: "I was never scared by *The Exorcist.*"" *Digital Spy*, Feb. 14, 2012, http://www.digitalspy.co.uk/movies/interviews/a365668/max-von-sydow-interview-i-was-never-scared-by-the-exorcist.html

Kevin Jagernauth. "Exclusive: William Friedkin Talks Making *Killer Joe*, The Problem With Exorcism Movies, *Sorcerer* & Much More." *The Playlist*, Jul. 26, 2012.

John Carucci, "De Palma reminisces on the Hollywood 'genius' era." *Associated Press*, Sep. 16, 2012.

Simon Callow, "*The Richard Burton Diaries* edited by Chris Williams—review." *The Guardian*, Nov. 29, 2012, https://www.theguardian.com/books/2012/nov/29/richard-burton-diaries-chris-williams-review

Paul Talbot, "The Unmaking of *Exorcist II: The Heretic.*" *Video Watchdog* #171, Nov-Dec. 2012.

Fred Topel, "Ahead of My Time: Linda Blair Revisits the *Exorcist* Movies." Craveonline, Feb. 15, 2013, http://www.craveonline.com/film/interviews/205015-ahead-of-my-time-linda-blair-revisits-the-exorcist-movies

Kier-La Janisse, "Q&A: Linda Blair speaks on the eve of FearNET's 40th Anniversary "EXORCIST" marathon!", *Fangoria*, Feb. 16, 2013, http://www.fangoria.com/index.php/moviestv/fearful-features/8599-qaa-linda-blair-speaks-on-the-eve-of-fearnets-40th-anniversary-exorcist-marathon

Philip Horne, "John Boorman: interview." *The Telegraph*, Mar. 24, 2013, https://www.telegraph.co.uk/culture/film/starsandstories/9946641/John-Boorman-interview.html

Michael Hogan, "William Friedkin, 'Exorcist' Director, Says Film's Sequels Aren't 'Worth a Bucket of Warm Spit.'" *The Huffington Post*, Apr. 15, 2013, https://www.huffpost.com/entry/william-friedkin-exorcist_n_3085477

Susan King, "William Peter Blatty reflects on 40th anniversary of 'The Exorcist'. *L.A. Times*, Oct. 8, 2013, https://www.latimes.com/entertainment/movies/moviesnow/la-et-mn-william-peter-blatty-exorcist-20131008-story.html

Simon Abrams, "Director John Boorman on Young Christopher Walken, *Lord of the Rings*, and Violence in Film." *Vulture*, Nov. 26, 2014, https://www.vulture.com/2014/11/director-john-boorman-on-violence-in-film.html

Rob Skvarla, "Exorcist II: The Heretic is the best and worst Exorcist movie." *Cinepunx.com*, Jun. 29, 2017, https://cinepunx.com/exorcist-ii-the-heretic-is-the-best-and-worst-exorcist-movie/

Matt Thrift, "John Boorman on Kubrick, Connery and the lost Lord of the Rings script." *Little White Lies*, Jan. 18, 2018, https://lwlies.com/interviews/john-boorman-lost-lord-of-the-rings-script/

Benjamin Lee, "Ellen Burstyn: 'Women on screen were prostitutes or victims—I wanted to embody a hero.'" *The Guardian*, Apr. 27, 2018, https://www.theguardian.com/film/2018/apr/26/ellen-burstyn-women-on-screen-were-prostitutes-or-victims-i-wanted-to-embody-a-hero

William Friedkin, transcript from "The Movies That Made Me: William Friedkin." Jan. 8, 2019, https://trailersfromhell.libsyn.com/william-friedkin

Christopher R. Weingarten, Brandon Soderberg, Steve Smith, Andy Beta, Andy Battaglia, Kory Grow, Piotr Orlov & Dan Epstein, "35 Greatest Horror Soundtracks: Modern Masters, Gatekeepers Choose." *Rolling Stone*, Oct. 17, 2019, https://www.rollingstone.com/music/music-lists/35-greatest-horror-soundtracks-modern-masters-gatekeepers-choose-126190/xtro-harry-bromley-davenport-1983-105371/

Quentin Tarantino, "Tarantino on *Deliverance*." *New Beverly Cinema*, 23 Apr. 2020, https://thenewbev.com/tarantinos-reviews/tarantino-on-deliverance/

Kia Khalili Pir, "Kitty Winn and *The Panic in Needle Park* (1971)." The Baram House, 2021, www.baramhouse.com/kitty-winn-and-the-panic-in-needle-park

Peter Bradshaw, "Max von Sydow: an aristocrat of cinema who made me weep." *The Guardian*, Mar. 9, 2021, https://www.theguardian.com/film/2020/mar/09/max-von-sydow-an-aristocrat-of-cinema-who-made-me-weep

John Boorman, "John Boorman: how a belligerent Ned Beatty won me over." *The Guardian*, Jun. 15, 2021, https://www.theguardian.com/film/2021/jun/15/john-boorman-how-a-belligerent-ned-beatty-won-me-over

Jordan Farley & Emily Garbutt, "*Exorcist* reboot director David Gordon Green says the movie will be a sequel to the original." *Total Film*, Jul. 22, 2021, https://www.gamesradar.com/au/exorcist-reboot-

director-david-gordon-green-says-the-movie-will-be-a-sequel-
to-the-original/

MEDIA

Exorcist II: The Heretic production featurette. A Professional Films/
Robbins Nest Production, 1977.

The Fear of God: 25 Years of The Exorcist. Producer: Nick Freand Jones.
BBC, 1998.

Intimate Portrait: Linda Blair. Executive Producers: Linda Ellman and
Christopher Meindl. Lifetime Productions Inc, 2001.

Death Be Not Proud: The Making of "The Exorcist III." Producers: Heather
Buckley and Michael Felsher. Executive Producer: Cliff MacMillan.
Shout! Factory LLC, 2016.

What Does She Remember? With Linda Blair. Producers: Cliff MacMillan
and Jeff Nelson. Shout! Factory Productions LLC, 2018.

SCREENPLAYS

The Exorcist by William Peter Blatty

Exorcist II: The Heretic by William Goodhart

Note: *William Peter Blatty on The Exorcist: From Novel to Film* (1974)
contains the first-draft screenplay of *The Exorcist* and a transcript of the
theatrical cut; *Classic Screenplays: The Exorcist & Legion* (1998) includes
the shooting scripts of the first and third *Exorcist* films. To date, no
versions of the *Exorcist II: The Heretic* screenplay have been published
in book form. All *Exorcist II* dialogue quoted in this book has been
transcribed by me.

Acknowledgements

I WOULD LIKE TO ACKNOWLEDGE the profound debt I owe to Danny Peary and the late Roger Ebert, whose informed and enthusiastic writings on film have been foundational texts for me. We all have our Damascene moments; mine was discovering Danny Peary's *Cult Movies III* in my high school library. I credit—or blame—Peary's *Cult Movies* series and his *Guide for the Film Fanatic*, and Ebert's *Four-Star Movie Guide* and online collection of movie reviews, for my ambition to write about film.

Father Lamont (Richard Burton) must cross a moat of nails to reach Kokumo (James Earl Jones).

My other influences include Pauline Kael, Leonard Maltin, Mark Kermode, Jim Emerson, Matt Zoller Seitz, Nathan Rabin, Elizabeth Sandifer, Lindsay Hallam, Lee Gambin, Tony Martin, Laraine Newman, Larry Karaszewski, Josh Olson, and Joe Dante.

Barbara Pallenberg's *The Making of Exorcist II: The Heretic*, Michel Ciment's *John Boorman*, John Boorman's *Adventures of a Suburban Boy*, and Bob McCabe's *The Exorcist: Out of the Shadows* were particularly valuable resources during the writing of this book. Special thanks also to Todd McCarthy and Paul Talbot for their writings on *Exorcist II*.

CaptainHowdy.com is a useful repository of material relating to *The Exorcist* series.

To John Boorman, Rospo Pallenberg, Linda Blair, and Louise Fletcher, I offer my apologies. No offence, if taken, has been intended.

To Ben Ohmart of BearManor Media, I will be forever grateful to you for placing your faith in me and for giving my project this opportunity. I hope that your faith and patience have been justified. To my editor, Stone Wallace, I appreciate enormously the time and help you have given me. Your encouragement and positive feedback are appreciated immeasurably.

Last but not least, I would like to thank Manfred Kauffmann, for encouragement early on; Simon Eadie, for help along the way... and my inspiration, Shirley Marr, for showing me it could be done. Nothing's forgotten.

About the Author

The author. Photograph by Cathryn Jupp.

DECLAN NEIL FERNANDEZ was born of Irish/Malaysian parentage in Glasgow, Scotland and raised in Perth, Western Australia, where he lives.

He studied film and filmmaking, history, and school-teaching at university. Besides cinephilia, his hobbies include writing, drawing, collecting old comic books, amassing books about Richard Nixon and Watergate, and obsessive support of the West Coast Eagles and the Perth Wildcats.

He works an administrative job by day and by night he tends to an increasingly unwieldy collection of films on VHS, DVD, and Blu-ray. Living space is becoming an issue.

He claims he will return that copy of Danny Peary's *Cult Movies III* should his high school library ever actually ask for it back.

Horrible and Fascinating is his first published book.

Father Lamont (Richard Burton) points to the evil Regan (Linda Blair) must face.

Index

Made in United States
North Haven, CT
14 August 2022

22713913R00153